You Be The Judge

by Randy G. Roy
with Carolyn E. Vaillancourt

Published by
Rylin Enterprises

Library and Archives Canada Cataloguing in Publication

Roy, Randy G.
    You Be The Judge / Randy G. Roy, Carolyn E. Vaillancourt

ISBN 978-0-9688462-2-3
1. Horsemanship - Officiating
I. Vaillancourt, Carolyn E.   II. Title

SF297.R69 2007   797.2'4   C2007-900271-4
First Published in 2007
by Rylin Enterprises

Printed in Canada
Porter Fine Printing Ltd.
Richmond Hill, Ontario

About the Cover

"Willie Be Good" was without a doubt one of the easiest, most uncomplicated, honest horses I have ever worked with. He never went to a show without winning; so reliable and loved by all who rode, trained or worked with him. This cover is a final tribute to an amazing athlete and companion who gave it his all.

"It's your turn now - YOU can be the judge!"

Running Fox

"An invaluable reference for now and all future generations"

King Weekly

"Truly a horseman's bible. Easy reading - something for everyone. An in depth comprehensive study of judging which is easy to follow and understand."

Horse Sport Magazine

"This book is a gift to the horse world. A wealth of information and entertainment."

Horse & Country Magazine

"Reading 'The Judge is Back' is like taking an amazing riding, judging, course-designing, conformation, equitation and hunter clinic in the comfort of your home."

Geoff & Teall

"The authors have masterfully covered hunters, equitation, conformation, courses and much more."

Bobbie Reber

Dedication

Carolyn and I would like to dedicate this book to all of our friends in the horse industry, and to the people who kindly contributed their questions. We hopefully give back to you something that will help you along your horse trails.

Contents

Preface

Thanks to our readers, *"The Judge Is Back"* is sold out. So my co-author, Carolyn Vaillancourt, and I, with the high demand for a reprint of this book, decided to write a new revised edition.

"You Be The Judge" is a brand new book with a new title, photos and content.

I have been asked so many times what is worse, e.g. two strides in the "in and out", trotting, cross-cantering or bucking, missing a jump or a strong and tense horse. In this book I will attempt to rate the faults in each area - hunter, hack, equitation and conformation, from the worst to least severe. You can use this as a guideline to place a class, but often many variables can alter the placings, so try to keep it all in perspective as to what is happening at the time. You also need to take note of each fault, whether it is major, judgment or minor, and the degree of severity of each when placing a class.

I can recall the few times in my entire judging career that it has come down to personal preference. Follow the basic rules, and then use what you prefer! GO with the best jump - the rest is a bonus. Rarely, if ever, do you get it all in the round - the jump, movement, attitude, evenness, looks and presentation.

It is apparent that many people think that judging is very political and that is has a lot to do with personal preference and 'who is who'. I hope this book helps you to see that this is inaccurate, and also helps to keep judges following the rules. I am aware of the concept that whoever is clapping at the ingate might be considered an influence on the placings, but the only constitutes one week of judging, and the judges only hurt themselves and their reputation. Following the rules keeps you honest. I must say that in defense of judges so many people are all too quick to criticize, and 'judge bashing' has become a popular sport in itself. This must end if our industry is to survive. The judge has a totally different view from their side of the ring, and I would like to say that the majority of judges are trying to do the job to the best of their ability, with honesty and integrity.

Randy G. Roy

Foreword
by George H. Morris

It is really quite an amazing story, how I met up with and subsequently worked with Randy Roy. It all began when I was growing up on Oenoke Ridge in New Canaan, Connecticut. Jack Monroe was a neighbour and one of my father's best friends. Jackie, his daughter, was my playmate and we would ride together at the Ox Ridge Hunt Club in Darren, Connecticut. Time went by, a lot of time, and we lost touch with one another.

Twenty years later at Man and His World, A horse show in Montreal, someone grabbed and hugged me from behind; it was Jackie Monroe Morald. She had married an Austrian, was living near Ottawa, and was building a large, first-class horse operation called Dwyer Hill Farms. Randy Roy worked for her.

Randy and I met at this show. He wanted to come to work and learn with me. It was rather a dilemma. Jackie, Randy and I sat down and came up with a compromise. Randy would come with me for a year, hopefully learn a lot, and then return to Canada to manage Dwyer Hill. All of this came to pass and more!

Randy Roy has really had a special and incredible background for years in the hunter/jumper business. I am very proud to say that with his background, with me in New Jersey and then with Ian Millar for so many years in Canada, he really understands the basics of showing hunters, jumpers, and equitation horses. He has learned all of this information the slow, old-fashioned way. The right way.

We are all lucky in North America to have Randy's knowledge put down on paper. "You Be The Judge" is structured, organized, and easy to understand. It should go down as MUST reading not only for judges but also for exhibitors, parents, owners, riders, trainers and grooms. It is one of those books we should review from time to time. Especially before we embark on a circuit of shows or go off to judge somewhere. The only thing worse than a dishonest judge is an ignorant judge.

A good judge is three things: scrupulously honest, knowledgeable, and a good bookkeeper. "You Be The Judge" certainly can't legislate honesty, but perhaps it can inspire such. The book can, though, teach most of the things one needs to know about horse shows. Learning how to formulate a system for judging and to keep a judge's card is especially important. There have been many great horsemen and horsewomen who were bad judges. They couldn't keep books.

Canada will applaud this book. We all will.

George H. Morris
Pittstown, New Jersey

Introduction
by Ian D. Millar

The fast-paced world of show jumping is considered a mysterious and exciting one to the general public. Yet, among it's participants, it is sport, business and a passion which takes them to levels they never expected to achieve.

To help enlighten those who love the sport and the world of horses, the authors have combined their expertise to write "You Be The Judge". The world of showing hunters and equitation has been demystified by this informative and exciting book. To look at the subjective sport through the eyes of two of Canada's premier judges is a view worth seeing.

The horse show judge holds the fate of all exhibitors in his or her hands. How do they make the decision of who should win? How do they separate 30 exhibitors in a class? "You Be The Judge" fills this information void. The secrets are out. The book's unique concept includes questions from exhibitors, judges and horsemen throughout the North America, questions which are answered by the authors from their perspectives as judges and horsemen. The book offers insightful information to its readers on the subjects of hunters, equitation, judging detail and rules of the sport, in a straightforward style.

The authors of this exciting book, Randy Roy and Carolyn Vaillancourt, are experts in their field. They both officiate at major competitions across the country, and have long resumes of their accomplishments in the equestrian world. Randy is the only Canadian to have officiated at all four prestigious indoor North

American venues - Madison Square Gardens, the Washington International Horse Show, Harrisburg and The Royal Winter Fair. This is Randy's sixth book, and a revised edition of his first sold out publication, "Here Comes The Judge". As a previously and successfully published author, Randy knows what the public wants. Carolyn has ridden, trained and judged horses for many successful years. The insight and information the authors reveal has never before been offered. In no other place can one find so much knowledge condensed into one publication.

"You Be The Judge" will include many photographs and illustrations to show faults and comparative knowledge for the reader. As in so many instances, a picture is worth a thousand words, and Randy and Carolyn have provided enlightening examples.

The reader should travel with the book as reference material, as well as exciting reading.

"You Be The Judge" is a **MUST** read for all horse enthusiasts, professionals and riders. A book like this has never before been offered to the public, and is sure to be eagerly awaited by those who want to know more.

Ian D. Millar

Special Thanks

First, I would like to make mention and give special thanks to my co-author, Carolyn Vaillancourt. Together, we were able to bring the judge back!

George H. Morris for his acknowledgment and continued support.

Ian D. Millar for his inspiration, and the years we were together.

To all the judges who participated in this book - thank you for your great input.

We want to thank the following for their wonderful photographs which have contributed greatly to the success of this book:

James Leslie Parker	Judith S. Buck
Cealy Tetley	Shoot Photographic
Coyote Photos	Clix
Time Flies Equine	Photos Pennington
Sandy Black	Niki Taylor

Chapter One

Hunters

Just Cruising

Introduction

Chinook

A properly prepared hunter walks or trots into the ring with ears forward and expression alert, is relaxed, lightly flexed through the poll and accepts the bit. The ideal mover is well balanced and carries itself over the course with long, smooth, rhythmic strides that appear effortless. It maintains the same pace the entire way around the ring. The preferred hunter is on the bit or with light contact rather than on a loose rein. Loose rein adjustments look obvious. If the horse is on a consistent contact, its response is much more subtle. The horse should establish a flowing hunter pace before leaving the opening circle.

Ideally, the horse meets each of the eight fences easily in stride, taking off without interrupting the rhythm, then curves its body through a crisp arc centered over the fence, is loose in the shoulders, and as the hind legs push off, draws its forearms and knees easily above the horizontal while keeping them perfectly level with each other.

In the air the horse drops its head to create a smooth curving line from nose through the neck and back to the hind legs, lands and continues in the same rhythm. Between lines pace is maintained with a slight bend to the inside, leads are switched smoothly without missing a beat. That is the ideal - but most horses demonstrate a major fault, several minor faults or a combination of both.

As far as form is concerned, a beautiful style is the ideal. The horse should jump in a bascule - round through the head, neck and the back. The legs must be up and knees tidy, but not tucked away so tight that they are limited. We like to see a little air between the fence and the horse. This is called scope. The hind end should follow straight along with the front end, neither swaying to the right nor the left. A big, round jumper is what we look for.

After briefly describing some of the more common jumping faults, we must stress that it is of the utmost importance for a judge to be able to differentiate between them and rate their degree of severity. If a horse, for example, jumps to the left only slightly, then it should not be heavily penalized. In this instance, the judge should note the fault and perhaps use it as a tie-breaker when another horse produces an equal performance without making a similar error. If, however, the horse jumps to the left and barely misses the standard, then naturally it has committed a major jumping fault.

Today, most judges both inside and outside the show ring are aware of these common faults. They must also be able to rate the seriousness of each fault. It is important not to over penalize any one of these faults. In reality, most of them are only minor deviations from the true classic hunter form.

In addition, a judge must maintain consistency in his placings by establishing in his or her own mind the faults he or she considers the most and the least serious. When a judge is consistent, then riders will know what kind of performance he or she is looking for.

The jumps are the most important aspect of a hunter's performance because no matter how pretty a horse is or how well it goes between the jumps, if it can't jump properly it should not win a hunter over fences class.

Newmarket

Introducing The Symbols

Symbols are basically a fast, easy vehicle that you use to recall whatever happens when a horse is on course. The symbols are categorized under the headings of major, judgment, minor and positive. These symbols best describe what has occurred, or act simply as a notation with regards to some feature of a horse's performance.

Many things can occur while a horse is on course and we have attempted to cover as many examples as possible. You have very little time to write while judging. Watching the round to draw the true comparisons is most important. Everyone ends up adopting their own notations and symbols, but we think it will be interesting for you to follow along as we go through the symbols we use. The meaning of each one is explained.

Oreo Cookie

Major Faults

The following faults are rated from the most to least severe:

Symbols	Interpretation
Fall	Fall of horse or rider (No courtesy jump allowed)
R	Refusal (Elimination after 3 refusals)
→ 4 ←	Rail down ← Behind → Front
LG	Hanging a leg over the jump, uneven front end. One leg completely drops down towards the ground while the other leg remains in the proper position. Hanging a leg is one of the most serious jumping faults, and can also be quite dangerous.

4

X	Disaster (indescribable)
T	Trotting
LG ↓	Leaving off of one leg
2ST	2 strides in the "in and out"
S→	Strong, tense and running away
KK	Kicking out over a jump or on the flat
BK	Bucking
STK	Using a stick
ST	Stalling, sticking, pausing - the horse arrives at the take-off point and hesitates before leaving the ground
O -	Leaving out a stride in a line
∧	Chipping, popping, missing the distance, adding a stride. All of these terms refer to a horse adding another stride at the supposed point of take off
A+	Adding a stride in a line
↕	Dwelling in the air, jumping high and hanging the front legs
1/2	Half halt or severely shortening of the stride
CC	Counter cantering
C.C.	Cross cantering

Degrees Of Severity

D	<u>D</u>	Ⓓ
Close-+ or deep to the jump	Quite close or deep to the jump	Very close or deep to the jump

Enterprise

Judgment Faults

The following faults are rated from the most to least severe:

Symbols	Interpretation
SPK	SPOOKS - the horse takes a look at the jump or is distracted by something outside of the ring
K	Poor use of the shoulders
	HANGING, KNEES DOWN - Hanging is not the same as hanging a leg. Hanging occurs when the horse's forearms are pointed towards the ground and the knees are not raised correctly
↓	HANGING, LOWER LEG - a horse can have its knees and forearm pulled up properly and still not fold its lower legs up in a neat and tidy fashion. This is referred to as hanging the lower legs and is also categorized under hanging
SW	Swinging or twisting occurs when the horse leaves the ground and swings its front or back legs off to one side. (*The degree of the fault must be taken into consideration when establishing an order of placings.)

6

SWRT - Front legs swing right ⌐^{SW RT}

SWLT - Hind legs swing left ⌐^{SW LT}

UE	Uneven splits with the front legs. The legs are not square and together.
	An UNEVEN horse prefers to land on one lead, and will often reach higher with that leg to attain the preferred lead. A horse is uneven when one leg is noticeably higher than the other
HP	The horse lands in a 'heap', i.e. stalls out as it lands and has to surge ahead to re-establish its pace
O	Reaching or unfolding too soon OPEN REACHING - instead of making an arc over the jump some horses will open or reach their front legs towards the ground. This leaves the judge with the impression of a very weak jump.
→	Runs to the jump
←	Runs after the jump
PH	PULLS HIND END - used when a horse sucks its back legs underneath its body in a quick and unbecoming manner
RT LT	Jumping to the corners
	RT - JUMPS RIGHT - When a horse jumps to the right side of the jump and not in the centre, where he should be
	LT - JUMPS LEFT - When a horse jumps to the left side of the jump and not in the centre, where he should be

SK	Skips the lead change (not a clean change), and did not take a trot step
↓R	Cuts down and rubs the back rail of the oxer with the front -> or hind <- legs
FR	Frozen in the air (dwells, no continuance)
H←	TRAILS HIND END - this symbol is for the opposite of PULLS HIND END (leaves its hind legs trailing out behind while in the air)

R R   Excessive rubbing R → (front)

R (behind) →

HITTING OR RUBBING - I use this symbol when a horse rubs a jump with its front legs. 'R' is used when the horse rubs the jump from behind. When the horse rubs the jump both in front and behind, the card is noted that with both symbols.

When judging, try not to penalize a rub too greatly unless the rub was the result of bad jumping form. A horse, for example, may hit a jump because it hung its legs, or because it jumped flat. However, you should make a note of a hard front rub. R R

F   Jumping flat or at the jump

FLAT BUT EVEN - This horse may make a nice equitation horse as it will not dislodge the rider. However, a very flat back does leave one with the impression of quickness and of being inverted. The knees are even, but instead of making a nice bascule over the jump the belly is barely missing the top rail. If a horse is really flat over a fence, circle the 'F' so that you remember to not place this horse over a horse who was just a little flat.

8

U   Inverted, hollow backed

STP   Steps over the jump

~ ~   Wandering off the line. Rough between jumps and around the ends. Stumble, wandering, tossing of the head or tail swishing, playing. Shortening in front of or between fences. Interruption of a smooth flowing pace. This symbol is my life saver. It saves you from coming up with a whole mess of symbols about some little thing that went wrong.

L   LONG STAND OFF - a long, standing jump can either be symbolized with a plus(+) or a minus(-) depending on the seriousness of the error. I use a plus when the horse leaves the ground a long way from the jump but still maintains its form, and does not run away on the landing side. Use a minus if the horse leaves the ground in weak form. Often a weak, long jump will cause the horse to chop down over the jump instead of completing a proper arc.

D   DEEP OR CLOSE TO A JUMP - Deep or close is not the same as adding a stride. A deep take-off point does not necessarily mean a bad jump. A deep distance occurs when the horse canters close to the base of the jump before taking off. In a case like this, the horse may and often does get away with a good jump. If the horse gallops up to a deep spot, leaves the ground positively, holds its form in the air, and then canters away in the same flowing rhythm, it is a good jump.

            However, it the horse pulls its way to the deep distance and then has to noticeably shorten stride before taking off I will circle the 'D', because in a case like this the horse usually struggles in the air

9

and then lands in a heap with no continuance of stride. A jump like this is very unattractive and should be penalized accordingly

↘↗   Cutting the turns in and out

→   Too fast

←   Too slow

→ ←   Uneven pace

Dreamcatcher

Minor Faults

The following faults are rated from most to least severe:

Symbol	Interpretation
P.G.	Pony gaited (short and choppy stride)
STF	STIFF / TENSE / INVERTED - these terms refer to a look of awkwardness or simply a style of jumping which does not comply with the easy, smooth performance of a hunter over fences

NS   No scope

M   Mouth open

H↑   High headed

S.L.   Switching a lead in front of a jump (or steps out of a lead)

L.C.   Late lead change

TM   Tight martingale

HO   Head out around the turn. A hunter should bend it's body in the direction it is travelling. If it is ridden with its nose toward the rail and shoulder bulging slightly toward the centre of the ring, he should be faulted lightly

SE   Sour ears

W.L.   Wrong lead starting the course (quickly corrected)

L   Long - a little long to the jump

D   Deep - too close to the jump

B.M.   Bad mover

R   Light rub

Engineer

11

Positive Features - *The Best You Can Hope For*

+	A + sign with a denotes an exceptionally good jump
TO	A well turned out horse
GM	Good mover
E	Even pace from the beginning of the course to the end
GJ	Horse that is a good jumper

Numerical Scoring

Applying a numerical score to each round assists the judge in the judging process. If you have a system that you are comfortable with it, do not change it! Remember to keep it simple.

Numerical scoring is requested by horse shows to be announced at the completion of each round during a hunter classic. It is often common practice at some of the larger American shows to run a leader board throughout the class, in order to keep the exhibitors aware of their current placings. Because of these instances, it is good practice to use the numerical method on a continual basis.

Throughout the horse's trip, the judge's card is marked. As the horse canters away from the last fence, the judge arrives at the trial score of how the horse's faults detract from the perfect '100'. The scoring system works like this:

A superb and very rare performance scores in the 90's. A horse with a few minor errors scores in the 80's. Most ribbon winners will have a score in the mid to high 80's. A horse that commits the same minor error repeatedly, such as rubbing almost every fence, will skip into the high 70's. The first time a horse makes any error classified under 'Judgment Faults', the score drops to the high 70's. If the horse repeats the error it drops to the low 70's. With the first error under 'Major Faults', the score goes to the 60's or lower. Trotting puts the score at 60, 55 for two strides in the 'in and out', 45 for a knockdown and 40 for the first refusal. Often horses will place in a tie position which is later broken after the rounds are further compared. It is important to give the rounds that have a close score extra time and thought. After deliberation, they are separated and placed. This ensures that the placings are correct and in a well thought out order.

It is possible to have + or - signs after the score to separate them. The exception to this rule is when the scores are announced publicly. In these instances, you must use decimals to separate the horse's placings, and no two horses can have an identical score.

Keeping a 'ladder' of the horse entry numbers, in order of placing, on the far right side of your card will make it easy to slot the entries in order. Once you have your ribbon winners on the list, and a few extra for the jog, the horses falling into place with scores lower than what is necessary need not be added to the ladder. The ingate will often ask for a standby list from you - a list of which entries need to stay around for the jog - and this makes the list easily accessible for you to pass on to the announcer or ingate. Time is always of the essence, and you don't have time to make a list as a horse is jumping around in your ring.

Also on the right hand side of your card, following the symbol squares, is an area very useful to make notes and comments on turns, pace and overall impressions. What is also valuable is the abbreviated description of each performer. This enables you to recall any horse or rider during or at the end of the class. A simple description of the horse when it enters the ring is a good idea, to help you recall the round at a later glance. This makes constructive comments (when asked for) on a personal level possible, such as "Oh yes, you are the girl who rides the chestnut horse with the lop ears. Well, over the second jump...".

Instant recall, regardless of the size of the class, is very important. It enables a judge to compare one horse with another. It eliminates error insofar as judgment is concerned. It aids in describing the round to a trainer or rider as you know exactly which horse is being referred to.

The abbreviated descriptions need to be short so that your concentration is not distracted from the horse on course. With the normal colours - bays, chestnuts, browns and greys - you need a short distinguishing sign along with it, as you will get many similar colours in a class. Don't panic if you don't instantly have the right recall note: add it as they go or at the end when you watch them leave the ring.

Samples Variations of Abbreviated Descriptions

LIV	Liver chestnut horse
BL	Black horse
CH-RING	Chestnut in a ring snaffle
AP	Appaloosa
RN	Roan horse
GR PLM	Grey horse in a pelham
CH ↑	Big chestnut horse
BAY ↓	Small bay horse
BR ← →	Long-backed brown horse
CH m	Mouthy chestnut horse
Bay Ⓜ	Bay mare
BR D-B	Brown horse in a D-bit
O/BR CH	An unbraided chestnut horse
SPOT	Pinto
PAL	Palomino
GR D.P.	Dapple grey horse
GR WH	White grey horse

GR DK	Dark grey horse
Bay Tail	Bay with a full tail
BR Sheep	Brown horse wearing a sheepskin girth
EYE	Horse with a white eye
Bay SKS	Bay horse with white socks
CH BL	Chestnut with a blaze
BR Star	Brown horse with a star
GR T.O.	Grey horse well turned-out
Face	A prominent white faced horse
Bay T.M.	Bay with a tight martingale
BR Off SKS	Brown with off white socks
CH SK ➜	Chestnut with front white sock

You will, naturally, make short forms for your own descriptions. You don't have to write a lot, though, in order to be able to visualize the horse and it's round. By the end of the third class over fences, you will easily recognize most of the horses in the class.

North Run's Proudfoot

Marking The Judge's Card

In judging hunters the judge needs to keep as accurate a record as possible of everything each horse does during its entire performance. This facilitates total recall in evaluating the horse's round, assigning it a score and ultimately placing it in relation to the entire class.

On the judge's card write short symbols as quickly as possible to allow maximum viewing time. Horses are judged from the moment they enter the ring until they exit. Many things can happen at the end of the round: bucking, missing a lead, a severe pull up or maybe a nice pat and reward for a job well done, so it is important to watch the entire performance.

You need to find each horse a slot as soon as it ends the course so that you can immediately concentrate on the next horse without missing their entrance. Don't search for a home for a horse and miss the next horse starting the course. Compare as one goes. Is it the best so far or the worst? Does it belong behind or in front of which round? Don't write a story about each jump - short, fast and simple is the key.

Use the 'ladder' to keep a running order. Don't wait until the end of the class to be fishing around for an order. Each horse should be 'placed' quickly and efficiently. Use brief and concise bookkeeping so that you can watch and concentrate on the next round.

I	Note description and specifications of class.
II	Signature. Sign your card after the jog is complete.
III	Left column entry number.
IV	The number of entries in the class, count down from the top and draw a line.
V	Far right column reserved for scores.
VI	Left of the scores reserved for abbreviated descriptions to identify horses.

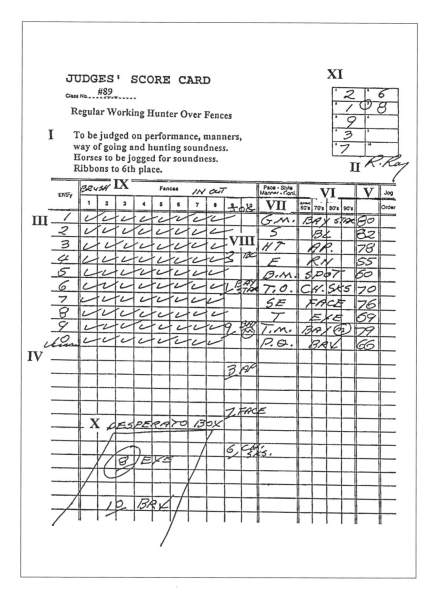

VII	Extra notes or impressions.
VIII	Jog order - underline the numbers and use a short abbreviated description. This will guarantee that you see the horses jog in the correct order.
IX	Jump description. Note the description of the first jump to be sure they jump the correct one, and note where the in and out is, if there is one.
X	Desperato box. This is reserved for very low scores.
XI	Final results. Again, check back with your jog order to verify and always circle reserve.

As a final check - from the lowest score of the final entry in the jog column - count upwards on the right score column to be absolutely sure you have not missed anyone.

North Star

Judging A Hunter Class

JUDGES' SCORE CARD

Class No. #21 . . . .

Pre-Green Hunter Over Fences

To be judged on performance, manners,
way of going and hunting soundness.
Horses to be jogged for soundness.

	121	68
	29	100
	79	
	33	
	18	

Entry	BRUSH Fences										Pace - Style Manner - Conf. Notes	Scores 60's 70's 80's 90's	Total Average	Jog Order
	1	2	3	4	5	6	7	8	9	10				
18											N.S.	BAY ✓	68	
79											G.M.	CH Ⓜ	72	
100							2 ST				T.O.	BR ↗	55	
29											G.J.	✗	76	
68											P.O.	GR D.R	66	
121											m	PAC	77	
87											I	PP	50	
33												BAY.m.	70	
											121 PAC			
											29 ✗			
											79 CH Ⓜ			
		18 BAY ✓												
		68 GR.D.R									33 BR Y.m.			
		100 BR ↗												

Class 21 - Pre-Green Hunter *(Poor Class)*

Number 18 - A small bay horse and an average mover. He is a bit flat when he jumps and looks like a limited jumper. I was right! He is really long to fence 2 and stalls off of the ground. At fence 3 he finds a deep spot and hangs his front end, at fence 4 he jumps flat and hits it in front, he is all right at fence 5, switches a lead in front of 6 and jumps to the left. He is fussy in the turn to the 'in and out' and low with his knees, but not bad jumping out.

Summary: Stalling hard at fence 2, hanging at fence 3, flat at 4, switched leads and jumping to the left at 6, low knees at fence 7. He receives a score of 68. Also, I note 'N.S.' for no scope.

Number 79 - The second horse is a chestnut mare, and a beautiful mover. She misses the first jump. The second jump is fine but she is deep to fence 3. Jumps a little to the right at 4 and gets a little bit deep to fence 5, but jumps it very well. Another good jumping effort at fence 6. A little bit long to the 'in', but positive and steady to jump 'out' in good style.

Summary: Missing the first jump and a few little errors add up to a score of 72. There is definitely quality here; an excellent mover and jumper.

Number 100 - A big brown horse who is beautifully turned out. He jumps high over fence 1 and hangs his legs. Jumps 2 through 6 are all basically the same. He gets lower with his body but still hangs his legs. Finally everything catches up to him and when he sees the combination he jumps really high, and again hangs his legs and adds a stride to jump out.

Summary: With a major fault - two strides in the 'in and out' - the score is an automatic 55.

Number 29 - This a Hanoverian, which I note by the brand. A good first fence and a really good second fence which I note with A+. His head is positioned a little bit out around the turn, and as a result arrives at fence 3 a little deep. He jumps well at 4 and 5. He is slightly to the right corner at fence 6. He is very deep to the 'in', but manages to jump 'out' well in one stride. This horse is a 'scopey' mover.

Summary: An excellent round for a pre-green class. He has a score of 76, the best so far.

Number 68 - A dapple grey horse, who jumps flat over the first jump and has to run to the second. Once again, he jumps flat and hits the jump in front and behind. I note "P.G." on my card for 'pony gaited' as he races around. The remaining jumps are all flat and limited. Then the rider reaches back with his stick and encourages his horse.

Summary: The use of the stick tells me that the horse cannot really do it on his own. I score him a 66.

Number 121 - A Palomino with a 'busy' mouth. He steps over the first jump, and jumps the second one fine. A late lead change occurs before the third jump, and he jumps this one inverted. Jumps 4 and 5 are steady. He then skips a lead change before fence 6. At the 'in and out' he jumps 'in' deep and has to invert to jump 'out.

Summary: A step jump with a skip lead change, and quite an upside down jump. However, there are no missed distances and he is relatively even. I move him to the top with a score of 77.

Number 87 - An appaloosa who looks fairly tense and edgy, which I note on my card with a 'T'. He runs to the first jump and clears it, but then has to half halt to the second. The third and fourth fences are another series of half halts. The rider is trying to slow down an aggressive canter. At fences 5 and 6 he settles down somewhat, but is still strong to the base. At the 'in and out' he is a disaster and runs off afterwards.

Summary: With the horrible 'in and out' and the running away he gets a low score of 50.

Number 33 - The last entry in this class is a brown horse with a tight martingale. He jumps the first jump fine and then counter canters the turn. Fence 2 is again fine, 3 and 4 are a little deep, with a hard rub in front at fence 5. Jump 6 is quite long and he cross canters the turn to the 'in and out', which are both satisfactory jumps.

Summary: The missing of two leads and a series of medium deviations gives this horse a score of 70.

Overall Comments

Here I have to go to my Desperato box to find the 5th, 6th and reserve placings. They really don't warrant ribbons. I don't have a solid winner, but I have followed the rules and here are the results. My second and third place horses both have great possibilities. They will easily come through and end up winning several classes as they work through their greenness.

Triple Warrant

Class 27 - *Amateur Owner Hunter*
(Average - Good Class)

Number 14 - The first horse in this class is a grey horse in a rubber bit. The rider picks up the pace nicely on the circle and arrives at the first jump a little long. He is a bit long at the second jump and has to open up early in the air. The third fence is good but there is a hard rub behind. He switches to his left lead at fence 4. At 5 there is another rub behind. I do not like to fault rubs heavily, but he has had two. He jumps slightly to the left at fence 6, is a little deep to the 'in' and a bit flat coming out of the combination.

Summary: He was long at fence 1 and opened up at 2, he had two rubs, and I did not like the flat jump at the 'in and out'. I keep him just out of the 80's with a 79.

Number 36 - A black horse with an exceptional canter. On his circle, however, he swishes his tail. Then he levels out and jumps a good first jump and steps over fence 2. He has a nice third fence and then has to increase stride to get down the line in good form at 4. At fence 5 he lands in a bit of a heap. The rider has to move him forward up the line to recover. This causes him to be a little long at 6. At the 'in and out' he jumps in well, but lands a bit shallow. The rider has to push him to get the line.

Summary: The worst jumping fault was landing in a heap after fence 5. The only real pace change was between 3 and 4; he stepped at two and was long at fence 6. I score him an 81.

Number 101 - A chestnut with white socks. As he enters I note he is high-headed. At the first jump he switches hard to the left lead. He switches to the left lead again at fence 2 and jumps flat, with a hard rub behind. Deep at 3, and head out around the turn (just a minor fault). Fences 4, 5, and 6 are good, but his head is still up. The rider interrupts this horse a lot. He brings him off the pace to the 'in and out'. Both elements are jumped inverted.

Summary: This wasn't a typical hunter round. The horse's head was up most of the way and his pace was uneven. He did not have

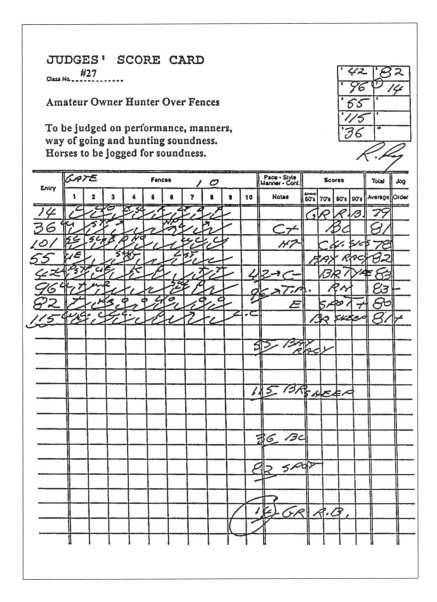

distance errors, but rider interruption spoiled the overall picture. I give him a 78.

Number 55 - A racy looking bay horse. He jumps fence 1 a little uneven and continues to 2 in an easy, relaxed way, and jumps it well. He swings his hind end slightly to the right over fence 3, straightens his hind end out and jumps fences 4 and 5 in good shape. Jump 6 comes up a little long and weak off the ground. He continues to the 'in and out' confidently, jumping both jumps in a positive and good style.

Summary: Two slight faults, uneven and swinging, right along with a long and slightly hesitant jump. I move him ahead of the black horse (#36), with a score of 82.

Number 42 - A typey brown horse is next on course. He has a four beat canter, so I note it on my card (C -). His head is up a bit as he approaches his first fence. He is a little deep and steps over it. He is uneven with his legs at the second jump. The rider is obviously lifting the horse's mouth off of the ground, which usually makes a horse 'steppy' and low with his back. He puts in a good effort at fences 3 and 4, but slows up in front of jump 5. He arrives a little close. He is good at 6 and very good through the 'in and out'.

Summary: I like him the best so far - he slowed up to the fifth fence and was 'steppy' once. He was uneven at the second jump, but he is better then #55 and scores an 83.

Number 96 - A roan horse with a tight martingale is the next amateur entry. He goes to the first jump (right up against the martingale) and then jumps up in the air rather than forward. He hits the front rail of the oxer at fence 2 from carrying his head a little too high. He then has three beautiful jumps in a row. He has a small swing to the left in front at jump 6, and then is deep to the 'in and out'.

Summary: This horse never leaves the martingale, except to jump. He is deep once, tilts to the left at fence 6 and has a front rub. This places him barely behind #42 with an 83 -.

Number 82 - A handsome well-marked Pinto ('spot') is next on course. He starts out with a good canter and has lots of pace to the first jump. They meet the jump right in stride and perform a good, solid jump. At the second jump, spot cuts down a little on the back rail and rubs it in front. Jumps 3 and 4 are similar, he opens up over the top a little bit. I feel that this is not because of lack of scope, but simply because he is too relaxed and uninterested. The fifth jump is long and reaching. Jump #6 is more together, but at the 'in and out' he opens up too early. He has a very even pace throughout the course, which I note with an E.

Summary: Cutting down once at fence 2, opening up too early several times, and a long distance gives him an 80 (but barely).

Number 115 - A brown horse with a sheepskin girth comes in and picks up a wrong lead. He is promptly corrected. The first jump is good, with a light rub in front. He inverts over the second jump and has a late lead change approaching the third fence, which he jumps well. The fourth jump is all right but fence 5 ends up a little tight. Fence #6 is passable, but he runs a little to the 'in and out'. He finishes with a late lead change on the closing circle.

Summary: I like him, and place him just ahead of entry #36 and just behind #55. He had two late lead changes, and was inverted and deep once. He also had a change of pace. The faults add up and leaves him with a score of 81+.

Overall Comments

No Desperatos sneak in for a prize in this class, which is good. A decent, close class with no major faults. My bookkeeping puts everyone in the proper order. A good winner with some '+' jumps, and all the others falling in closely behind. Slight errors keep them all in the average category, but at the same time quite adequate and all legitimate ribbon winners.

Kato

Class 32 - Open Working Hunter
(Exceptional Class)

Number 88 - The first horse is a chestnut horse with big ears. He jumps the first jump very well (I make note of this with an A+). The second jump is good, he is deep at the third, but easily makes the line and jumps fence #4 well. A little front rub at the 'in' and the 'out', but jumps clean. He switches his lead in front of fence #7 but doesn't shift away from the centre. He jumps the last fence well and has a late lead change at the end of the round.

Summary: A solid jumping round with good distances. A little close to fence #3, rubs one of the jumps, switches lead at #7 and has a late change at the end of the course. He scores an 86. Many good rounds may follow, but I feel he really deserves a good score.

Number 71 - Second to go is a liver chestnut horse. The first two jumps are great. He gets a little bit strong going to fence #3, and is fine to #4. At the 'in and out' he arrives somewhat closer than planned, but jumps it well. The last two jumps are well executed and he finishes his circle in a relaxed way and leaves the ring nicely.

Summary: He is placed just behind the first horse, with a score of 85. He was good, but somewhat strong.

Number 112 - This entry is a grey mare who carries her head slightly high. She touches the first jump, but jumps in good style. Jumps #2 and #3 are good. A little rough in the turn to fence #4. She is not happy about the bit and raises her head in protest (probably needs a martingale). She jumps fence #4 and the 'in and out' very well. Again, a little resistant to the contact in the turn, but jumps the last two fences in top form.

Summary: She easily goes to the top with a score of 87. However, the fussiness with her head could lower her placing.

Number 46 - This is a bay horse with a breastplate. He picks up a great canter early and goes right down to the first jump, handling it very well. The pace never varies from the beginning to the end. All

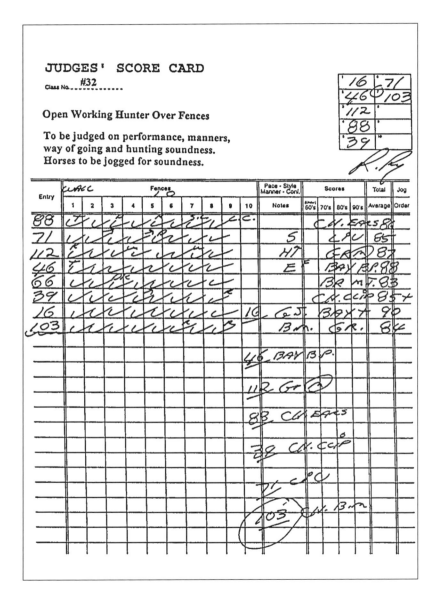

the jumps are quite good. The only impression I am left with is that he is a little flat, tight with his legs, but there is not a lot of roundness or scope.

Summary: The even, clean jumps all add up to an 88 score and a new class leader.

Number 66 - The fifth entry is a brown horse with a mud tail. The first two jumps are good. The third jump comes up a bit early and he doesn't handle it perfectly with his front end. The rest of the trip is good.

Summary: A good round, nice pace with good jumps. However, the one close distance and the questionable front end put him at the bottom with a total of 83. A good score, but in this company minor errors lower the overall score.

Number 39 - We are now looking at a clipped chestnut horse. As expected in this division, the first three jumps are good with nothing to note. At the 'in and out' he has to lengthen to jump out. It seems as if he hadn't focused on the 'out' until the last moment. The last three jumps are good, with a light rub behind on the last jump.

Summary: The obvious change at the 'in and out', and a light rub will put him ahead of #71 (a little strong), and behind #88 (close jump and a late change). He scores and 85+.

Number 16 - This is a beautiful looking (+) bay horse. As good as he looks, he moves and jumps beautifully as well. Nothing to note, just great jumps. I sit back and watch the round.

Summary: Such a superior jumper, a horse with a wonderful look and great movement. A score of 90 is a top score, and he receives it easily. An undisturbed, effortless and pleasing round.

Number 103 - The last entry is a grey horse with a lot of high movement. However, he is a great, scopey, effortless jumper. He jumps up so hard in front over the oxers that he ends up touching fence #2 behind.

Summary: The rub and rough movement gives him a score of 84. I do not hold the movement against him too hard.

Overall Comments

These are seasoned, experienced show horses. One would expect flawless performances, good jumps and high scores. It is great to judge such quality. Only minor errors separate the placings in this class.

Tour Guide

Questions & Answers

Q: **Is the colour of the horse a factor in a hunter class? If not, if you have two equal performances and one is grey and one is pinto, do you go with the more conventional colour?**

A: Firstly, there are no two rounds that are equal. The horse's colour makes absolutely no difference to the performance - the best one wins.

Q: In regards to manners in a pre-green or green class, my concern is what we are doing to our young horses to get them quiet (i.e. longeing and medicating). To me this should be a jumping contest that allows for a little expression of playfulness, not which is the quietest and most mannerly. How do you judge these classes?

A: The best jumper should win, but allow a young horse to be a young horse. He is not a seasoned children's or amateur horse, and will have his moments of acting slightly "childish". Imagine trying to keep a child from running or giggling.

Q: How much do you penalize a horse that plays on course?

A: This depends on the "playing". If a horse swishes his tail or pins his ears during a lead change, or simply throws his head, it may be slightly forgiven, depending on the quality of the class. Playing in the form of bucking or extensive shying is not acceptable behaviour, as danger comes into play.

Q: Do you have any comments regarding tack?

A: Tack needs to be fitted properly.

- no long, loose martingales (running martingales cannot be converted into standing martingales!)
- nosebands should be snug and 1" below cheekbone
- saddlepads should fit the saddle
- bit should be polished and tack should be clean
- bits must be of a legal type

Q: A hunter has a great jumping round, but at the end of the course misses a lead change. How do you place him?

A: If he had the best jumping round, then he is the winner. But if there is a close jumping round to his you need to place him second. Regardless, you will need to take note of the missed lead.

You Be The Judge

Q:When using the numerical scoring method, I have noticed that judges use duplicate scores. Can you explain this?

*A:*As a class progresses, a judge may give a duplicate score to a horse who is not in the running for a ribbon. There are only 10 numbers in the 80's, and often horses will need to be separated by a percentage. The judge will note this on his card.

Q:Do you like the numerical scoring system?

*A:*This system is good for the public, as it helps them to understand your order of placing.

Q:Do you count strides, and if so, how do you deal with adding and leaving out strides?

*A:*You can tell if the horse is making the set lines or not, whether he is short or long strided. Safety is the number one issue.

Q:During my back to back rounds, I have a great class the first round and a poor performance in the second. How does this influence the judge?

*A:*It shouldn't. However, some judges may second guess if the first round was actually as good as they first thought. An honest judge will pin the classes individually as he/she sees it. They are two separate classes.

Q:What is worse - a horse that misses his lead behind and cross canters, one that counter canters the turn, one that does a skip lead change, a late lead change, or trotting for the lead change?

*A:*We have 5 possible placings here, as follows, from best scenario to worst:

1/ Late lead change

2/ Skip lead change

3/ Cross cantering

4/ Counter cantering

5/ Trotting the change

*Q:*A horse jogs into the ring for the ribbon presentation, gets loose and runs or jumps out of the ring. Do you still pin him?

A: As the horse had already jogged, he has filled the requirements for the class. Had he not jogged yet, and left the ring, he would be disqualified for leaving the show ring.

Q: If my horse is unbraided for whatever reason, should I tell the judge why, so as not to offend him?

A: Often the ringmaster will pass us a note to this effect from a competitor. It is usually fine, and the horse will be judged equally. It is respectful of the division, horse show and judge, however, to turn out your horse as well as possible, and to date braiding is expected. Low hunters and schooling classes are acceptable classes in which to show an unbraided horse.

Q: After you call the jog order, do you indicate where you would like the horses to jog?

A: Good question. The judge should look at the ring and tell ingate personnel or announcer which way to jog, so that you can see the horses properly from the side. Also, it is important that the riders jog their horses right to the end of the ring so that there isn't a pile-up of horses at the end of the line, most of which you haven't been able to see jog.

Q: If a rider heads to the wrong first jump, circles away and goes to the correct first jump, how do you judge this rider?

A: This is a major fault. Crossing the track is treated as a refusal. Sorry! The judging starts the moment the horse enters the ring.

Q: Will using artificial aids such as spurs, standing martingales or carrying a crop affect the judge's opinion of the overall round?

A: Not if you are focusing on the horse and the round. As long as the aids are not abused and the performance is there, these aids are not offensive.

You Be The Judge

Q: Do you want a horse in a frame coming into a line of fences?

A: No. Just let go and allow horse to travel in balance. An overly framed horse looks forced and unpleasant.

Q: When do you eliminate a horse and rider?

A: When a rider has had three refusals, has fallen or is showing abusive behaviour in the ring.

Q: I have heard hunter judging referred to as a "MacDonald's" system, insofar as you know exactly what you are getting - no surprises!

A: What people are saying is that it appears to always be the same winners. However, the gate is always open for a new winner. Often the seasoned and consistent riders sitting on quality horses are in the ribbons regularly, but they can have off days and can be beaten. The class is not pinned until it is over!

Q: Have you ever excused a rider for showing their horse a jump in the ring? How do you determine "showing the fence"?

A: Riders should be excused for breaking this rule. If the horse stops moving forward, is standing too close the jump, or has his nose on it, it constitutes "showing the fence". This is a judgment call, but quite an easy one to make.

Q: When a horse enters the ring with the illegal equipment, (i.e. boots or bandages), when do you eliminate him?

A: First, call the steward in order to make sure that certain equipment has been allowed (due to bad weather). If the equipment is still illegal, let the horse complete (which it has probably done by the time you sort this out) but make sure you do not give him a score.

Q: If you do not like a hunter or equitation course, do you say anything to the course designer or show management?

A: Only if the course is dangerous for the competitors. Your job is to judge, not course design. If asked, you could suggest moving a distance, etc. Often the course designer will ask your opinion as the first class of the day is going, as you watch the lines more intently than he does, and at this time you may have suggestions as to the footing problems or distances.

Q: **When a horse finishes the course, and the rider puts the horse's nose in a fence or walks up to one and shows him the fence, what do you do?**

A: The horse is judged until he has walked out of the ingate. This example would constitute elimination.

Stetson

Q: **Have you ever missed seeing a jump while judging? If so how do you handle the situation?**

A: Honestly, this has happened to most judges at some point. In watching all the rest of the course the judge will have a good idea how they ride or jump, and they must give the rider the benefit of doubt for the jump they didn't see.

You Be The Judge

Q: **What happens when a horse steps into the ring wearing boots or a tail bandage, someone points this out to the rider, and they leave the ring to get properly attended to (or the groom enters the ring to undress the horse)?**

A: Sorry! You are being judged from the moment you enter the ring. Often you are forgiven, but it is completely left up to the judge's discretion, and you may be eliminated. So beware and be prepared!

Q: **When there is a dotted line for the start of a course, which means you cannot travel beyond it to start your course, does that also apply to when you have completed your course and may want to go back to a trouble spot?**

A: Yes, it does. Elimination is the reward!

Q: **When judging hunters, how much does the rider count?**

A: Try to take your focus off of the rider. The ride should be invisible and not distract the judge's eye from the horse's performance.

Q: **Can a hunter judge act a course designer at the same show? If so, do you think it is a good idea or too much to handle?**

A: Yes, the judge can be the course designer at the same show. This works at smaller shows, but at large shows where there are more than one hunter ring the individual will find it difficult to focus on both jobs and not be able to do either well. You should accept one job or the other.

Q: **In a handy hunter class how do you place the horse that makes tight turns and inside options, but gets close to some jumps or doesn't jump as well as the horse that goes wide and safely?**

A: "Handy" means promptness and accuracy in what was trappy hunting territory. You should go with the one that makes the effort to be handy, as that is what is required, even if they get out-jumped by another horse. You must, naturally, still keep in mind that an unsafe jumper is still at the bottom of the list.

Q: How much does turnout have to do with the end results?

A: Turnout is all part of the presentation and the best look definitely breaks a tie.

Q: As a rider is travelling towards the first fence something goes wrong (i.e. horse plays, switches lead, etc.) and the rider circles as if they are making their courtesy circle. How do you judge them?

A: In reality, the rider is allowed a courtesy circle before attempting the first fence, but in this instance, this is not courteous and would be scored as such.

Q: What is the best way to come into a hunter class - walking, trotting or cantering?

A: Whatever works the best for your horse. Show off your horse's best gait. Walk him to relax, or canter to get going.

Q: A rider enters the ring without a number on. The ingate personnel indicates this and the rider leaves the ring to put his number on, and re-enters the ring. What do you do?

A: Same case scenario as any other reason the horse leaves the ring. He won't be judged. Once you step in the ring you are being judged.

Q: When you give a standby list, is it in order of preference, and should you have that point announced?

A: It is wise to announce at the end of the list that it is in no particular order. You may need the option to make changes to your order. After the first list is given, you will add to and delete and from this list in order to update it, and the numbers added are just added to the bottom of the list. Therefore, by the end of the class, there is no possibility of the standby to be in order.

You Be The Judge

Q: **What about the hunter that goes around really well, but stares out of the ring at all the surroundings?**

A: Ponies are notorious for this. You need not hold it against them if they don't change their pace or spook as a result of it. It just shows they are interested and not the most offensive of faults. However, it is the ideal for the horse or pony to travel in a straight line, slightly bent to the inside around the turns.

Q: **In a broken line, would you penalize a horse or pony for adding a stride?**

A: We live by the strides, and God forbid someone should add or leave out a stride in a line. However, if in a broken line the rider safely and nicely adds a stride in a line while putting in a beautiful trip, he can be the winner on my card.

Q: **How do you feel about judging "back to back to back" trips (triple rounds)?**

A: Management often asks the judge to judge three classes at once. This is popular with trainers and riders, as they can complete one horse's show day over fences quickly and move to another ring, but it does make the class seem mechanical and takes away from the presentation. It takes the drama away from the class - who remembers how which horse went in which class? On top of being difficult to run three cards at once, it makes for a dull competition.

Q: **What does a judge do with regards to a horse that makes a noise in a hunter class?**

A: This is considered an unsoundness and therefore the horse is eliminated. Often outdoors you cannot hear him or you are enclosed in a vehicle and you can't hear. Under these circumstances, the horse gets away with it. Indoors it is hard to mask. When you hear a noise you need to follow the rules - the horse is eliminated for an unsoundness.

Q: **When judging hunters do you find it difficult to not pay**

attention to an overly active rider, and does this hinder the performance?

A: You be the judge of that! You must focus on the horse's performance. This is your job, and you don't want to miss anything because you were watching the rider's performance instead.

Q: **In a short stirrup hunter class, do you look for suitability?**

A: Yes. You want to see a good match for the rider as it is the very beginning stage, and a good fit not only looks good but would be more comfortable. Small riders on big horses don't look right and likewise, big riders on small ponies don't work.

Q: **When you jog back to back classes and only have a few entries, do you have to jog them twice or is once enough?**

A: You must jog each class separately! To expedite things you might jog them into the ring for the first class and the back towards the ingate for the second class in the new order.

Q: **How do you feel about "no jackets" in the hunter ring on a very warm day?**

A: This is a show management decision. I am fine with it as I am judging the horse, not the rider, and rest assured that if it is that warm out, my jacket is off too!

Q: **Has a judge ever given a score of 100 to a hunter?**

A: As a matter of fact, USEF judge Leo Conroy gave a perfect score to Rick Fancher and 'Asczar' at the 1997 Capital Challenge Horse Show in Maryland. To Leo, this round was perfection. The second judge gave Rick a 95. Different angles, different horse show.

Q: **What is the highest score you ever gave?**

A: I gave "Roxdene" a score of 98 at the Washington International Horse Show. In hindsight, I could probably have given her a 100. My judge's card had no other notations on it than perfect jumps!

You Be The Judge

Q: **With your short descriptions for recall in a hunter class, how many, as an example, bay horses could you differentiate between in a single class?**

A: A list of the possibilities:

Bay PL (plain)	Bay GM (good mover)
Bay M (mare)	Bay Fat
Bay Type (typey)	Bay M (mouthy)
Bay Racy	Bay Sheep (sheepskin girth)
Bay Sks (front socks)	Bay Pad (large pad)
Bay T.M. (tight martingale)	Bay Crest (cresty)
Bay Star	Bay M.T. (mudtail)
Bay Snorty	Bay ↑ (big)
Bay ←→ (long back)	Bay Ears
Bay ↓ (small)	Bay Tail (full tail)
Bay Sks (socks)	Bay O/Br (no braids)
Bay T.O. (turn out)	Bay + (very nice)
Bay Sk (sock-front)	Bay)((Hanovarian)
Bay BL (blaze)	Bay Tongue (tongue out)
Bay Rom (roman nose)	Bay BL (big blaze)
Bay Tack (new tack)	Bay Plm (pelham)
Bay Snip	Bay R.B. (rubber bit)
Bay D-B (D bit)	Bay Face (white face)
Bay K (klunky)	Bay D.P. (dapple)
Bay R.M. (running martingale)	Bay P.G. (pony gaited)
Bay Sks (sock-behind)	Bay - (bad)
Bay Clip (clipped bay)	

Q: **How do you feel about a horse coming into the ring covered in sweat?**

A: Firstly I judge the round, and they often win, so whatever it takes to get them ready. I cannot penalize a horse for being sweaty if it has a good round. It would be the same as not using him because he is a bad mover or is unattractive, all of which you cannot do.

Stocking Stuffer

Q: **In a hunter class, are you allowed to eliminate a competitor after a major fault? I have seen this happen when a show runs late - a judge asks a rider to leave the ring if he feels they are not in contention for a ribbon.**

A: I have never done this. The competitor has paid an entry fee, and may compete until they are eliminated through the rules, i.e. fall, three refusals.

Q: **Do you feel badly when someone has gone well and doesn't place as a result of large classes and top competition?**

A: You feel badly if they have had a great trip and are beaten by a fine margin. This is one reason numerical scoring being announced is great for the competitor, as they see how very close they were in points, which is encouraging.

You Be The Judge

Q: **How receptive are you to opening up cards and keeping track of as many as six classes at once?**

A: It is not preferable, especially with large classes. The ingate person is crucial to make it work, so that you know right at the start where each competitor goes on which card. There is nothing worse than finding out you judged the horse on the wrong card after the fact. Holding open a number of cards is a recipe for inaccurate judging, and therefore not the best scenario.

Q: **When horses jog back into the ring, do you let them take their own track or do you designate a route?**

A: Usually the riders figure out the best route, but if there are obstacles in the way, or a group of young riders, it is best to ask the ingate to instruct them on where to jog. You must make sure they are not jogging straight at you!

Q: **Do you agree or disagree with jogging?**

A: I absolutely agree. Horses need to be serviceably sound to show. I could, however, forego jogging in the unrated classes, as horses could then be put away right after they show.

Q: **If a rider loses a stirrup in a hunter class, how does it affect their placing?**

A: I am judging the horse, and if he is not disturbed by the lost stirrup and goes well I pin the round accordingly, ignoring the lost stirrup. If I focused on the rider I would lose sight of how the horse is going and jumping.

Q: **With the large amount of warmbloods showing in North America these days, has the picture of the ideal hunter changed?**

A: An interesting question, as most assuredly the look of the hunters has changed a lot with so many European breeds showing in the hunter ring.

As a judge you must look for the same good jump, movement and evenness. As far as looks go, you sometimes don't get it all in one package, and whatever horse goes the best on that day is the winner.

Ideally, you are looking for the best looking horse as well, but the European horses have definitely found their way into the hunter ring, and our thoroughbred "picture" hunter has been subjected to some alterations. The best performance both on the flat and over fences needs to prevail.

Q: **Is it possible to have a small hunter division in Canada? Smaller horses are usually shown in junior hunter classes, and adult riders often show horses which are too large for them. Smaller horses have to work harder to make the distances set for medium and larger horses, and as a result are not as competitive.**

A: There are certain areas that have just small hunter divisions and most all of the USA shows have small hunter divisions. They actually jump the same heights and distances as the large horses. We in Canada just do not as a rule have enough entries to split the division, therefore all sizes compete together. The small horses are judged the same and are very competitive.

Q: **A horse canters into the ring, halts, walks around and then picks up a canter and goes to the first jump. Is this considered a false start?**

A: I don't like it. It is more of a "jumper" type of entrance, so I would take note of this type of start. It is definitely not a smooth, attractive hunter start.

Q: **At the end of your course, can you pull up to avoid a lead change, or come right back to a trot before the end of the ring, or if the ring is large enough is it possible to circle in the other direction if you landed on that lead?**

A: This scenario would indicate to me that you have a lead change problem, and that you will attempt anything to avoid a bad ending. I would prefer a nice circle, cantering on the correct lead, but if it is all done smoothly I would not penalize it.

You Be The Judge

Q: **If a horse or pony enters the ring and completes his round wearing a tail wrap, is he eliminated?**

A: Yes. The same rule applies to polo wraps and boots. Be sure to check all ends before entering the ring.

Q: **In a two round class, i.e. hunter classic, a rider is injured during the round and cannot return to ride the second round. Is it possible to substitute riders so that the horse can compete in the second round?**

A: No, it is not possible to substitute riders. The class, although over two rounds, is considered to be one class, and the same horse/rider combination must complete both phases.

Q: **If a horse comes into an over fence class in a non-rated division or a class that does not jog, and trots lame in front of you, can you eliminate it or simply not judge it?**

A: You are the judge and you have the choice of whether or not to judge it. Personally, I choose not to, and if asked I would say that I felt that he did not look sound at the trot, and that is a part of the performance that I have to take into consideration.

Q: **Do you allow a courtesy jump after a horse is eliminated?**

A: No. The rule reads that three refusals or a fall of horse or rider all constitute elimination. You must leave the ring. It is not proper to ask the judge for a courtesy fence - the judge needs to adhere to the rules as well.

Q: **How do you handle a situation such as a horse spooking or bolting as a result of some unforseen circumstances e.g. a loud noise outside of the ring?**

A: I allow as much as I possibly can. If it occurs in the ends of the ring or at the end or beginning of the course, I virtually ignore it. When it happens in a line or right in front of a jump, therefore altering the distance, I have to take that into consideration. Unfortunately, it often results in being eliminated from the placings. Most people attribute this to horse showing and look to the next class or show. I have been asked if the horse can go again and the answer is no! It is something we all have to deal with, as unfortunate as it is.

Q: What do you think about training a hunter in the ring while the show is in progress?

A: Once a competitor enters a recognized show, we would hope that their horses are prepared because their homework has been done at home. Unfortunately, horses sometimes find a way of making us look unprepared and often it is necessary to reprimand a horse in the ring. It is crucial, however, that all discipline be done in a professional manner without abuse.

Tight horse show schedules do not allow time for 'training' in the ring, so if you have a more serious problem it should be taken to the warm up ring, not dealt with in the show ring. I might add that training a hunter in the ring often leaves the judge with a poor impression of horse and rider.

Q: Do you penalize a horse or rider when they pick up the wrong lead at the beginning of the course?

A: As a general rule, at an 'A' recognized show a rider in an equitation class or a horse showing in a hunter class should be penalized for this. However, in the short stirrup, pony, children's or adult amateur hunter classes, the individual situation should be taken into account.

The exception to the rule would be when judging at a lower rated show in any type of classes where a mistake of starting on the incorrect lead may be the lesser or two evils. These exceptions assume that the adjustment to the correct lead is made promptly.

Q: When do you stop judging?

A: Judge all of the class. It is important to always be courteous. Do not get up and walk away or start talking to someone. Remember, someone is always watching and they have no idea that their child or customer is not in contention for a ribbon.

You Be The Judge

Q: **How do you deal with long waits?**

A: When judging, reality is that there are going to be breaks in the ring with no horses, whether they are due to trainer or rider conflicts. The judge needs to be very patient. Take advantage of these breaks by looking over your cards, or give yourself a moment to rest your eyes. While these breaks are sometimes unavoidable, the trainers and exhibitors need to pay special attention to the day's schedule and try their best to be efficient and organized. 'Over dressing' a horse at the in-gate (oiling hooves, polishing boots, etc.) may try a judge's patience after a day of long breaks.

Q: **How do you handle an irate exhibitor or trainer?**

A: First, assess the situation - do they truly desire to know what they should or should not have done to improve their performance, or are they just looking for a person to vent their anger at? If the latter, I feel it is most likely counter-productive to speak with them, at least not until they become rational. Let me point out that a judge has absolutely no obligation to speak with the competitor, unless they choose to. The judge's decision is final.

If you choose to speak with the individual, it is imperative that you have your judge's cards with you. As the rules state, a steward must be present, who will oversee the discussion. You should speak with them at an appropriate time, such as at the conclusion of the day (sometimes the problem in question solves itself after a cooling off period has elapsed). It is important that you never discuss the round of another exhibitor - if asked, I would terminate the conversation at that point. I also feel that judge's cards should not be posted.

Q: **What is the proper release in a hunter class?**

A: The best answer to the question of whether or not a release is correct is the quality of the horse's jump. Whether you are talking about judging hunters or equitation, the jump is always the most important piece. It is possible to have poor jumping with a good and accurate release, but not possible to have a good jump if the release is incorrect. Jumping with the head up, legs down or hitting the jump either in front or behind is often directly related to the rider, and specifically to the rider's hands and release. While these faults are related mostly to not enough release, there are another host of jumping faults relative to too much release - a quick horse, hitting the jumps and flat jumping, just to name a few.

In hunter classes the release itself is not specifically judged. If the release is too distracting, or causes specific jumping faults the results from the poor release will be penalized. In equitation classes the release itself, in addition to the result, are judged and penalized if done poorly. In all three jumping disciples the jump and its quality are the primary concern. Perfecting a release that will allow your horse to make a beautiful jump, with a relaxed top line, long and low head and neck and accurate use of his legs will stand you in good stead whatever division you are competing in. Remember that when you are showing horses your job as the rider is to become invisible and show your horse off to his best advantage. This sport is and always has been about the horse and the jump. Perfecting just the right release will help you as a rider to do your job.

Geoff Teall, Chairman of the Trainer's Committee

Wellington, Florida

Q:**Something outside of the ring is spooking the horse e.g. a piece of brush, jumps, signs, etc. Can you move it before the end of a class?**

A:Yes, if it is outside of the ring.

Q:**If a horse comes into the ring, picks up a canter and spooks or breaks stride, then picks up the canter and goes around well, is he penalized for the break at the beginning?**

A:Yes. This is a major fault as the horse needs to keep cantering. A break of stride is a major fault, as is trotting during the course.

You Be The Judge

Q: **Can the judge change his/her mind after a score is announced?**

A: Before the end of the class the score can be changed, as long as it is announced.

Q: **How do you feel about the long walks into the ring before the rider starts their course?**

A: Some horses need that time to stay relaxed. Others do it when it is not needed, simply because it is somewhat of a trend. I cannot complain, as it is the rider's choice how they start their course.

Q: **In back to back classes a horse goes well in the first class, and then in the second class has a mishap and gets hurt. The horse cannot jog. What happens for his placing in the first class?**

A: An unfortunate situation, but if the horse doesn't jog, it cannot get pinned.

Q: **During a large pony hunter over fences class, the first pony goes around and adds a stride in each line, yet has a wonderful trip. None of the other ponies in this class are as good. Should the adding pony be your winner or should your average ponies getting down the lines win over him?**

A: The average ponies are the winners. The pony that jumps well needs to step it up and make the distances in order to win.

Q: **In the Short Stirrup hunter division, a pony is so quiet that the entire audience has to cluck at this pony to keep it going. It seems as if the child is only sitting on the pony for decoration. Should the pony get credit for doing the course anyway?**

A: The pony responded to your voices of encouragement, so I believe the pony should get credit for a job well done. I probably was clucking along with the audience. It is not proper, however, for what is termed "outside interference" to play a part in a round, and that has to be considered.

Q: **The entire day of the horse show it has been raining. A Regular Working hunter gallops down the first line and jumps a water puddle which causes him to take a stride out of the line, yet all of the fences jumped during the round are beautiful. Do you drop the horse out of your winning order even though it had one of the nicest trips?**

A: If the horse left out a stride, he must have been long to the second jump, as the distances are fairly open in a Regular Working hunter class, and that would affect the placing. You could still give him a ribbon just because the other good rounds that did the right number of strides, as long as they jumped well.

Q: **When jogging a class of Amateur Owner hunters a horse stumbles and trots five steps unevenly, and then is sound again. How would you call it?**

A: If the horse looks sound after recovering from the stumble, he is considered sound. The difficult situation would be if he jogs around, then stumbles and comes up lame for the second jog in back to back classes. You would then have to call it as is, even though it is an awkward situation.

Q: **During An Adult Amateur Hunter Under Saddle class, one of the exhibitors bumps into another exhibitor's horse and causes the horse to break out of the canter and into the trot. Should this cost the exhibitor the win because his/her horse was treated unfairly?**

A: No. This was in no way their fault, and if quickly corrected it should not affect the placing.

Q: **During a hunter class, a very good moving, good jumping horse hits a fence so hard that the rail jumps up and lands at the lip of the jump cup. All the other fences of his round are flawless. The other horses in the class do not jump or move as well. How do you place them?**

A: Sorry. This is a major fault and will affect his placing accordingly.

You Be The Judge

Q: **If a horse makes a noise, or in your opinion in unsound of wind, how do you deal with it?**

A: Simply do not call him back for a placing, as it is an unsoundness, and is therefore not eligible for a ribbon. This is a rule and, this unsoundness is treated the same as any. Even if there are not enough horses to cover all the ribbon placings, this horse should not be included in the line up.

Q: **In a hunter class, I know that the horse is judged, but any tips on the rider and how they should present themselves to enhance their performance?**

A: While the rider himself is not judged, he can do a lot to present his horse favourably to the judges. In fact, it is up to the rider to show his horse to the ultimate advantage. By appearing relaxed and demonstrating as little motion as possible, the rider shows how easy and enjoyable his horse is to ride. Dressed in the traditional hunt field attire - conservative, clean and well-fitting, with gloves and tail, polished boots - a well turned out rider reflects his own good form on his mount.

Q: **Can you comment on what you expect from the Hunter Round?**

A: Hunter judging begins the moment the horse and rider enter the ring and lasts until they leave. The rider's opening circle, executed before he attempts the first jump, gives the judges their first impression of the horse, for better or worse. Here, more than anywhere, the careful turnout of horse and rider is critical. Nothing tops a pretty horse that moves well and has a relaxed, confident manner.

First impression quickly gives way, however, to the hunter's real job - the jump. The judges look for consistent jumping efforts, each jump cleared confidently, easily, and in good style. They award top marks to the hunter that maintains his pace from beginning to end, and penalize any sudden changes. Heavy penalties accrue as well to any horse that hits, knocks down, or refuses a jump. In addition, the horse is expected to stay straight in the middle of each jump and go easily through the corners. The most beautiful horse with the smoothest round and the best jumping efforts will win the class on that judged round.

Q:Could you possibly explain to me being a parent who pays the bills, what the judge is looking for and help me to better understand this hunter world?

*A:*In hunter competitions, the horse is the centre of the judges' attention. Judges look for the horse in each class that comes closest to the ideal mount for a ride to hounds. The perfect hunter is beautiful, with a small head and a correct and proportionate conformation. But the judges look for more than simply the best raw material.

The horse should be well-turned-out, completely clean, with a healthy shine to his coat. His mane should be dressed in small, evenly-spaced braids, and his tail braided and well combed. Essential as well to the overall effect is clean and supply tack (saddle and bridle), set off by well-polished metal (bits, stirrups, and incidentals).

A quality presentation also involves the horse's movement and carriage. Because long days in the hunt field require a good reserve of energy, the ideal hunter has as little action in his legs as possible. A relaxed horse - light and graceful across the ground, with a long, low neck and a good expression (ears forward and alert) - ranks as the most desirable.

Probably the most important criterion is jumping style. The horse should jump with his front legs folded high and evenly, his head and neck stretched out and down to insure a well-balanced jump. For high marks, the judges expect the horse's body and legs to remain straight as he executes a perfectly-centered jump. Because a top hunter does not appear nervous or difficult to handle, his expression should say that he enjoys his job (ears forward), and his jumping should appear effortless.

Mistral

Numerical Score Sheets

- Bring copies of your own score sheets to show where numerical scoring is expected
- These sheets keep you from duplicating your scores, and are a quick and handy reference
- Provides an instant standby order and jog order
- Shows the cutoffs so that you can provide that information to the in-gate personnel
- Unclutters your judge's card

ENTRY #	COMMENTS		ENTRY #	COMMENTS		ENTRY #	COMMENTS	
		95			79			70.50
		94.5			78.75			70.25
		94			78.50			70
		93.5			78.25			69.75
		93			78			69.50
		92.5			77.75			69.25
		92			77.50			69
		91.5			77.25			68.75
		91			77			68.50
		90.5			76.75			68.25
		90			76.50			68
		89.5			76.25			67.75
		89			76			67.50
		88.5			75.75			67.25
		88			75.50			67
		87.5			75.25			66.75
		87			75			66.50
		86.5			74.75			66.25
		86			74.50			66
		85.5			74.25			65.75
		85			74			65.50
		84.5			73.75			65.25
		84			73.50			65
		83.5			73.25			
		83			73			
		82.5			72.75			
		82			72.50			
		81.5			72.25			
		81			72			
		80.5			71.75			
		80			71.50			
		79.75			71.25			
		79.50			71			
		79.25			70.75			

Summary

One of the most difficult things about judging is not having the best horse win. A horse of lesser quality can have a winning round. Try not to dwell and deliberate too long and don't complicate and clutter. Simple, prompt, easy referral and good bookkeeping will make it work.

Really good classes can be difficult to judge as the horses can all go well. It could be their best round ever and they will not even win a ribbon. Just one error, even a slight one, could mean being out of the ribbons in good classes. The judge, through proper bookkeeping and recall, places the rounds accordingly. A minor fault such as having to move up a line, a late lead change, or being a little close to the jump can become critical. The opposite also applies in a bad class. Missing a lead or adding a stride could be considered a minor fault when compared to a bad or dangerous jumper.

Most important of all, never lose sight of a really good jumper. A little playfulness, arriving a little deep, switching a lead or any other minor faults can be underscored when comparing a quality horse to lesser ones.

Scoring the eight fences is not the only part of the judge's job. The quality and correctness of the horse (and rider) are of prime importance. What is the horse's carriage and balance like? Does he 'stroke' over the ground or does he move high, wearing himself out? Is he a 'living' horse or a 'zombie' that mechanically steps through the motions? Is this an athletic horse with something to spare or a 'splinter-bellied' one just making it over the fences?

You would much rather own, ride or pin a good horse who might play on a turn or change his lead galloping to a fence than a horse who mechanically has a better round but is not a better horse. Jumping ability, way of moving and rideability (manners) are major concerns when judging. Soundness (or lack of it) shows up in these factors if you are sharp.

Try judging a class for fun now that you have the format. We are sure that you will be more sympathetic, tolerant and understanding.

Chapter Two

Hunters Under Saddle

Just Cruising

Introduction

This chapter deals with the movement of the horse - ideal movement - deviations from, and how and what the judge looks for. An ideal mover is one that carries himself in good balance, moves well from the shoulder, with as little knee action as possible. His hocks are well under him, he appears alert but not sharp, quiet but not asleep and can be ridden on a light contact.

Judging An Under Saddle Class

The Equine Canada Rule Book states,"Hunters under saddle are to be shown at a walk, trot and canter both ways of the ring. At least 8 horses, if available, may be asked to hand gallop but never more than eight at one time (pre-green and green horses not to gallop). Light contact with the horse's mouth is permissible...". Completely loose reins used to be the style. However, now it is suggested that some contact be maintained with your horse.

I prefer to see a rounder frame. A horse should be slightly flexed at the walk (his nose pulled in just a little bit). He should be somewhat more flexed at the trot. The extra flexion will help show off really good shoulder movement. At the canter, the flexion should be back to where it was at the walk. The neck should be slightly above the horizontal at all gaits.

Focus on and compare your top horses. If you have a large class, put your good horses in the centre of the ring after they complete the first direction. This allows you to watch the remaining ones to be sure you have not missed anyone. This way you can view your best horses at one time and draw a true comparison.

The Under Saddle class is always important. If you feel there is not enough room for the class to run efficiently and safely, ask that the jumps be moved. This avoids collisions and gives all a fair chance. Crowding can make for bad classes and can encourage ear pinning and kicking. Young riders and horses cannot cope with small narrow lanes.

For best viewing, the outside of the ring is the best place to sit.

This way you will see the whole picture, not missing any 'events' happening behind your back. It is always a good idea to ask the announcer to have the riders turn their numbers slightly to the outside, to enable you to view them quickly and easily.

Try not to penalize horses for minor errors if extraneous circumstances are the apparent cause. For example, don't lose your winner if it drops its lead as a result of being kicked by an unruly horse. Do not penalize the horse that shies from someone kicking or shaking a chair in the spectator's tent beside the ring.

If the class is a Pre-green or Children's class, you can often allow for late transitions and even a quickly corrected lead with a top mover. When asking for a hand gallop you are looking for more than an extended canter. There should be a long, forward stride that covers the ground but the horses should not be running away. After the hand gallop, asking for a trot is a good choice. It is an opportunity to see if the horses can settle and relax after the gallop. When asked for a halt, they should stand squarely and be relaxed, with no movement. If you ask for a trot after the canter, look for an easy and relaxed trot.

If you are comfortable with your winners, don't overwork the class. It is advisable not to take too long at each gait or you may lose your winners. An Under Saddle class should not take more that 10 - 15 minutes to run. However, do more if you feel you need to.

Nevada

Major Faults *(rated from the worst to least severe):*

* Fall of horse or rider
* Any unsoundness, even if they look fine in the other direction
* Wrong leads
* Strong or running away
* Kicking or bucking
* Switching leads or cross-cantering
* Very poor mover
* Tense
* Jogging, not walking
* Sour look or pinning ears excessively

Minor Faults *(rated from the worst to least severe):*

* Flipping or tossing of the head. Note whether or not it is a resistance to contact or merely a fly. Does he fuss and then settle? If the horse is trying to resist contact it is more serious.
* High headed.
* Overbent, too much flexion.
* Swishing of the tail.
* Over extending, or rushing the trot in an attempt to make it extended. This can make a very nice mover look rough and hard. It can also put him on his forehand and out of balance.
* Under or barely trotting. The horse appears to be barely capable of trotting and is sluggish.
* Horse's nose stuck way out in front of him.
* Circling the judge. It is offensive when a rider tries to over show his horse by circling endlessly in front of the judge.
* Ears back. (Half-mast is allowable. Horses can't always be alert. I call these easy ears. If a horse is relaxed and a good mover he can win a top prize.)

Positive Features - *What You Are Looking For:*

* Moving straight, even, freely and in a balanced frame.
* Pleasant horse, alert with his ears forward.
* Light contact, not floating reins.
* Long effortless stride.
* Clean and well fitted tack.
* Horse well groomed, turned out and braided.
* Noseband and browband snug so that nothing flops around.
* Smooth transitions. Not too prompt, no rocket departures and no abrupt downward transitions.
* Horses should be obedient, alert, responsive and move freely.

Trilogy

"You Are Now Being Judged"

We would like to acknowledge Don Stuart's expertise and contribution towards judging an Under Saddle class.

"ALL WALK PLEASE"

The walk should be long and relaxed. Riders rarely perfect or execute the walk correctly. Take the time, slow down, and watch - it is a required gait!

"TROT PLEASE"

Don't rush into the trot as soon as it is called for. I see a lot of competitors who blast their horses into a trot. They will appear strung out and rough looking. A few strides like that and you can ruin the overall impression you have made on the judge. A rider who throws himself out of the saddle is distracting to watch.

Overextending - the rider looks as if he's out of control or struggling to keep up with his horse as he posts. The free-flowing, balanced look is gone because he has asked for too much extension. The other rushing look comes from the rider pushing too hard. Instead of overextending, the horse trots faster and faster to keep his already precarious balance. This can give the impression of a shorter stride.

"ALL CANTER"

Canter very quietly (don't hurry) - you want your horse to start off quietly, collected and round. When judging, I occasionally see people pick up the wrong lead. This error can be exaggerated by the rider trying to get a flying change when a simple change will do (and usually works).

I like to see a rider canter in the three-point. A rider in a two-point gives the impression of having a horse that's too fresh.

A good canter is relaxed with the horse slightly flexed, the stride slightly extended and in good rhythm. It is a definite three-beat gait. A four-beat canter usually means the horse is strung out and travelling too slowly.

I like to see a horse that looks 'through the bridle' - alert, ears up, paying attention, his neck a little above the horizontal, his head position steady.

When a transition back to the walk is called, I like to see a gradual transition.

"REVERSE AND WALK"

If not carefully watched riders may use a small turn to help re-establish flexion and responsiveness. They should do a large circle so that they are away from the others. This will allow for better viewing.

"LINE UP IN CENTRE RING"

If a horse trots really well a rider might make one last pass in front of the judge before lining up. If a horse is nervous and won't stand, riders often walk in a small circle.

Further Testing

If you are comfortable with your winners, don't overwork the class. However, do more if you feel you need to. As mentioned above, when asking for a hand gallop you are looking for more than an extended canter. There should be a long, forward stride that covers the ground. The horses should not be running away. After the hand gallop, a good choice is to ask for a trot. This will enable you to see if the horses are settled and relaxed after the gallop. You could also ask for the trot after the canter, looking for an easy and relaxed trot.

The Judge's Card

Avoid excessive writing. Watch attentively so that you can draw a true comparison. It is good practice to immediately write down the number of the first horse that strikes you as a potential ribbon winner. This number then becomes your frame of reference. You then add the other numbers above or below it.

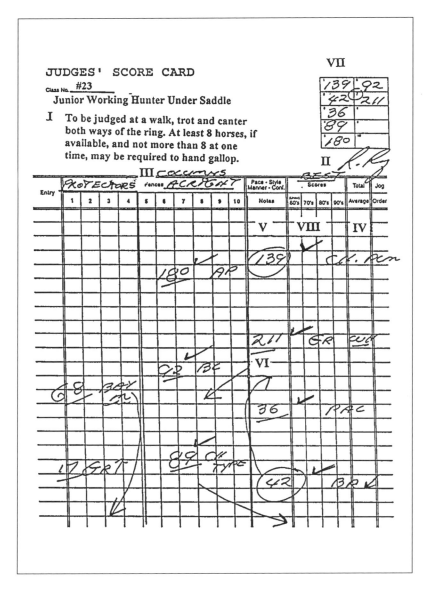

I   Class specifications and description of class

II   Sign the card

III   Columns

Protectors	**Alright**	**Best**
Emergency numbers! In poor classes you have these for all the tail end ribbons (or if you lose a good winner because of a mistake).	These are OK hacks with good manners. They often get ribbons. (You sometimes move them over to the best column).	These are the real ribbon winners and you hope to have them in this column.

IV   Again, use a short abbreviated description to go beside each number so you instantly know which horses you are comparing and how you are placing them.

V   I circle the top performers to show I am totally satisfied with their performance. Only mark the top ones as the rest have moved around or are not in the best column.

VI   ← Losing ground moving out of the best or all right column
            ↓ Going below their column partners
            → Gaining ground - moving into the all right column or best column
            ↑ Going ahead of their column partner

VII   Results. As you fill in the numbers, look up and down the line to be sure that you have written down the correct numbers and to see if the horses are all standing in a mannerly fashion

VIII   Check mark (✓). This simple check beside each number is to make sure you have placed each number in the proper result line up. As you write each number beside the placing, check (✓) it off the card. This check system assures you that every number is used and in the correct placing.

Closing Remarks & Last Minute Tips

I don't think I will ever forget judging the Washington International Horse Show. The Under Saddle classes were outstanding, but one class in particular stood out. It was the Medium Pony Under Saddle, with 25% conformation to count. I was required to line up ten ponies. Well, I had no choice but to line up fourteen. The fourteenth pony in line could easily have won the hack anywhere. To complicate things even further, the first twelve in line were grey ponies! Such a challenge, but it's great to see such top performances.

When showing, use the crowds. Get out of the crowd when your horse is hacking well, hide in the crowd when he is not.

Use the ring. Judges don't usually watch the short ends of the ring. Therefore, use the ends to reorganize and collect your horse, then lengthen down the long side to show him off.

Deal with jigging. If you have a horse that jigs you can spend a little extra time at whatever gait precedes the walk rather than walking immediately. For example, if you have just reversed halt a few seconds before you walk on, and if you're trotting or cantering take a few extra strides before doing your transition. Another horse might beat you on promptness, but jigging will count more against you than those few extra strides.

Hawthorne

Deal with stress. Use cotton in the horse's ears to cut down the stress level. Try this in the schooling area first to make sure he accepts it and won't start shaking his head.

Watch the footing. It may be deeper in certain rings and you may have to use a little more leg because your horse will have to work harder.

Questions & Answers

Q: **What sort of contact, if any, do you use for the under saddle class?**

A: I like to see my hack class entries ridden on a light contact. The contact should allow them to remain round and balanced while they move freely forward, and demonstrate the quality of their movement and the ease with which they can be controlled. The riders should demonstrate a long enough rein length to make it obvious that the horse accepts the bit willingly and stretches onto the long rein. There is, however, no point in throwing the reins to a horse who falls onto its forehand, becomes inverted, speeds up or looses its rhythm.

Q: **If your winner does something wrong at the end of the class (i.e. bucks, breaks stride), what do you do?**

A: In good company, this type of error would eliminate the horse from the ribbons. If the error was minor, there is room to move the horse down in the ribbon placings.

Q: **If a horse does not pin during the over fence classes, will his chance of placing on the flat be affected?**

A: No. The under saddle class is judged under its own criteria. The best mover may not always be the best jumper, and visa versa. The best mover with the best manners wins.

Q: **Does it matter in an under saddle class if the rider is on the wrong diagonal?**

A: No. The horse is being judged, not the rider. Often the horse will travel better and more comfortably on a certain diagonal, and the rider can use this to his advantage.

Q: **If you have an unruly horse in an under saddle class, disrupting the class, what do you do?**

A: You may certainly excuse this horse, especially if its unruliness is jeopardizing the safety and performances of the others in the class. The easiest way to excuse this horse is to ask the ringmaster or announcer to have the horse in question line up in the centre of the ring for the duration of the class. If it does not comply, the horse should leave the ring, and the class can then resume.

Q: Do you ask for the hand gallop anymore?

A: If you have a good group and they are all hacking well, time is not an issue and the surroundings are adequate, you may ask for the hand gallop. You risk losing your top horses with the hand gallop, and therefore sometimes the test's risk outweighs the benefit. If used, only eight horses can perform the hand gallop at once. Remember, it is not allowed in pre-green or green classes, and not recommended for very green rider classes, as accidents can happen. Safety first!

Q: Can you call for a halt in a hack class?

A: Yes. In certain 'hack' classes it is called for to show obedience. In under saddle classes you are judging movement, and is therefore not a necessary requirement to call for.

Q: If there is not enough room in the ring to run an under saddle class comfortably can you ask for the jumps to be moved, or do you need to make do with the ring as it is?

A: You should absolutely have the jumps moved. You want to run a safe and efficient class and you need to see the horses clearly, and in order to do this, the path must be clear. Often, moving just one line of jumps is enough.

Q: If you ran a class with only a few entries (e.g. four) and one of the horses is lame, what do you do?

A: There is no option. You just place the three sound horses. Lame horses are eliminated. You also cannot pin the fourth horse because it would still accumulate points. The same scenario if a horse jogs into an over fences class lame. It is eliminated!

Q: **If you are running a hack off for champion or reserve champion, do you have to work the horses both ways of the ring?**

A: Yes, as you need to see them travel in both directions to judge a fair class.

Q: **If a horse or pony enters the ring wearing a martingale, do you ask them to remove it or simply eliminate them at the beginning of the class?**

A: You can be a nice person and call the rider over or ask the ringmaster to inform them, as long as the class has not been started. Once started, they have to be judged as is.

Q: **In an under saddle class, often horses in the line up will act up and won't stand. Does this have any bearing on the results?**

A: It certainly does. A horse can move down in the ribbon placings for not standing quietly - this is a requirement of the class.

Q: **If a horse travels lame in one direction of the ring during an under saddle, but seems to work out of it or travels sound in the other direction, can you use him?**

A: No. A lame horse is a lame horse.

Q: **Do you take points off a horse for rough transitions during a class, or do you really watch the transitions?**

A: You should really watch the transitions. They need to be smooth and well executed. You want to see easy transitions that are connected to a pleasing performance. Prompt and rough is not as pleasing as a bit slow and smooth.

Q: **In an under saddle class, have you ever had a horse or pony jump a jump that is in the ring? How would you judge an incident like this?**

A: You hope to never see this, but it has happened. Hopefully the horse or pony is not a ribbon contender. If it is, you would have to decide if it was unavoidable due to the jumps being in the wrong place. This is a very subjective call.

Q: Do you find it hard to judge the under saddle classes if the footing is deep or muddy?

A: Most horse's movement will change in this type of footing. They tend to move with a higher step to simply get out of the footing. The one who moves the best at the canter often decides the winner, as this is the gait out of which the horse jumps.

Q: The class is in the final stage and called to a walk and asked to line up. A few riders trot their horses to make one final pass in front of the judge, and then line up. What does this do for them?

A: This action is of no benefit. The placings are already in order in the judge's mind and that final added pass is not needed or appreciated. The rider has been asked to "walk and line up", not "line up at any gait you choose". Trotting into line will deter from their performance, not add to it.

Q: I have heard so many different opinions regarding contact on the horse's mouth in an under saddle class. Some say the judge likes a loose rein, others say flexed contact and a frame. What do you recommend?

A: The Rule Book recommends a light contact. Dangling reins or overly flexed and stiff contact are extremes. A comfortable, pleasant contact is nice so that you can easily guide your ride with your hands.

Q: Which gait is the most important in an under saddle class?

A: All the gaits are important. Many judges use the trot as the tie breaker, but don't forget that the canter is the gait at which hunters perform when jumping. This gait is very important. Make sure to watch and judge the walk as well.

Q: **If a rider falls off in a flat class, what is the proper procedure?**

A: First, bring the class to a halt. Once the loose horse is caught, the rider and horse are excused from the ring. It is a good idea to let the class walk for a moment before continuing at the gait they were at, so that they can regroup and organize calmly.

Q: **When do you write down the numbers for an under saddle class, the first direction or the second way of the ring?**

A: In the first direction I try to write down, as promptly as possible, the numbers of the horses that I consider ribbon winners. This way I can spend the rest of the time watching to make my final decision on the placings.

Q: **What is the proper way to reverse?**

A: Traditionally, turning your horse inside to the rail to reverse should be done efficiently, not meandering aimlessly around the ring. Turn your number and pick up a well-balanced walk immediately. This is a good time for the rider to balance their horse and for the judge to check over their card to make sure the ribbon winners are listed.

Q: **What about a quickly corrected lead or late transition?**

A: With a good group of horses I would have to penalize a wrong lead fairly strongly. However, if it happens to be a very good mover in a pre-green class or green class, I would be more forgiving. Within the more experienced divisions (i.e. junior or amateur) and a good group, this error would move the horse down considerably in the ribbons. In regard to late transitions, allow yourself a reasonable amount of time to be sure you have proper clearance for a canter departure, or wait to trot until there is a good opening. Late upward transitions are more tolerated than late downwards transitions. I feel that transitions that take too long going down a gait communicate to me that the horse may be strong and not very obedient. You should, however, be far more demanding in equitation classes with prompt transitions.

You Be The Judge

Q: **What bit do you like to see used in the under saddle class?**

A: Whatever bit your horse goes best in. You are judging movement, not tack. To me, a horse in a plain snaffle or D-bit whose performance is as good as one in more bridle (for example, a pelham) would get the edge. I am not offended by more bridle, but less is best. When a horse or pony comes into the ring overbridled, I instantly have the impression of a strong horse or runaway pony. If as the class progresses none of the above happens, I pin it accordingly. I also think that the trainer and rider need to decide what bit enhances the overall picture.

Q: **How do you enter the hack class, and which direction should you take?**

A: The correct way to enter the ring is at a walk, travelling on the left rein on the rail. Your horse should be previously prepared and ready to show at this point. If the class is not called to immediate order, wisely go on to work your horse. You might just want to walk and work your horse in the ends of the ring. If your horse is fresh you could canter before you trot. Be cautious not to overwork your horse before the class starts, and walk once you know you've been seen.

Q: **What about carrying a crop or wearing spurs in an under saddle class?**

A: Ideally, the picture you want to present would be best without a crop or spurs. If a crop is carried, it could draw a judge's attention to the fact that this horse may be a little sluggish. If you feel your horse needs an artificial aid, the spurs are a more subtle way to obtain the right amount of impulsion.

Q: **Is it difficult to judge an under saddle class for conformation when they don't strip off their saddles?**

A: It is more difficult to judge a horse's conformation when they are not stripped, because you are not seeing the same picture as you would without a rider and tack. The horse's back and wither will be partially hidden and covering part of a top line that may be very good or less than desirable. The overall balance of the horse is interrupted by the rider's leg and saddle causing you to view it in two parts instead of as a whole. Also, the rider's size and the way they fit the horse may influence the general impression. The rider, when on the ground, is in a better position to present the horse correctly which in turn helps you to view it at its best.

Q: **When you start an under saddle class do you always call the horses to a walk, or is there something else you may ask for?**

A: First of all, I make sure they are all going in the correct direction, so I ask them to walk on the rail to the left. Two other things before I start - I ask them to spread out and to turn their numbers slightly so that I can see them. Then we are ready to start.

Q: **If a horse pulls a shoe in an under saddle class, can the class be held while the shoe is replaced? I have seen this done in 3 and 5 gaited classes.**

A: Sorry, not in the hunter ring. As in the over fence classes, you have to continue to the end of the class, exit the ring and have the shoe put back on.

Q: **In an under saddle class you realize that your horse is just unruly and you want to leave the ring. Do you have to ask the judge's permission or can you simply exit as best you can?**

A: You do not have to ask permission. Just leave when you are near the gate. If this is not possible, line up in the centre of the ring and wait for the gate to be opened. Try not to get in the way of the other competitors.

Q: **What is the difference between a Hack class and an Under Saddle class? Are they the same thing?**

A: In a word, NO. According to the Equine Canada rule book, a Hunter Under Saddle class is judged on the horse's way of going i.e. "they should move in a long low frame and be able to lengthen their stride and cover ground", and "they should be obedient, alert and responsive". Further, they are judged on soundness, movement, manners, condition and conformation.

They are to be shown at the walk, trot and canter in both directions, and may be asked to back. Faults in an Under Saddle class include wrong leads, too fast or too slow, being above or behind the bit, tripping or falling, and bad behaviour such as kicking. A horse in poor condition should also be penalized. The top 8 to 12 horses may be asked to hand gallop. In this class horses are not to jump.

In a Hunter Hack the horses are first required to jump two fences, not necessarily in a line, at the height of 2'9". Horses being considered for an award are then asked to return and are shown at the walk, trot, and canter in both directions, on a light contact. The same faults and merits are looked for as in the Under Saddle. The placings are determined on a ratio of 70/30, jumping to flat. The Under Saddle is what we commonly see as part of a hunter division. Although horses are not required to jump in this class, they must successfully complete at least one jumping class of the division in order to participate.

A Hunter Hack class is not usually seen at a typical "A" circuit hunter/jumper show in Ontario any more, although it is still very popular at the Trillium level. The Hunter Hack is usually teamed with a Pleasure, Show and Road hack to make a division. For more information on these and other classes, refer to your Equine Canada rule book.

Q: **What type of contact are you looking for in a hunter under saddle class? Do you have an image of how you would like a hunter to carry his head and neck? Do either of these two things vary with divisions (i.e. do you look for anything different with a first yearn green hunter versus an amateur owner hunter)? How do contact and carriage enter the formula along with quality and movement to decide your final placings?**

A: To start with, the winner of the Under Saddle class should move well. My definition of a good move is a long, low athletic stride in a relaxed manner. I prefer a horse that appears elastic and supple, that moves lightly with a reaching swing from his shoulder versus one that moves too flat and only from its elbow. I like a horse with a strong push behind that reaches well under itself without high hock action. These traits should be noticed at the trot, canter as well as the walk. The walk, too often being overlooked, should be long and relaxed rather than tense and ready. In under saddle classes the walk is the transition gait between the trot and canter. The true hunter look is horse with good movement, manners, balance and expression. I like to see the neck stretch out in a natural looking carriage. A neck worn much below the withers creates a horse moving on the forehand and a neck raised too high creates the look a hollow back. I like to see the rider have a light feel of the horse's mouth. The degree of flexion depends on its confirmation. Never should the contact with the horse's mouth appear muscled or contrived. The wagging of the bit or horse's head to create flexion is never acceptable. Lastly, I feel that many horses have good symmetric trots but not as many have a great canter. Since hunters jump courses while cantering, this is the most important gait. Keep horses in the ring partially because of their trots, but hopefully the final selection will be determined by the fluid, athletic look of the canter.

Ron Danta, Rebmert SC

Member of USHJA Trainers Committee

Q: I am a novice parent wanting to know what the under saddle class is all about?

A: In the Hunter Under Saddle class, the judges consider movement and manners. Conducted on the flat with a group of horses each horse must walk, trot and canter. A top show hunter moves fluidly and effortlessly, with minimum movement or action of his knees. This means that the legs stay straight and reach out as far as possible in a pointing motion.

In the manners department, judges want to see a horse that works quietly in a group, with only light contact on his mouth. He should appear relaxed, confident, and happy, with his ears up, his neck stretched out, and his head down. Heavy penalties are leveled on a horse with his ears back, his head high, or his tail swishing.

Q: **Can you carry a crop in an under saddle class?**

A: It is not against the rules, but makes a horse seem dead to the leg, and should not be needed.

Q: **During an under saddle class, the judge calls for the walk, and a horse that you had planned to use in the ribbons stumbles badly, what do you do?**

A: Move him out of the ribbons. The horses need to stay on their feet, just as in an over fence class. Stumbling or tripping can dislodge the rider and cause a fall.

Q: **Often you will see the judge ask for the horses to try trot at the end of a class, e.g. after they canter the final direction. Why is this asked for?**

A: It is often used at the end of a class for the judge to break a tie between horses.

Q: **A rider competes in an under saddle class without a number on. Are they scored?**

A: A competitor cannot be scored without a number on. If the number falls off during the class, this is an exception, and I would score them.

Q: **Do you watch the horse's line up in a class, after asking them for the final walk and line up?**

A: Absolutely. I need to make sure that they are mannerly. It is also the time to double check your numbers.

Q: **How many horses do you consider to be the most before you would split a class?**

A: Even though it is time consuming, it is proper to split if there are more than 20 horses in a class. This way, all competitors get proper consideration.

Q: **What type of contact are you looking for in a hunter under saddle class? Do you have an image in your head of how you would like a hunter to carry his head and neck in a hack class? Do either of these two things vary with different divisions (i.e. do you look for anything different with a first year green hunter versus an amateur owner hunter)? How do contact and carriage enter the formula along with quality and movement to make your final placings?**

A: When I judge an under saddle class, I have a vision in my head of the class's origin, which is hacking home from the hunt. With that in mind, besides, having a beautiful mover, I would want to ride a horse that covers the round in a longer, low frame with light contact.

That doesn't mean heavy on the forehand or downhill, but balanced and engaged. I am more concerned with manners and obedience for the A/O division, and could credit a little more brilliance in an open division. Again, this goes back to who would be hacking home from the hunt. I would say frame and contact could count up to 25% of the overall performance.

Julie Winkel, Reno, NV

Licensed Official

A: To start with, the winner of the under saddle class should move well. My definition of a good mover is a long, low athletic stride in a relaxed manner. I prefer a horse that appears elastic and supple, that moves lightly with a reaching swing from his shoulder versus one that moves too flat and only from its elbow. I like a horse with a strong push behind that reaches well under itself without hock action.

These traits should be noticed at the trot, canter, as well as the walk. The walk, too often overlooked, should be long and relaxed rather than tense and ready. In under saddle classes the walk is the transition gait between the trot and canter.

The true hunter look is a horse with good movement, manners, balance and expression. I like to see the neck stretch out in a natural looking carriage. A neck worn much below the withers creates a horse moving on the forehand and a neck raised too high creates the look of a hollow neck. I like to see the rider have a light feel of the horse's mouth.

The degree of flexion is never acceptable. I would expect more solidity in the hacking of horses in upper divisions as opposed to the divisions for greener or younger horses. Remember, the under saddle class is a hack class and the horses must hack well and move well.

Movement alone is not enough. Last I feel that many horses have good symmetric trots but not as many have a great canter. Since hunters jump courses while cantering, this is the most important gait. Keep horses in the ring partially because of their trots, but hopefully the final selection will be determined by the fluid, athletic look of the canter.

Ron Danta, Rebmert SC

Member of USHJA Trainers Committee

A: In a hunter under saddle class I look for a light contact to the horse's mouth. "Light" is a soft connection of the rein to the mouth versus no connection at all. I like to see hunters working through their back with a round top line and soft frame. The horse should carry its neck slightly up and out from its withers with a soft arc and nose slightly ahead of vertical. Its back should be round and its hocks underneath itself. I feel there should be a consistent way of going under saddle whether it is a first Year hunter or an Amateur Owner hunter.

Ultimately my top horse under saddle should be carrying itself from behind in a soft frame allowing it to move freely from the shoulder with little to no bend of the knee, slight suspension of gate and covering the ground effortlessly.

Nancy Green-Free, Buckley, WA

Chair of USHJA Riders Committee

Summary

As in the over fence classes, remember that talent wins. The best moving, best mannered horse should stand out in the crowd. Keep your classes short and concise. Overworking the horses often ends in losing your winner!

Any horse that does not complete a class over fences is not eligible to compete in the under saddle class. It is a good idea to keep a list of these horses during the over fence classes, and inform the ringmaster and ingate of the horses not allowed to compete in the under saddle. This saves the possibility of having to re-issue the ribbons afterwards.

Chapter Three

Equitation Over Fences

Missy Clark

Introduction

The equitation over fences class is not simply judged as a beauty contest for the rider. The modern day class is one of riding ability, technique and sensitivity, combined together to produce an accurate and skilled performance. Today's equitation rider must be prepared to execute an exact ride over a technical course, a course which asks many questions and demands precision. All of the symbols under the Hunter section also apply to the Equitation division. First of all, the rider has to find a correct distance to all the jumps. After this is accomplished you can comment on the rider's position. Form follows function. The ability to execute a round effortlessly, beautifully, in control, and with style will make the ultimate winner.

In an equitation class over fences it is of utmost importance to try to record as many rider faults as possible. Many young riders will approach the judge and ask what he or she is doing wrong and how their problems can be corrected. Therefore, it is necessary that your bookkeeping is adequate enough to point out some of the things that you felt kept them out of the ribbons. Considering that these young riders are in the midst of such a competitive field, most of them are very receptive to suggestions for their own improvement.

Brian Walker

The Look

The basic solid foundation is apparent, with a good release. The rider stays in the centre of the horse, and jumps with the horse, neither too far ahead not too far behind. The lower leg is against the horse holding the base of support. The position is not perched or

Natalie Gascho

forced, and the rider has a look of confidence knowing that the jump has been properly executed.

The manner in which riders negotiate the course, the smoothness, and the most effortless and natural round are features that the judge is looking for. The rider's seat is well out of the saddle and is in perfect balance with their horse. They are letting the horse jump 'up' into them and they are doing nothing to interfere with the horse's outstanding efforts. The rider's weight is well into their heels and the lower leg is exemplary. It hasn't slipped back, forward, nor is it gripping the horse's side too tightly.

A proper leg position is most important. This is the base of support and any fault in this area causes many other problems. The lower leg must be secure, with the rider's weight dropped into the heel. The ankle is supple, not forced into a stiff position. If the lower leg is too far forward the body's balance is thrown backwards, causing the rider to have to 'catch up' with their upper body over the fence. Often the rider will get 'left' over the jumps, which is very abusive to the horse. If the leg is too far back, the rider's weight is too far ahead of the motion, perching, causing problems with the horse's centre of gravity. This can cause faults in the horse's jumping form - hanging legs and rubbing the jumps.

You Be The Judge

The rider's eye level is up and focused straight ahead in the direction they are travelling with their horses. The rider uses his 'eye' early in the turns to plan the route travelled and the distances to the jumps. The jumps come up very quickly in equitation classes, and the rider needs to be constantly looking ahead to plan the next line of jumps and the path that they will take. Leads and diagonals are felt, not looked for by dropping the eye and head, which not only looks unattractive but breaks the concentration of the ride.

Do

* Use a short crest release or an automatic release. The horse must be given the freedom to use his head and neck over the jump.
* A short crest release works with a horse that has a long stride and will enable him to be compressed as soon as he lands, without making any obvious movement with the rider's hands.
* Good corners are just as important as good fences.
* Concerning showmanship, the rider that takes the shorter, more difficult option, and executes it with the same smoothness, can gain the edge over the more conservative ride.
* Turn yourself and your horse out impeccably, and make sure your tack fits your horse.

Alexa Law

Don't

* A sharp, 'shove' release makes the horse flat and forward.
* Don't ruin a good round with a rough exit.
* Above all, never display temper in the ring.
* Falling forward can cause the horse to unfold his front legs early or reach for the ground too quickly.
* Do not do too much forcibly, or too noticeably.
* Try not to 'try' too hard, as it appears false and forced.
* Don't cut the corners, use all of the ring. Poor turns look hurried and not in control.
* Do not over flex and bend in the ends of the ring and on the approach to the jumps.

Matthew Mulligan

The Upper Body

Wayne McLellan heading into a turn while working on the flat, inclining his body slightly in the direction of the turn and using his eyes well.

The Eyes Have It

One of the most serious faults in an equitation class is poor use of the eyes. A rider with a good eye level looks slightly above the jump at all times, looks up and around the turns for the next jump and never looks down while in the air. If the eye level is raised properly, the rest of the body will follow the eyes.

The head should be raised slightly and the shoulders square, with a slight (not exaggerated) hollow in the lower back. By looking up, you won't fall into the turns, make any obvious adjustments to the jumps and will hopefully meet the jump evenly and in the centre.

If the rider looks down, his horse will probably bulge into, run through or cut the turns. At worse, he may even miss the jump! Since the body follows the eyes, if the rider is looking down through the turns, the shoulders will naturally follow. As a result, the back will hunch and the rider will be off balance.

You Be The Judge

Shifty eyes, or wandering eyes that look around the turn, then back, then ahead, then back again, are really distracting to the judge, and make for an uneven, unfocused round. When a rider over-uses his eyes, turning them - and usually his head - too early over the jump to look at the next one, it appears forced and strained.

A major no-no is looking down for diagonals and leads. I must emphasize that riders need to be taught to feel where they are, in regard to leads and diagonals, before they start showing in the more advanced equitation classes. The rider should be able to look straight ahead, and with the proper aids, feel for the diagonal and the lead they are on.

The head position follows the eyes and needs to be up and focused in the centre of the jumps, and slightly following the direction of the turns.

Toska Kocken shows how it's done, with an upper body that is poised and comfortable.

Front and Centre

A rider is off-balance when they lean to the right or left on approach and/or over the jumps. By sitting squarely and directly in the centre of the saddle, the rider balances both themselves and the horse. When the rider leans in on the turns, weight is then thrown onto the horse's inside shoulder, which in turn will cause the horse to cut in or run through the turn to support the rider's weight.

Dipping to one side over the jumps has the same adverse effects. If the rider leans, he will probably make the horse jump to the side of the fence. As a result, it will be difficult for the horse to get to the next fence on a straight track, or execute a proper turn on the landing side. The horse may also twist behind or start "laying on his side" to compensate.

Looking down and off to the side can put a horse off balance and result in poor jumping form.

Jumping The Gun

This is an all-too-common rider error. The rider jumps ahead off the ground, gets up the horse's neck too soon and leaves the horse weak and off-balance. Riders tend to do this upon seeing a long distance - a distance that the horse may have negotiated successfully had the rider not thrust all of his body weight onto the forehand, making it far more difficult for the horse to jump. If the rider maintains an upright position and the horse fits in another stride, the error is not nearly as noticeable.

*Here, the rider's eye level is down and to the right,
pitching the upper body forward and causing the legs to
swing back.*

Beware of Ducks

This equitation fault is not the same as jumping ahead. Usually there is a smooth, even approach to the jump, but as the horse begins to leave the ground the rider snaps the upper body forward, then unfolds it suddenly in the middle of the horse's arc. I find this action particularly offensive, because of the drastic contrast between the soft, flowing approach and the harsh, jerky body movement in the air.

Ducking will inevitably make your horse quick and flat over the jumps, so slow down and allow him to jump up into you.

Falling Behind

This error occurs when a rider falls behind the forward motion of the horse over the top of the jump. I refer to this error as being left in the back seat. It most often happens when a rider finds too long a distance and can't quite catch up, or is really deep to the fence. Being left behind indicates a weak lower leg that is unable to hold the rider's body in the correct position, which is forward and off the horse's back. When left behind, not only does the rider commit an equitation mistake, he also causes the horse to jump flat or punishes him by catching him in the mouth in an attempt to regain his own balance.

This jumper rider is displaying excellent use of the eyes and upper body, properly focussed and positioned over the fence.

The Rider's Topline

There are several common rider flaws seen between the neck and the tailbone which can ruin an otherwise pretty picture. For instance, a roached back is a rounded back that is often simply a result of too short a stirrup. Rounded shoulders, on the other hand, weaken the effectiveness of the rider's back.

The opposite of a roached back is a hollow back, caused by a rider closing his hip angle too much, carrying his buttocks too far behind him and his shoulders too far back. This creates an unnatural concave profile and may make your round look stiff and artificial.

The Hands

Zero Release

Instead of executing the proper crest release, some riders merely set their hands (no give in the air) which definitely inhibits the horse's jumping freedom. As a result, the horse is unable to use its head and neck properly, and in more drastic instances this error will make the horse tense, causing it to invert its neck and jump very flat.

Zero Contact

In the other extreme, some riders approach the jump with absolutely no contact. I must stress here that I like a sensitive contact, but when I see a rider with long, slack reins, I don't feel that there is any communication with the horse's mouth.

Opposite ends of the spectrum:
(left) the shove release, which is too much of a good thing; and
(right) the 'zero' release.

Rotating Release

The rider gives the impression of taking the horse off of the ground, lifting it over the jump, then letting it down on the other side.

High Hands

This is a common equitation error that mainly occurs on the approach to the jumps, when the rider carries his hands too high above the withers as though he was trying to hold the horse 'up in front'. For equitation, the hands should be carried slightly above the withers (not resting on) at a forty-five degree angle.

Fixed Hand

A fixed hand is one that does not follow the motion of the horse's head; i.e., are set in an immobile position.

Open Fingers

Open fingers are ineffective and weak. In this instance, the reins get progressively longer as the rider proceeds around the course. The reins are constantly being gathered up to re-establish contact. The rider's fingers should always be closed firmly around the reins.

Flat Hands

Hands that are not at the proper angle (i.e. parallel to the ground) are not as effective.

Shove Release

The rider's hands creep towards the horse's ears over the fence.

Uneven Contact

One rein is noticeably longer than the other, which can affect how the horse carries his head.

Dropped Hands

Conversely, some riders carry their hands too low on either side of the withers, both over jumps and on the approach. Low hands force the rider's balance onto the horse's forehand and often it looks as though they are trying to force the horse's head down and into a frame.

You Be The Judge

Note: The proper frame comes mostly from the leg, not the hand. You encourage a horse up into the bridle with a strong leg. Never force the horse's head down with your hands.

Rough Hands

The rider perpetually takes too much contact in an abrupt manner (e.g. the rider constantly raises his hands and then rests them on the horse's neck). Another version of rough hands occurs when a rider rides with one rein shorter and higher than the other, using this short rein as a pulley rein. Contact and feel of the horse's mouth is more affective when it is distributed evenly with both reins. Contact should be subtle and steady, not harsh and erratic.

Three equitation no-nos: (above) the high-handed 'lift' release;
(below left) open fingers on the reins
(note the effort on the part of the horse, however!);
(below right) elbows out.

Long Reins

Not only should a rider maintain a sensitive contact on approach to the jumps, he or she should also use a slightly shorter rein for a jumper than a hunter. (A jumper rider needs to readily regain contact to negotiated more difficult courses.)

When I see a rider jumping with long reins, it looks as though the reins are in their lap, and their elbows are often jutted out in an awkward fashion like they have wings and are about to take flight! The entire look is sloppy and I fault it accordingly. Long reins contribute to an uncontrolled performance.

Too Short a Contact

Not only is it important to give your horse freedom while jumping, it is just as important to maintain a sensitive (not harsh) contact through the turns and down the lines. A rider who rides with extremely short reins and a harsh contact appears to be choking the horses. Consequently, the horse looks tense and strong and the overall ride has no fluidity. Short reins also draw the rider's seat out of the saddle.

The Seat

Front Seat

Too far ahead over the pommel.

Back Seat

Too far back, touching the centre.

Sits Into of Drives

It is incorrect for a rider to sit into or drive the horse forward with their seat and back. In an equitation class, I expect to see the rider encouraging the horse's stride with a firm lower leg.

*The driving seat might be acceptable in a grand
prix or on a cross-country course, but it has no place
in a hunter equitation class.*

Lower Body

Lower Leg Slides Back

When the lower leg slides backwards, it is not necessarily the sign of a weak leg, but can be caused by a variety of factors. One of these is the rider who lays over the neck, causing their base of support to slip behind them. Another is the rider who supports their body by pinching with their knees, thus allowing the leg to fall behind the girth, resulting in a weak, swinging leg.

Toe-out

Some riders exaggerate the proper toe-out position. This can weaken the lower leg. Toe-out is not a drastic error, but the rider would lose points in an equitation class. Ideally, the toes should be at a 15-degree angle from the horse's sides.

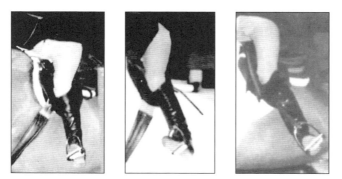

(Left) Stirrups too long.
(Middle) Leg back, and foot jammed too far into the stirrup.
(Right) This pinched knee causes the lower leg to swing back.

Leg Ahead

When the leg moves toward the shoulder of the horse, it puts the rider behind the motion and is often a result of lack of weight down in the rider's heel. As with the lower leg that slides behind, the lower leg that shoots ahead can also have a variety of causes. A rider with their 'feet on the dash' appears defensive (they may be riding a horse that stops). He or she often rides with a deep seat that is too far behind the motion. In this instance, the leg is awkwardly propped in front of the rider and gives the look of a brace against which the rider is pushing or holding.

(Left) Here, the stirrups are too short and the leg is climbing.
(Right) The leg has been shoved ahead, and the rider is in danger of losing her stirrup.

You Be The Judge

Weak / No Leg

A weak or non-existent leg is ineffective. A rider with such a leg problem is not hard to spot, because they are often jostled about in the saddle on the approach to the jumps. While jumping, I can see air space between the leg and the saddle. Either the leg simply dangles loosely or it swings back and forth. The support of the upper body comes from the leg and if the rider neglects to discipline their leg, a sloppy, insecure performance in the ring tells all.

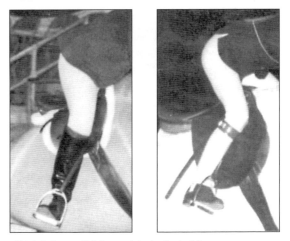

(Right) A parallel foot, with the heel riding up.
(Left) Toe turned too far out, and leg too far back.

Standing In The Stirrups

If at the canter the rider appears to be posting, he or she is likely standing in the stirrups, rather than using the whole leg and sinking their weight into their heels.

Other foot problems include stirrups that are too long or too short, a foot that is either parallel (to the horse's side) or a heel that is riding up. Stirrup loss anywhere on course is a good indicator that one or several of the above have occurred.

Put together all the elements of correct equitation you have learned from this section, and you should be able to make quite an impression in the equitation ring this show season.

Cathy Roy exhibits proper lower leg position aboard
Just Cruising, and the rest follows beautifully.

Judging Symbols For Equitation Classes

All of these symbols have 3 degrees of severity. They are separated by underling or circling, as follows:

WK - symbol for a weak ride

WK	WK	(WK)
A little weak	Quite weak	Seriously weak

Faults, listed from the worst to least severe:

Symbol	Interpretation
STP	Stirrup loss anywhere on course.
LFT	Left behind. The horse arrives at the correct take-off distance and the rider is left sitting in the tack.
WK	Weak off the ground - A hesitation that makes the horse look as though he has stalled or barely come off the ground.
O/R	No release. Instead of executing the proper crest

release some riders merely set their hands (no give in the air) which definitely inhibits the horse's jumping freedom. As a result, the horse is unable to use its head and neck properly, and in more drastic instances this error will make the horse tense, invert it's neck and jump very flat.

← Behind - Conversely, this symbol notes the rider who falls behind the forward motion of the horse while in the air. We refer to this error as being left in the back seat, and it most often happens when the rider finds too long a distance and can't quite catch up, or is very deep to the jump. Being left behind indicates a weak lower leg that is unable to hold the rider's body in the correct jumping position. When left behind not only does the rider commit an equitation error, they usually cause the horse to jump flat or punish the horse by catching it in the mouth to regain their own balance.

→ Jumps ahead off the ground - the rider gets up the horse's neck too soon and leaves the horse weak and off balance. Often the rider jumps up the horse's neck before it has left the ground. This is an all too common riding error. Riders tend to jump ahead upon finding a long distance, a distance that the horse may have attempted had the rider not thrust all their own body weight onto the forehand, making it far more difficult for the horse to jump. If the rider maintains an upright position and the horse still adds another stride, the error is not nearly as noticeable.

O/L Weak/no leg. The rider's leg is ineffective. A rider with such a problem is not hard to spot because they are often jostled about in the saddle on the approach to the jumps. While jumping you can see air space between the leg and the saddle. Either the leg simply dangles loosely or it swings back and forth. The support for the upper body comes from the leg, and if the rider neglects to discipline their leg, a sloppy, insecure performance in the ring tells all.

LG→   Leg ahead and not at the proper angle (the leg moves toward the shoulder of the horse, puts the rider behind the motion and is often a result of lack of weight down in the rider's heel). As with the lower leg that slides behind, the lower leg that scoots ahead can also have a variety of causes. A rider with the 'feet on the dash' appears defensive (they may be riding a horse that stops). He/she often rides with a deep seat that is too far behind the motion. In this instance, the leg is awkwardly propped in front of the rider and gives the look of a brace against which the rider is pushing or holding.

LS   Loose, sloppy, not tight, not in proper contact or position.

STF   Stiff, rigid appearance. The rider is not relaxed and poised. Tense looking.

RG   Rough, uneven, somewhat erratic pace.

R/R   Rotating release. The riders gives the impression of taking the horse off the ground lifting it over the jump, then letting it down on the other side.

↑⤻   Lifting the horse off the ground.

E   Eyes. One of the most serious faults in an equitation class is poor use of the eyes (E-). A rider with a good eye level (E+) is a rider who looks slightly above the jump at all times, looks up and around the turns for the next jump and NEVER looks down while in the air. If eye level is raised properly the rest of the body will follow the eyes. The head will be square with a slight (not exaggerated) hollow in the lower back. By looking up, the rider won't fall into the turns, won't make any obvious adjustments to the jumps and will meet the jump fluidly and in the centre. If the rider does look down, their horse will probably bulge, run through or cut the turns. They may even miss the jump! The body follows the eyes, and if the rider is looking down through the turns the shoulders will follow; the back will bunch and they will be off balance.

DK   Ducking. This equitation fault occurs over the jump. It is not the same as jumping ahead. Usually there is a smooth even approach to the jump but when the horse begins to leave the ground the rider throws the upper body forward in a quick manner. As a result, their body will snap up in the middle of the horse's arc. This fault is particularly offensive because of the drastic contrast between the soft fluent approach and the harsh rushed body movement in the air, and can make a horse quick and flat over the jumps.

L/O   A rider who lays over the horse's neck appears top heavy. This error occurs when the rider throws the upper body too far ahead of the vertical while in the air and/or on the landing side. The rider is using the horse's neck for balance. Instead of pressing weight into the heels and using the lower leg to support, the heels are up and the base of support has slipped behind. In addition, all that extra weight placed over the horse's withers makes it more difficult to jump and will often cause the horse to throw its legs behind rather than raise them into the correct jumping form.

O/C   No contact. The opposite of 'no release', some riders on their approach to the jumps ride with absolutely no contact. There is no communication with the horse's mouth, which makes for a myriad of problems. A sensitive contact is the ideal.

Dropping back in the saddle too soon.

← LG   Lower leg slides. When the lower leg slides backwards it is not necessarily the sign of a weak leg, therefore this fault is categorized by itself. A sliding lower leg can be caused by a variety of factors, one being a rider who lays over the neck causing their base of support to slip behind them, another being a rider who supports their body with the knees (knees pinched) and thus allows the leg to fall behind the girth.

↑   The rider stands up over top of the jump instead of following the horse in the air. The rider appears upright almost in a standing position. This equitation error occurs both on the flat and over jumps. Often riders who stand in their stirrups are neither ahead nor behind the motion. They simply appear to be perched in the saddle rather than flowing with the horse's forward motion. Such a rider is too erect with the upper body and the overall picture is stiff and rigid.

↓   Sits into or drives - A rider who sits into or drives the horse forward with their seat and back. In an equitation class I expect to see the rider encouraging the horse's stride with a firm lower leg.

R/H   Rough hands. The rider perpetually takes too

much contact in an abrupt manner (e.g. the rider constantly raises their hands and then rests them on the horse's neck). Another sign of rough hands occurs when a rider rides with one rein shorter and higher than the other, using this short rein as a pulley rein. Contact and feel of the horse's mouth is more effective when it is distributed evenly with both reins. Contact should be subtle and steady, not harsh and erratic.

~ C   Uneven contact. One rein is noticeably longer than the other.

R/ ↗   Shove release. The rider's hands creep towards the horse's ears.

← K   Knee pinched and henceforth a weak swinging leg.

O.   Open fingers. Hands are not effective and are weak. In this instance, the reins get progressively longer as the rider proceeds around the course. The reins are constantly being gathered up to re-establish contact. The rider's fingers should always be closed firmly around the reins.

C ←   Too short a contact. Not only is it important to give your horse freedom while jumping, it is just as important to maintain a sensitive (not harsh) contact through the turns and down the lines. A rider who rides with extremely short reins and a harsh contact appears to be choking the horse. Consequently, the horse looks tense and strong and the overall ride has no fluidity.

C ↓   Dropped hands. Conversely, some riders carry their hands too low on either side of the withers, both over jumps and on the approach. Low hands force the rider's balance onto the horse's forehand

and it often looks as though they are trying to force the horse's head down and into a frame.

Note: The proper frame comes mostly from the leg, not the hand. You encourage a horse up into the bridle with a strong leg - never force the horse's head down with your hand.

C↑   High hands, mostly on the approach to the jump. This is a common equitation error that occurs when the riders carry their hands too high above the wither as though they were trying to hold the horse up in front. For equitation, the hands should be carried slightly above the wither (not resting on it) at a forty-five degree angle.

FH   Flat hands. Hands are not at the proper angle, seem parallel to the ground and not as effective.

C →   Long reins. Not only should a rider maintain a sensitive contact on approach to the jumps, they should also have a slightly shorter rein for a jumper than a hunter, as a jumper needs to readily regain contact to negotiate more difficult courses. When a rider jumps with long reins it looks as though the reins are in their lap, and their elbows are often jutted out in an awkward fashion. The entire look is sloppy and faulted accordingly.

← OB →   Off balance. A rider is off balance when they lean to the right (O/B →) or left (← O/B), both on the approach and over the jumps. By sitting squarely and in the centre of the saddle the rider balances both themselves and the horse. When the rider leans in on the turns, weight is thrown onto the horse's inside shoulder, which in turn will cause the horse to cut or run through the turns to support the rider's weight. Dipping to one side over the jumps has the same adverse effects. If the rider leans, they will probably make the horse jump to the side of the fence and then will not be able to execute a proper straight line or turn on the landing side. The horse may also twist behind or lay on his side to compensate.

T/O   Toe-out. Some riders exaggerate the proper toe-out position. This can weaken the lower leg. Toe-out is not a drastic error, but the rider would lose points in an equitation class.

R   Roach back. A rounded back that is often the result of too short a stirrup.

Courtney Donaber

Testing Over Fences

Further testing is either required or the judge may have the option. If required, you need to note how many riders you must test and the possibility of testing more if you have close rounds. How many tests are required in that class, and what level of class is it? Is this a small show where the competition is not of great quality or is it a final with top riders? The following are some ideas for further testing, starting with the easier ones and ascending to the more difficult ones.

Testing Ideas

* Put together some simple fences with a change of lead.
* Exiting to the ingate and walk out on a loose rein.
* Halt at a place designated by the judge.
* Rein back (remember to mention how many steps).
* Trotting a fence (make sure it is a fence that can go low enough and still have a top rail).
* Walk a fence (again, low enough with a rail on top).
* Gallop a fence.
* Counter canter a fence.
* Put together two jumps that will make a new line (be sure they are going in the same direction as the initial round).
* Halt between two jumps and canter out (be sure there is enough room allowed for the caliber of competition that you are working with).
* Demonstrate a change of lead between two fences (ideally you have a six stride line and it can be a simple or flying change).
* Riding without stirrups.
* Switching horses and riders for important events - consider the difficulty factor and try to match horses and riders fairly.
* Verbal testing (e.g. parts of the horse, tack, course preparation, etc.). This is always good as it encourages riders to read more literature on the subject.
* Free style testing (the riders make up their own test). For example, the rider needs to demonstrate the following: counter canter a fence, a halt, a hand gallop fence and jump any six jumps in any order. Same direction as the first round.

You Be The Judge

It's great to judge as you don't know which test they will show you, and it's up to them to demonstrate the winning ride.

* No schooling - this makes them have to be ready and they have to show a little riding talent.

* Announcing the test with the riders in the ring so they have to deal with it themselves. This eliminates trainer assistance.

* When designing your ride-off test, make sure the number of jumps are in the correct order and are the same direction as the first round. An example of a test: Trot fence #1, canter fences #4, #5 and #8, exit the ring at a sitting trot.

* On the judge's card, reserve an area for bonuses such as turn backs, inside turns, promptness, etc. I simply put a check mark by the number in the centre of the card to note the extra effort.

Judging An Euqitation Over Fences Class

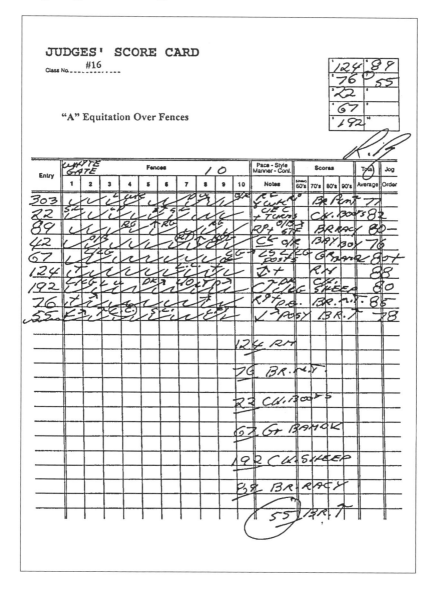

You Be The Judge

Entry 303 - The first entry is a girl riding a big brown horse in a pelham. The first line is well ridden, but she is a little bit strong at the third jump. After being long, she doesn't react fast enough and leaves weakly off the ground at fence 4. She recovers and negotiates fences 5 and 6 just fine. She is a little close at fence 7, into a broken line. The rider has to really move forward for the in and out, and she jumps out holding onto her horse's mouth, with no release.

Summary: A somewhat rough round, a weak jump, and she had to run for the in and out, demonstrating a poor release. This adds up to a score of 77.

Entry 22 - The second rider in this class is a girl riding a chestnut horse with front boots. A good first jump, but the horse switches leads from left to right. The second jump in the line is good. Maybe slightly deep to fence 3 but with the turn back it is barely worth noting. Fence 4 works out well, but approaching fence 5 she looks away from the direction in which she is going. Another switch of leads from left to right, jump 7 is good, and the broken line to the 'in and out' works well.

Summary: I notice her contact is somewhat uneven - the right rein is shorter than the left. This may be why the horse switched leads from left to right when she steadied for a distance. I note that she has excellent turns, all well rounded, smooth and even. The eyes wandering off the track once, and two switches of leads, I score her a very acceptable 82.

Entry 89 - This entry is a brown horse that is thin and racy looking. All the jumps are good, with accurate distances and accompanied by a confident ride. I put in the centre column 'Ri+' for a good rider. However, every turn back I note as rough, as the horse bulges out and never totally gives in on the turns. This makes the rider look stiff and abrasive as she has to use her body along with her leg to make the turns. She is also off balance, leaning off to the right.

Summary: Not being in the middle of her horse and the obvious rough turns, but a good rider, I give her a score of 80.

Entry 42 - This is a bay horse ridden by a boy. I notice right away that he rides with a very short rein. As he jumps the first two jumps he has very little release - he stays with the short rein and the contact as if he is afraid of losing the controls. The horse is scopey and rideable, so the jumps are quite passable. At fence 6 he jumps off to the right, and then has to go far out in the turn to compensate for it. Quite rough after jump 7 and too far out, arriving at the 'in' quite long, but scope gets him out of the long spot and he jumps 'out' well.

Summary: A low score of 76, with the hard jump to the right, rough approach to fence 8 and being long without a very generous release anywhere.

Entry 67 - This girl is riding a grey horse with back bandages on. I would have to say that the horse is one of the best equitation horses I have ever judged. The round was faultless on the horse's part, effortless and enjoyable to watch. However, the rider has some obvious faults. Topping the list is her loose swinging lower leg, followed by a somewhat loose looking ride and posting at the canter. Over the last jump her leg shoots ahead of her and lands her in the tack a little early.

Summary: Well, my constant referral here is for the rider to find the jumps first, and then I comment on the ride. I score her just an 80+; as outstanding a round as it was, her equitation faults cannot allow her to score any higher. She is just ahead of rider #89, who had rough turns.

Entry 124 - This is a tall boy riding a roan horse. He rides in a three-point position, and looks very well positioned as he picks up a good forward canter to the first jump. He catches a good distance to jump #1 and follows his horse lightly off of the ground. He regains his three-point position beautifully and rides nicely down the line. Except for a couple of strides, and with a late lead change, the whole round is a pleasure to watch.

Summary: He undoubtedly leaps into the lead with a score of 88. Not all riders can execute the jumps in a three-point position, however this rider has demonstrated it exceptionally well.

You Be The Judge

Entry 192 - Here we have a girl riding a chestnut horse, wearing a sheepskin girth. She jumps the first jump and her leg appears loose, which proves true as she arrives off the base to jump fence 2. This causes her horse to land and play at the end of the line. Fence 3 is fine, and she ducks over 4. She is a little ahead of fence 5 and lays over the horse's neck at the sixth fence. She jumps too much to the left over fence 7. This puts her too close to the in and out. The rider carries her hands too high, which makes it seem as if she is throwing away her release.

Summary: I am going to squeeze her in for a score of 80. Nothing drastic, nothing great. Behind rider #67,who had the great even round, and just ahead of rider #89, with the rough turns. I added a minus sign to the score of 80 that rider #89 received.

Entry 76 - This is a girl riding a brown horse sporting a mud tail. She comes in with a lot of intent, picks up a healthy gallop and goes right down to the first jump. She lands going right away from the jump and has to move forward to get the line. A well-ridden, positive round with lots of pace. I note 'P.G.' for little short strides or 'pony gaited', which the rider has compensated for and offset with pace.

Summary: This girl could be and will be a winner, but in this class the two lines with the pace increase puts her in second place. She receives a very credible score of 85.

Entry 55 - This last entry is a tall girl riding a big brown horse. As she canters to the first jump I notice that she rides vertically and is over-positioned. At jump #1 she goes from the vertical position to a much too forward position over the jump. The change from 'in the tack' to 'out of the tack' is too drastic. She jumps the second fence standing up a little and has a very rough and late lead change. She switches lead at fence #5 and gets left behind at the 'in and out', although she recovers and jumps out all right.

Summary: Although she is a bit over-positioned, she has a tall, well-distributed look. The late and forced lead change is her most serious fault. This leaves her with a score of 78.

Erynn Ballard

Overall Comments

A good class - all my ribbon winners are scores of 80 or above. I have an outstanding winner, with another top rider right behind him. A fun class to judge, as they all rode well and didn't miss any jumps. This has allowed me to concentrate and comment on their riding techniques. I enjoy it when the riders are the winners, and not the course.

Alyssa Smith-Avery

Questions & Answers

Q: **In an equitation class, do you take into account how a horse jumps?**

A: You watch the rider, however you are also focusing on the horse insofar as evenness, rideability, distances from which he leaves the ground at the jumps and hard rubs or rails down as a result of the rider's position and technical ability. It is a bonus if the horse jumps in good form, as that means the ride was right! Often you will see horses that jump flat used as equitation horses as they are easier to stay quiet on in the air.

Q: **When asked to demonstrate extended gaits, should the rider steady along the short sides and proceed to lengthen down the long sides, or should the extended stride be maintained all the way around the ring?**

A: The best way to show off an extended gait is down the long side of the ring. The judge is watching the gait more down the long sides, rather than at the ends of the ring. The rider must balance around the turns and shape the ends without cutting the corners.

If the horse is extending around the end there is a strong possibility that it will fall out of the gait.

***Q:*When a halt is called for in an equitation class, and the horse reins back from the halt, how do you score it?**

A: It would depend on the quality of the performance. If the rider is far superior in the class and the horse steps back from the halt from nervousness, then you may be a bit lenient. A proper halt, though, is what you are looking for. The horse should stand squarely on all four legs, without tossing his head or showing strain. Stepping back is certainly noted, but perhaps not serious enough to eliminate a rider from the ribbons.

***Q:*When testing riders called back in an equitation class, are you limited to the number on the specifications for the class, and are you limited to just one series of tests?**

A: You are only obligated to test the minimum, but you may add more if they are close in performance and you feel they are eligible to be tested. You may test further if you feel the top riders are tied and you need to do more to separate them.

Laura Tidball-Balisky

***Q:*Do you as a judge ever walk an equitation course?**

A: Absolutely. It is advisable, as you get a true feel for the course and the lines. When a test is required and you have to design the test, it is advisable to walk any new lines to be used to make sure they will work out.

Q: **What is the idea behind bringing the riders into the ring to announce the test?**

A: In order to keep trainers from telling their riders how to ride the test. This allows the riders to plan their own strategy. It is very important that the riders remember the number of each jump, as the jumps are often jumped out of order in the testing stage.

Q: **After each rider completes their test do you allow them to leave the ring?**

A: No. It is not fair to leave the final competitor alone in the ring as their horse may get nervous or excited being left alone. All the riders should have the same atmosphere in which to be tested. Once a rider has completed their test, they simply return to the line-up.

Q: **How do you feel about a rider that talks to his horse while on course?**

A: Silence is golden. The only ones that should hear the rider are the rider and the horse. Any clucking, 'whoa' or talking takes away from the performance, and actually amplifies the problem they are having.

Q: **Do you like verbal testing in an equitation class, or does it put the riders on the spot?**

A: It is not a common practice, as it is time consuming, and time is dear during a day at the horse show. If you have the time, however, it is a good test, and doesn't put any more pressure on the riders than riding the course does. Questions which make the rider more aware of their horses, such as parts of the horse, tack, stable management and performances, are good examples to use.

Sydney Vince

Q: **If you have a rider that performs beautifully in an equitation class, but is turned out poorly, how do you penalize them?**

A: Turnout of horse and rider is part of the whole presentation, so if there are two equal performances this could be the deciding factor. However, if the round was far superior to the others in the class, the turn out would become secondary and the rider would still win, as the performance takes priority.

Q: **If a junior rider's chinstrap comes undone during a round, and they have to stop and do it up, how does this affect their round?**

A: It is mandatory that a junior rider stops to do up their chinstrap before proceeding on course if it comes undone. If this rule is not followed, the rider is eliminated. As a judge, you must disregard the interruption and judge the round from the point where the rider stopped. If they don't stop on their own you may have the announcer excuse the rider from the ring. Again, safety first.

Q: **If testing is optional what factors do you consider when deciding to use further testing?**

*A:*If you have a clear-cut winner, you can pin the class. If your top are very close, you certainly have the right to test further. You may test for second or third place separation as well, but usually the riders fall into place without that being necessary. Keep in mind the length of the day. If you tested every class when it wasn't necessary for placing the class, we would all be at the ring after dark!

*Q:*Should a rider use a two-point seat position in an equitation class?

*A:*With the technical difficulties proposed in today's medal and equitation classes, it is advisable for the rider to use a modified three-point position. The upper body is inclined at about 10%, and the seat is light, but in contact. The rider needs his upper body to ride the tight distances and turns in the course, backing up the shoulders to shorten the stride and balance the horse. The two-point position (with the seat out of the saddle and the body inclined at a 20% angle) is too much of a 'hunter' seat for the equitation ring. A 'perched' ride is not an effective ride.

*Q:*Is there a certain 'dress code' for the equitation ring?

*A:*The proper dress for the equitation ring is a neat, proper and clean riding outfit. A navy blue or dark green or grey jacket is acceptable. Gloves should be worn, but are not mandatory. Boots should be polished and fit properly. The rider's hair should be up in the helmet, contained within a hairnet (for the girls). Neatness is expected, and adds to the polished look.

*Q:*If a rider is eliminated in a ride-off of a medal class, is the rider eliminated from the entire class?

*A:*No. The rider is in the ride-off as further testing for a group of usually the top riders. They would end up placing last of those in this phase of the class, which may be second, third or fourth place.

Melanie Walters

Q:When asked to counter canter a jump after starting the course should you execute a simple or a flying change?

*A:*The flying change would be preferable, as a simple change involves trotting which is considered a major fault.

Q:Which is worse in an equitation class - counter canter or cross canter?

*A:*A well-executed counter canter, balanced, rhythmical and with correct flexion is a valuable exercise and accepted movement. A cross canter or disunited canter is a mistake indicative of loss of balance and rhythm. Someone who executes a balanced and rhythmical turn in counter canter and meets the jump correctly, gets my nod ahead of a disunited canter that makes finding the jump difficult.

However, if someone comes around a turn on the wrong lead (i.e. wrong flexion and unbalanced) without attempting a correction, and another attempts to do a flying change and fails for one reason or another winding up disunited, the latter may come out ahead.

The judge has to look at the total picture and how the next jump was met, which ultimately is the most important part of the exercise. There are world famous horses who, while executing a very tight turn at speed, may take a few disunited steps. It is their somewhat unorthodox way of handling a fast turn - and in no way should become a training goal.

Q: **How do you feel about a bad jumper in an equitation class?**

A: The equitation division is the only division where the rider rather than the horse is judged. In the hunter or jumper divisions a rider does have an effect on how the horse performs. A very skillful rider on a limited horse will improve the horse. In the equitation division the horse has an effect on the rider. It takes a very skillful rider to compete on a bad jumping horse.

A competent equitation judge will raise his eyes to the level of the rider, but a bad jumper does detract from the overall picture. A bad jumper is much harder to hold a solid position on when jumping. They also allow for a much smaller margin of error on the part of a rider. For example, a leg hanger must leave far enough away from the base of a jump to be able to negotiate the obstacle. In equitation classes, faults are not penalized unless they are the fault of the rider, but a bad jumper is much less scopey and therefore it is more difficult to have a clean round. Courses today are technical and tend to test the rider and horse. It takes a great deal of manufacturing and finesse to get a bad jumper around an equitation course in an attractive and polished riding style. In a class where the competition level is high an excellent ride on a horse that jumps well will present the smoothest and most skilled picture.

A judge must judge the round in front of him and cannot make concessions for a horse or rider. An equitation round on a horse that is a bad jumper will have to be far superior to the rest of the competitors to win. The rider will have a much more difficult job to do. It can be and often is done, but to be a consistent winner at a top level of competition a bad jumper does detract from a rider's position and demands a very technical ride.

Q: **When there is a knockdown in an equitation class, how do you judge the situation?**

*A:*A knockdown in an equitation class does not automatically constitute a low score. Circumstances must be considered. Was it the fault of ineffective riding? Was it a poor jumping effort by the animal despite good riding? Was it the fault of the horse and rider fighting each other?

When the knockdown is primarily caused by the rider, I consider this to be a major error. However, when a knockdown is the result of poor jumping effort on behalf of the horse, I analyze the performance of the rider in successfully getting to the jump. It is particularly important to assess the rider's ability to ride off the corner, as it is invariably the first fence on a line that is the culprit. If I feel that the rider has accomplished this task, I would not hesitate to use this entry in my call back below first place. Depending, of course, on the quality of the class.

In the third scenario, when a knockdown is caused by the horse and rider fighting each other, invariably they will not be in my call back order. However, if there is sufficient proof to me that the rider is making a supreme effort to fulfill the proper aids, then I feel that serious consideration could be given for a late call back, depending on the degree of competition in the class.

In my opinion, the outcome in any of the above situations, comes down to the number of clean, quality performances.

*Q:***What do you think about switching horses in Medal classes?**

*A:*As a judge and coach, I believe that switching riders onto different horses is the ultimate riding test. It demands that a rider be skilled, confident and experienced. If we are to assume that the winners of our various medal finals are to have a future competing at an elite level then it is appropriate that we test the skills that apply towards this goal.

When judging a medal class, I may take the top four riders and have them switch horses. Usually I would have my top two riders switch and my third and fourth rider switch. However, the best test of all is to have all the top four riders ride all four horses (as is done in the CET Regional an other medal competitions). This is very time consuming and not practical given the time schedule of the average horse show.

Switching horses is a great test for 'weeding out' what I call a 'one dimensional rider'. Many riders are comfortable on a certain type of horse, whose temperament suits their riding style. Such riders become very accomplished on their own familiar mount but become a 'fish out of water' on a strange horse. For instance, a rider who is effective on a hot, sensitive horse, may be lost riding a strong, dull, or cold-blooded horse. Catch riding is an art at which few excel.

There is always risk involved in this test, though. For reasons of safety and good horsemanship this test should be reserved for special times, such as regional or national finals. It is not a good test for novice riders or where green horses are involved.

*Q:*What do you think about outside assistance, coaching, clucking, etc.

*A:*Not much! Coaches should not be allowed to coach their riders from the sidelines. Riders should be left alone to fully concentrate and focus while they are in the show ring. Interruption by the coach acts as a disruption, and mistakes are likely to follow. If the judge or steward notice outside assistance they should deal with it in accordance to the rule book.

*Q:*When asked to trot a fence, where should you trot, and should it be a posting or sitting trot?

*A:*The distance away from a fence that one should trot would differ depending on the exercise incorporated with the trot jump. For instance, if you are cantering through a turn, or on a roll-back turn, you should make the transition to the trot as close to the trot jump as possible without making it look like a last minute, 'I almost forgot' idea.

If the trot fence is coming out of a line or off an opening gallop to an oxer, then the downward transition should be as prompt as possible on the landing side, without looking rough. The difference in distance away from the jump that a rider picks up the trot, in these two situations, exhibits the level of control a rider has over his horse.

Whether one should sit or post trot is not stipulated. The ideal solution for the perfectly mounted rider would be to do a posting trot literally throughout the exercise, the jump being merely a rise function of the trot. However, most young, less experienced horses would be more likely to successfully negotiate the trot jump ridden at the sitting trot, with the rider better able to keep a more balanced rhythm. The worst error a rider could make would be to begin at the rising trot and change to the sitting trot as this almost always results in a last minute canter stride.

Corie Bannister

Q: When to test further in a Medal Classes?

A: The first round of a medal class will determine how much further you should go in your testing of the riders. If the course designer has given you a challenging course which asks a lot of questions, how the riders handle this course determines the next steps for testing.

If, for example, after the first round you have four to six very solid performances, that is, each rider had a plan, executed it well and had the form to match the performance, your scores should be very close. In the Equine Canada Medal class the over fence portion is worth 60% of the score. In the flat phase (worth 40%) you ask questions such as lengthening and shortening of stride, counter canter, and work without stirrups. The two scores are then added together on your card. If the top four riders are very close in scores, now is the time to test.

The Equine Canada Rule book states "from a maximum of four of the contestants the judge may call for any two or more requirements". This change of wording from 'must' to 'may' has definitely changed the Medal Class. If the show is running late, the management may choose to eliminate the testing phase.

The judge should determine what he/she is going to use in the third phase prior to the start of the class. You have the opportunity to walk the course at this point, which is invaluable if you are designing a shorter course from the available jumps. You may choose to use two unrelated jumps to make a new line. This is a good indication of the rider's ability to reason and demonstrate their understanding of the horse's ability to respond. The third phase should incorporate both flat work and jumping, with or without stirrups.

Remember to have the test announced over the public address system, so the riders as well as the spectators are aware of the test.

Q: **In an equitation over fences class, do you prefer a deep seat or a forward seat?**

A: Whatever suits and works best. I don't really like an exaggerated forward seat as it could mean a weak ride. Too deep a seat means they are always having to catch up at the jumps.

Q: **How much do the turns count in an equitation over fences class?**

A: As much as you mark good jumps accordingly, note good turns. It is really important to keep it all fluent and smooth. Give credit for good, efficient turns along with the jumps to make the best overall picture. Rough turns spoil the round and effect the placings.

Q: **When you call for a ride off in an equitation class are you** allowed to use a jump in the test that the riders have not jumped in the initial round?

A: Absolutely not. Be sure you know the course and the numbers of the jumps. Extra jumps in the ring cannot be introduced in a ride off if not jumped in the initial round.

Q: **When an equitation class over fences calls for a flat phase to count (i.e. 40%), can a rider move up or down a lot after the jumping phase?**

A: That depends on how good of a group you have, and how "testy" you make the flat phase. How well the riders perform on the flat very often dramatically alters the placings. When a flat phase calls for 40%, try to ask for some more difficult gaits and transitions which will allow good riders to move up or hold their placing.

Q: **In a ride-off test when you ask the riders to hand gallop a fence, how do you determine which fence to use?**

A: I have two suggestions. One is that it is a fence going away from the ingate, so you can determine whether the rider is making it happen or not. The second suggestion is to make sure it is an oxer, as they might hit a vertical and have it down or possibly make a mistake. An oxer is much more inviting to gallop to.

Q: **In a junior equitation class over fences a rider's chinstrap comes undone. Are they allowed to circle after pulling up to do up the chinstrap, or do they have to go straight to the next jump?**

A: A great question! I would answer this by saying that if it happens after a line of jumps, in the corner or far enough away from the next jump, they should just canter to the next jump. If they are too close to the fence a circle would be in order and not penalized.

Q: **In an over fence equitation class do you prefer the riders to enter the ring at a posting or a sitting trot?**

A: I am asked this so often, and I really do not have a preference. Whichever is the most efficient and prompt way to go to the first fence. Going directly at the canter would probably make the best impression on me, as a long, slow sitting trot entry does nothing for me but say, "get on with the job!".

Q: When you ask riders in a ride-off to exit the ring (e.g. at a sitting trot after the last fence), do you want them to make a circle at the trot or are you looking for an immediate exit of the ring?

A: It's up to the rider if I do not specify. I would be more impressed, however, if you come down to a sitting trot immediately after the last fence and proceed right out of the ring.

Q: When you have announced the ride-off test, and the riders are outside of the ring, do you stipulate how the riders should enter the ring?

A: Absolutely. It is required that they walk into the ring to proceed with their test. They must exit the ring at a walk as well.

Q: When showing in equitation a rider has her hair pulled neatly back in a pony tail with a bow tying it up. Another rider has as nice a round over fences as the rider with her hair outside of her helmet. Should the hair change her placing in the class?

A: Absolutely not. You pin the ride not the hairdo!

Q: In a USET class a rider goes around the entire course without having any trouble finding the jumps easily, although at every fence this rider opens his/her body before the horse has fully landed from the fence. You like the presentation of this rider and the way in which he/she found the jumps but the position unfolding bothers you. How do you place them?

A: Remember, form follows function. Find the jumps first.

Q: When you test the top four equitation riders do you think that the last one to go, or any of the others, has an advantage?

A: Yes. My solution is to have the riders waiting for their turn to turn their back to the one on course.

Q: **Starting their equitation class over fences, many riders enter the ring at a sitting trot. Is this required?**

A: Not at all. It is actually preferable to go straight to the canter and to the first jump.

Q: **What are some questions to ask the riders in a test?**

A: How many strides in a 96' line and a 72' line?

- Are running martingales allowed in a hunter class?

- Tell me two major faults in a hunter or equitation class?

- What am I looking for in a handy hunter class?

- What position am I looking for at the hand gallop?

- Can a hunter jog back in to the ring with a saddle on or a tail wrap?

- Is making a noise considered an unsoundness in a hunter?

- Can a hunter jog back in a halter or another bridle other than what he showed in?

Q: **When you ask a rider to drop their stirrups, is it acceptable if they cross them before continuing?**

A: It is a rule to allow the riders to make their own choice, and given them time to do so, before continuing.

Ashley Reber

Summary

Winning in equitation over fences should result from who rides the best and not who looks the best. The best round is more often than not the winner. I try to be as innovative as possible with the test when I judge equitation. We owe it to the industry to try new things.

Chapter Four

Equitation On The Flat

Toska Kocken

Introduction

Who is the best rider? Who presents themselves the best? The one who is actually riding will place ahead of the perfectly mounted rider who poses. You are looking for a rider who presents a horse well and has a good rapport with their mount. First and foremost the rider gets the job done and looks the part. The one who can do that is going to place ahead of the rider that looks stylish but is merely a passenger.

The riders must show the judge, in the short time in which they have to do so, that they know how to work their horse correctly and that the horse is comfortable and obedient. You look for the positive ride. The equitation riders should think about how they affect their horses, not about the pieces of their own position, and complete the entire job with precision.

Judging Faults

* (Some of the symbols listed under Equitation Over Fences also apply to Equitation On The Flat)

Faults listed from the worst to least severe:

Fault	Interpretation
DG	Posting on the wrong diagonal.
W.L.	Cantering on the incorrect lead.
STRP	Lost a stirrup.
TW R or S	Twisted rein or stirrup.
STF	Stiff, tense rider.
LS	Loose, sloppy rider.
O/C	No contact.
E	Eyes wandering or looking down.

C →	Long reins which communicate an uncontrolled performance.
C ←	Short reins which draw the rider's seat out of the saddle.
F/H	Fixed hand - one that does not follow the motions of the horse's head - set in an immobile position.
↑	Standing up in the stirrups (e.g. at the canter the rider appears to be posting).
P/T	Poor transitions either upward or downward.
H↑	"Above the bit" indicates the horse's evasion of the rider's legs, seat and hands.
O/F	Over flexed, forced, too much collection.
K←	Knee pinching.
FT →↑	Foot is either parallel → or heel is riding up↑ .
STRP → ←	Stirrup length looks either too long → or too short ← .
H/B	Hollow back - a rider closing his hip angle too much and carrying his buttocks too far behind him and his shoulders too far back.
R	Roached back (rounded back) often a result of too short a stirrup.
RS	Rounded shoulders - weakens the effectiveness of the back.

Erynn Ballard

Positive Features (Ideal Positions)

The ideal leg position places the leg just behind the horse's girth. The steady leg provides a sound foundation for the upper body. Viewed from the side, the rider's knee and toe are on the same vertical line. The rider's calf is against the horse. When viewed from the front, the rider's legs are snug against the saddle. The inner knee bones are in contact with the saddle, the inside of the lower legs are against the horse's sides, and the toes are turned out slightly.

In the proper position, the hands are just over and slightly in front of the wither and in a direct line from the rider's elbow to the horse's mouth. The forearms and wrists should be straight and the thumbs just inside the vertical, only a couple of inches apart.

The upper body can be positioned in the two-point or the three-point position. The two-point position or 'galloping position' is used mainly over jumps. The rider's legs are in contact with the horse but the rider's seat is held out of the saddle to free the horse's back. The upper body is inclined approximately 20 degrees in front of the vertical. The rider will then be with the motion of the horse. (The two point position is a popular hunter round position.)

The three-point position is one in which the rider's legs and seat are all in contact with the horse. This position offers more security than the two-point position. In the three-point position, the rider can reinforce his aids, making them stronger. The three-point position is more popular on the flat as it demonstrates a better position and a solid communication with the horse. For an experienced rider, the three-point can provide an advantage over fences for tight turns and precision riding. It allows for maximum control of the horse and engagement of all the aids.

Bending - a properly bent horse is one who's body is slightly curved around the inside leg, in direct relation to the turn. (e.g. when going to the left, the horse's body is bent to the left.) The horse's body is bent from nose to tail. The rider must maintain impulsion around the turns, and not allow the horse to drop it's weight on the inside shoulder which encourages the horse to cut the turn.

The Walk:	In an equitation class, the walk should be slow, and slightly contained. The rider should have a feel of the horse's mouth.
Working Walk:	It should be a little more lively, more animated. The horse should appear as if it is going somewhere. The walk should be workmanlike, with contact and slight flexion.
Sitting Trot:	Use a decreased pace, it is easier to sit to! Look as smooth as you possibly can. Have a little more contact and a little more flexion in this slower pace than in the ordinary trot.
Posting Trot:	Let go of the flexion a little bit, but do not lengthen the stride. It is an 'ordinary' trot, posting.

You Be The Judge

Extending the trot:	Use a working trot, and rise with a little longer rein to let the head and neck 'out' slightly. There should be enough extension to show the judge that the horse's stride is opening up and the legs are reaching further out. There should be no increase in the pace. It should definitely not look as if the horse is going to break into a canter at any moment.
Canter:	The working canter is an ordinary canter with contact and a little flexion. Use less flexion in the canter than at the sitting trot. The canter is a stronger gait and you have to cover some ground.
Extending the canter:	Show a lengthening of the stride. Sit a little bit deeper to create the lengthening stride. Lighten the contact slightly, but do not totally abandon it. It is not a hand gallop because you are sitting. Open up the stride and make it long and fluid. The stride should cover more ground than the ordinary canter.
Counter Canter:	In the counter canter the horse leads with its outside foreleg, and its body is flexed slightly towards the outside of the ring. It should be just as fluid and controlled as the canter. Sit, maintain the contact, but keep the gait going. Do not move under the pace so that you lose the gait. It should not look like the rider is 'protecting' the canter, but maintaining it.
Hand Gallop:	Definitely forward in movement with a long, looser frame. Really cover the ground, with the rider in a two point position encouraging the horse forward.

Judging A Flat Class And Marking The Card

This is a "B" equitation on the flat class. As the riders all assemble in the ring and are working at will, I often get a head start and jot down a few numbers. I like to do this as it gives me a feel for the class, and I am more comfortable knowing that I have an idea of the calibre of the class - will I ask for extra or stick to the basics? Also, with a few numbers written down it helps expedite the class once started, and if I have to bring some riders into the middle I already have a head start and can spend more time watching.

The first number I write down is #613. This is a girl riding a grey Hanoverian. She goes into the middle of the 'good' list, and I am assured that she could win a ribbon. She becomes my frame of reference. Another good possible ribbon winner is #230, a girl riding a lop-eared chestnut. I put her behind #613, as she doesn't seem quite as effective. #948, a male rider, very stylish and well positioned, catches my eye. I put his number ahead of #613. I then see #912, a boy on a black horse with a somewhat parallel foot, but a good position otherwise, and I squeeze him into the bottom of the list.

Topping the 'all right' column is an unbraided bay horse, #319. The girl's stirrups seem a bit short. Then I notice a very attractive rider on a good moving brown horse, who seems to be tossing and fussing about something (flies or contact?). I write her number down, #421, and I'll see how things progress. The seventh exhibitor, #507, is a pinto ridden by a girl with a fixed hand. Even though there are only six ribbons, I need to add a few as these bottom ones have faults that can escalate when they are asked to move in the opposite direction. The last two numbers that I choose are #780, a chestnut horse with white socks that is quite high-headed (the rider appears to be avoiding contact with the horse), and #202, a big brown horse ridden by a girl with wandering eyes. This last entry goes into my protector column.

After working at the walk, trot and canter, they all reverse. I notice right away that #421 has settled down and is working

You Be The Judge

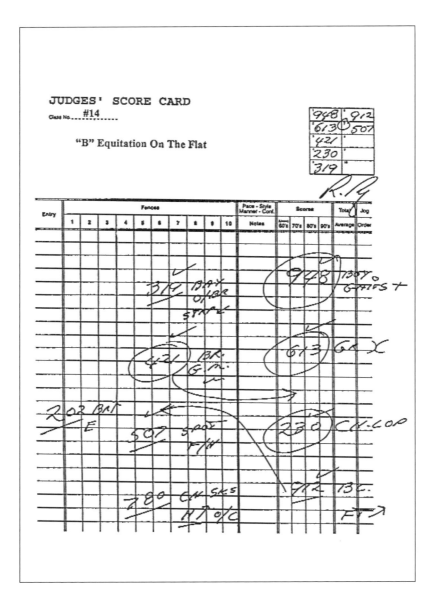

beautifully - I move them right over to the good column in third position, as she is really a top rider. However, the beginning of the class will keep her away from a first or second placing. I circle my top ones in the right hand column as I watch them in the final direction, to be sure they still belong there. #912 is getting a little bit excited and the parallel foot means no leg contact (or a hot horse). As he progressively warms up, he moves down to sixth and across to the all right column.

I have four good ribbon winners, so I am satisfied. I ask the class to walk and line up. I fill in each number in the result boxes, and check the numbers off down on my card to make absolutely sure that all are accounted for and placed correctly.

In this case, I was comfortable with the placings. I did not have to test the group beyond a sitting trot. They showed themselves enough to separate the winners without me having to prolong the class.

Testing The Rider On The Flat

Test	Explanation.
Halt	Prompt, smooth, immobile, standing still and square on all four legs.
Back Up	Steady, on the bit, no raising of the head (often a designated number of steps are called for), invisible hands and legs, straight with the horse's mouth closed.
Working Without Stirrups	Rider drops or crosses them. Posting without stirrups is the most difficult as it shows the true strength and effectiveness of the lower leg. Riders may also asked to pick up their stirrups while working and need to do so without looking down, and not

	twisting the stirrup to place it correctly on the ball of the foot.
Mount / Dismount	Consider the rider's size in relation to their horse. The rider should mount without pulling on the horse's mouth or poking the animal in the side. When mounting properly the rider holds the reins tightly enough so the horse won't walk forward. They should grasp the mane or crest to prevent pulling on the horse's mouth when mounting, and the rider should turn the toe of the boot into the girth rather than pressing into the horse's side.
Turn on the Forehand	This is an exercise executed from a halt, employed to teach the horse obedience. The horse's hind quarters are moved in regular, quiet steps in a circle around its forehand.
Turn on the Haunches	Can be executed from a halt or walk. Requires the horse to move into the bend.
Change Horses	Ability to cope with an animal at the spur of the moment without the benefit of practice time.
Shoulder-In	The horse moves forward and sideways down the track. Its forehand is a little inside the track with its shoulders turned in, while its hind quarters remain on the track. Its body is bent around the rider's inside leg, away from the direction of travel.

Haunches - In and Out	The horse is flexed and bent in the direction in which it is moving. The forehand remains on the outside track. The haunches are shifted to the inside, so that from the front one sees four tracks. Haunches-out is a reversed haunches-in. Here the forehand is brought to the inside. The hind quarters remain on the outside track.
Work With Long Reins	Let the reins slide through your fingers so there is a loop. Guide the horse with your leg and upper body.
Work With Light Contact	Take up the contact but keep a gentle feel of the horse's mouth and not too short a rein.
Work On The Bit	Close up on the reins, shorten, with a good feel of the horse's mouth.
Reverse Trot	Change direction across the ring and demonstrate a change of diagonals.
Reverse Canter	Change direction by the use of a flying lead change. The complete change of direction should be performed at the canter.
Canter to Counter Canter	Cantering on one lead, demonstrate a flying change to continue on the counter canter lead.
Counter Canter to Canter	Counter cantering on one lead, demonstrating a flying change to continue changed lead.
Figure 8 At The Trot	Two nice rounded circles demonstrating the change of diagonals.

Figure 8 At The Canter — Again, two nicely executed full circles with usually a simple change of lead if announced and allowed. Otherwise use a flying change.

Change Leads In A Straight Line — Simple or flying changes, if not stipulated. Demonstrate the correct number asked for, or as many as possible if not told. Often simple changes are as risky as flying changes.

Natasha Smith Avery

140

Questions & Answers

Q: **How do you balance your horse in the corners without allowing him to drop his shoulder?**

A: Travelling to the left, work with an inside bend around the inside leg, with the horse's head and neck slightly bent to the left. Use your outside leg to keep his quarters following without allowing them to fall to the outside. When learning this skill, start a bit at a time, at the walk. When you have accomplished balancing and bending at the walk, go the trot, and then to the canter.

Q: **Are gloves mandatory in an equitation class?**

A: No, they are not listed as mandatory dress, but they do nicely finish off the look of being neat and well turned out. The hands become a bit more 'invisible' under gloves, as the hands blend into the sleeve of the dark jacket. This is a bonus for the rider!

Q: **Are you allowed to wear a running martingale in a flat equitation class?**

A: Martingales (running or standing) are only allowed when it is a flat phase of an equitation over fence class, such as a medal. They are not permitted in the basic seat equitation flat classes.

Q: **When you, as a judge, call for a rein back in a class, is it wise to say how many steps you would like the riders to execute?**

A: It is a good idea to specify how many steps you would like the riders to back up, as it becomes a more accurate test. Letting the rider back up as far as they want makes the test only show that they can back up, without the test of accuracy.

Q: **In a flat equitation class, when you call for a halt followed by a reverse of direction, what if they walk when they reverse?**

A: It is wrong. They need to stay at the halt until the next gait or maneuver is called.

Q: How do you respond when a rider asks you a question such as, "What didn't you like about me on the flat?" or "How can I improve?".

A: I like to answer the question with a question. This makes the rider think about how they are riding and what they can do to improve. For example, you could say, "What do you think you need to do differently?". Once they have given you a reasonable answer, if they are correct, this will steer them onto the right track.

Q: What about turn out of the rider?

A: It is all a part of the total presentation. A beautiful rider can be detracted from by poorly fitted attire. You really need to look the part! Some things to avoid:

- boots and clothing improperly fitted

- hair not neatly contained in a hairnet

- poor or flashy coloured clothing

- white gloves

- dirty boots or clothing

Q: Judging alone versus judging together. Are two opinions better than one?

A: Let me answer this simply by saying two things, if you are compatible then great, if not, then it can be a nightmare (the show may end up prolonged or you may not end up with the correct, agreed upon results). Personally, I tend to rely on my own opinion. When I have to confer with someone else it only adds to the length of time to get the results. Moreover, it means that you have to work doubly hard. The days are already difficult enough with the hours of concentration required.

Q: What about a really bad moving horse?

A: Raise your eyes and focus on the rider. However, very often a bad mover does not always follow with a smooth flat ride and may appear somewhat rough. The smoothness of the gaits allow for a poised, still, comfortable ride. In contrast, often the offensive mover dislodges and gives one the impression that the rider is having to work at being properly positioned. In conclusion, a bad mover does not enhance a rider's position, but it should not eliminate them if they ride well.

Q: How do you prefer riders to enter the ring in an equitation on the flat class?

A: The rider should enter the ring displaying an air of efficiency and style. To do this, they must be totally prepared, suitably mounted and immaculately turned out.

When entering the ring the rider should have the horse in a workmanlike frame, and once in the ring go straight to work. This is the opportunity to catch the judge's eye and make that important first impression. It is important to stay by yourself. The riders could work at a balanced posting trot, canter or counter canter after they enter the ring, until the class is called to order. They should make the most efficient use of the time allowed before the class actually begins.

First impressions are lasting impressions. Therefore, a rider's entrance to the ring can be of considerable significance when judging a large class.

Q: How do you deal with a lame horse in an equitation class?

A: The question of what to do with a lame horse in an equitation class falls into the area of the judges experience as horsemen. Equitation rules do not call specifically for soundness as a judgment factor, however there are many reasons why a judge should leave a lame horse out of the final cut and out of the ribbons. Obviously the degree of lameness must be a considering factor. A very slight lameness where the horse is in no obvious pain is not quite the same as a severely lame horse hobbling around the ring.

The rider is being judged on his or her performance on a balanced, well trained and properly prepared horse. It is the overall picture that is judged and not just a rider propped up on a horse. Lameness definitely detracts from this picture since the horse lacks balance and cadence.

Since equitation involves horsemanship, the rider should be penalized for not noticing or caring that their horse is in fact lame. The most serious consideration in any equitation endeavor must always be the health and welfare of the horse. The Equine Canada has a Code of Ethics which states that all members, including riders, trainers and officials must "uphold the welfare of the horses, regardless of value, as a primary consideration in all activities", and that "horses be treated with kindness, respect, and the compassion that they deserve, and that they never be subjected to mistreatment." Equestrian sports are continually under the scrutiny of animal rights groups. Keeping this in mind, it should be very clear that the sport does not encourage individuals to show horses that are in obvious pain.

Q: How important are transitions in equitation classes?

A: The purpose of equitation classes are to judge the riding ability, and to coordinate his or her fundamental skills with those of the horse. This coordination is only possible if the rider is able to successfully communicate with the horse, and both have done their homework. The success of the communication between the horse and rider is visible in the correctness and accuracy when performing the tasks demanded by the judge.

Transitions are essentially a multifaceted task. In equitation classes, transitions show coordination of skills, balance, discipline and mental focus. Also, the training of transitions carries through to other facets of riding. Like any skill involving coordination, correct transitions are not developed overnight.

The judge's expectations vary according to the age and level of the rider. The 'Equitation C' rider does not have the benefit of years of training. Consequently, he or she is not expected to be able to perform transitions at the level of an 'Equitation A' rider. The C rider is required to do transitions that demonstrate control and focus. A lack of discipline and control will often manifest itself in roughness that is penalized. A rider at this level cannot be expected to have smooth, clean and accurate transitions.

The 'Equitation B' rider is at the transitional stage between the young and the skilled rider. This is a time when the rider is developing more skill, therefore, a higher degree of accuracy is expected by the judge. The rider should have a well-developed sense of control, balance and discipline.

The 'Equitation A' and Medal rider should be able to demonstrate his or her ability to communicate with the horse and draw upon the training of both. This is clearly shown by clean, smooth and accurate transitions. Beautiful transitions can only be executed when the horse and rider are in balance and each is communicating as well as cooperating with the other. The judge expects to see beautiful transitions from the 'Equitation A' and Medal rider, and will judge accordingly.

Q: **What about a small child on a horse? Do they have an advantage?**

A: The horse is the backdrop for the rider. Being properly mounted, size wise, will enhance the judge's impression of the equitation ride. A horse that is too large for the rider will distort a small rider's proportions, making the leg look shorter as a horse that is too small for a rider will look awkward and poorly fitted. However, a quiet, well-broken horse may be a better choice than a small, quick pony for a small child. As long as the rider is capable of handling the horse, the quiet horse is a good vehicle to show off their talents.

Q: **Before a flat equitation class, as the riders come into the ring some will show an extended trot, counter canter and execute different manoeuvres. Does this have any impact on the placings?**

A: No. Have no fear, I will find the best riders without the showy entrance. Riders can come in and practice different things before the class is called to order, but I judge them once the class has started.

Q: **In the flat equitation class, does the best rider or the best mounted rider win?**

A: I have so often had good riders on misbehaved horses not win just for that reason. You need to be well mounted with a horse that is mannerly and obedient so you can execute the best ride.

Q: **When asked to line up from the canter, could you share with us the best way to execute this?**

A: You are expected to keep cantering to the centre of the ring, which should be announced as to which direction this is to be done. Halt from a canter, not from a trot or a walk.

Q: **In an equitation on the flat, or an under saddle class, do you have to walk, trot and canter them both directions of the ring? Would a sitting trot be enough one way and would a counter canter constitute the canter?**

A: Trotting each way can be sitting, extended, collected or posting. Canter can be either extended, collected or counter canter. You can do just any one or a combination of all or any of the above. It's the judge's call.

Q: **In beginner equitation classes, do you keep it really simple - walk, trot, canter, or can you ask for more?**

A: Simplicity is best. If I ask for more it may be for a halt to show me that they all can stop, and if needed, it is good in case one falls off or runs away!

Summary

When the riders all assemble into the ring and work at will, they have the opportunity to sit trot, counter canter, extend the trot, flex and bend. In a good class they may all appear to be very professional and workmanlike. As the judge looks around panic can set in, as they all appear to be winners, and you have only six ribbons to place. Remember, they are showing their best skills to you at this point!

Write down some numbers of your preferred riders, who will be potential ribbon winners. You will be amazed how they will sort themselves out into an order as they work along under your instruction. Panic will subside as you see the numbers you have down are where they should be or close to it. You can relax and be sure of your judgement by asking for some difficult tests. The riders will truly earn their placings. Remember you are the trained expert, and it is your job to pick out the best of the class, and you have done just that!

Chapter Five

Conformation

Fair Swap

Introduction

The Equine Canada rule book states that in judging hunters on the line, they should be evaluated on "conformation, quality, substance and suitability to become a hunter".

The judge is to base his evaluation on conformation, way of going and soundness, but there is no specification on how much individual emphasis is placed on each aspect, or the relative importance of each. I believe that there is too much emphasis placed on conformation. I lean more towards movement. The intention of breeding programs, and the judging of them, is to produce performers from the breeding divisions.

Spit and polish time only comes when a horse is brought to a show in proper condition. That means that he is clipped, trimmed and braided, and is scrupulously clean. Riders should remember that they are promoting themselves and their horses. It is always better to overdress both the rider and the horse. Judging horses and ponies on the line can be really difficult and awkward simply because we are not subjected to it often enough. The principle idea of this chapter is to put you at ease by going over the basics and outlining a procedure that can enable you to view, sort out, and put an order to a class of horses or ponies.

Class Procedure

Lining Up

* Plan the ring yourself.
* Show the ringmaster what you want.
* Have enough room to view all competitors.
* Have the horses off the rail so you can stand back and view them from each side.
* Allow for space between horses so that you will not get kicked, but still allow for proper viewing.
* Jog away from the gate (this enables the handlers to control the trot better).

* Handlers should be handling on the opposite side from you, so that you can fully view movement when jogging.

* Jog all of the horses in the class before you line them up in order. You owe it to them.

* After the original order is made and lined up, try not to move horses around too much, as your original line up has the most ammunition.

* It is possible, and a good idea in a large class, to keep your top horses in the ring and excuse the remainder, so that you only have to take your second look at the top of the group. This works well if you are judging with a second judge, as it gives you a better perspective helping you to arrive at more equal placings.

Jogging

Models	VS	Breeding Classes
Usually there are jumps in the ring.		Empty ring for more room.
Have fewer numbers - Jog one after the other .		Walk down towards the ingate and jog back individually.
Advise the ringmaster to hold the next one until you glance up to signal ready.		Young horses get too excited jogging as a group.

* When judging alone, start at the front of the line. This will allow late arrivals to enter the ring.

* When there are two judges, start at opposite ends so that you are not continually colliding

* When judging alone, you can pull each horse out one at a time. This way you can give them another look, and make sure you are satisfied.

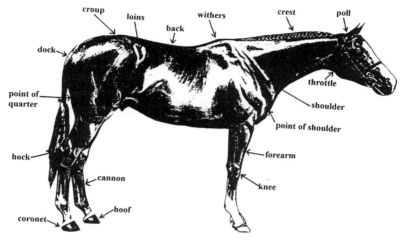

Body parts of the horse.
Painting of "Fair Swap", by Myfanwy MacDonald

Individual Inspection

Start your inspection with a side view. Back away from the horse and get an overall view. Note the top line, head, shoulder, neck, legs, wither, back hind quarter and tail set.

Head

* Not too large or small.
* Ears should be in proportion with the size of the head.
* Jowl joins nicely to the neck and is not too thick.
* Large eyes are better than too small.

Front Legs

* Should be square and underneath, not camped out in front or under behind.

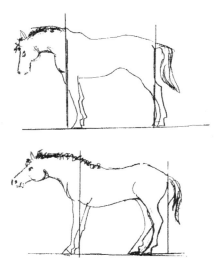

Top drawing shows horse standing under in front and camped out behind.
Bottom drawing shows the opposite, camped out in front and under behind.

Neck

* Not too cresty or ewed.

* Not too muscular or studdish.

* Not too short or long. The neck should be in proportion with the rest of the body.

Shoulder

* Should be long and sloping.

* If it is too straight and short it can restrict the length of stride.

Wither

* Not protruding or mutton.

* Simple definition and fits smoothly into the top line.

Back

* Short is better than too long.

* Note if it is sway backed.

The Judge is Back

Hind Quarter Leg

* Leg should stand parallel to the point where the tail joins the hind end.
* Note whether the hind legs are sickle hocked or if the hind leg is too straight.

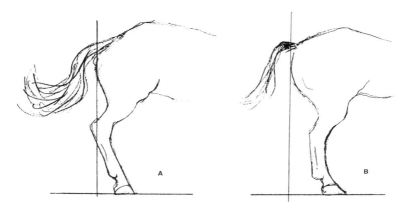

Figure A: Sickle hock. Figure B: Straight hind leg.

Tail Set

* Should fit into the top line and sit high rather than dropping off the horse's rump.
* Move in closer to examine the foot and legs. Look for obvious conformation defects such as ring bone, osselets, sidebone, bowed tendons or windpuffs.
* Is the foot the proper size and connected with the pastern?
* Then move to the front of the horse. Look for splints, the shape of the foot, and whether or not they toe in or out. Are the knees benched, crooked or bowed? Are there any blemishes or scars?
* Move to the back of the horse. Look for bowed or cow hocks. After completing this detailed inspection and jogging the class, make a new line-up according to what you have seen. This gives you the opportunity to see your top placing horses closer together for a true comparison.

Quickly go down the line to glance at each one, giving them a second overall view to be sure they are in the correct order.

At this point go back towards the front, and focus one more time on the top ones. How do they compare as you stand back and view them? As a rule, I leave them. The first detailed inspection has arrived at this order. Unless they are extremely close in all areas and one is showing himself better, then rarely do you need to move anyone.

Conformation Faults

The following faults would usually keep a horse out of the ribbons:

Crooked leg   Offset.

Ringbone   High - pastern joint and can be seen one inch above the coronet.

               Low - found at the coronet.

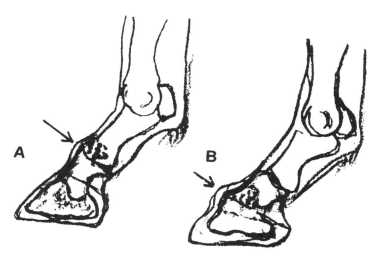

Figure A: Shows high ringbone.
Figure B: Shows low ringbone, affecting the coffin joint.

You Be The Judge

Osselets   Appears as a bulge on the front of the fetlock.

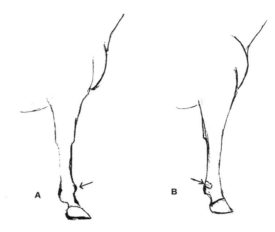

Figure A: Shows an osselet, found on the front of the fetlock.
Figure B: Indicates the location of a windpuff.

Sidebone   Just above the horse's heel on either side or both sides of the foot.

Bone Spavin   Inside of hind leg and on the lower part of the hock.

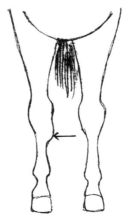

Arrow points to a bone spavin, viewed from the front of the hind legs.

156

Thoroughpin   Just in front of the point of the hock. Round ball-like swelling.

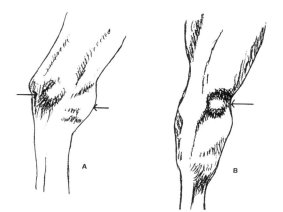

Figure A: Arrow on the left indicates a secondary bog swelling.
Arrow on right points to a bog spavin.
Figure B: Arrow indicates the position of a thoroughpin.

Bowed Tendon   Severe strain to the tendon sheath which results in scar tissue, appears between the fetlock and the knee.

Bog Spavin   Front of the hock, swelling on the hock joint.

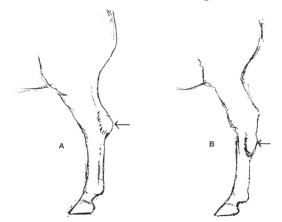

Figure A: Arrow indicates location of a capped hock.
Figure B: Arrow indicates a curb.

Curb	Just below the point of the hock, inflammation of one of the ligaments of the hock.
Splint	Bony growth below the horse's knee and usually on the inside of the front leg. Can also occur on the outside of the leg or on the hind legs.
Capped Hock	Swelling at the point of the hock.
Capped Elbow	(Shoe boil) Swelling caused by a shoe hitting the elbow while the horse is lying down.

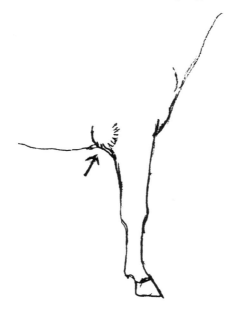

Arrow points to a capped elbow.

Bucked Shins	Swelling of the front of the cannon bone.
Club Foot	Both the foot and pastern axis are excessively steep.
Toes In	Pigeon toed.

Toes Out	Less serious than "Toes In" as there is less interference.

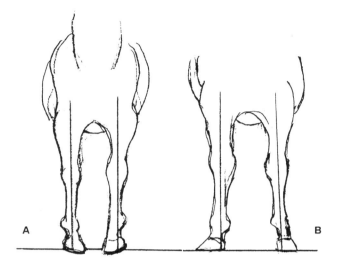

Figure A: Indicates a horse that toes in.
Figure B: Indicates a horse that toes out.

Calf Knee	Knee set too far back.
Bucked Knee	Knee sprung, hangs over the front of the cannon bone (over at the knee).
Sickle Hock	Angle of the hock joint so acute from the side that the horse is standing under from the hock down.
Straight Hind Leg	Hock joint is so erect that it causes excess. concussion to the leg.
Bowed Hocks	Horse's hind legs bent outward placing the hocks too far on the outside of the body.
Cow Hocks	Hocks too close together and turned in so they point toward each other.

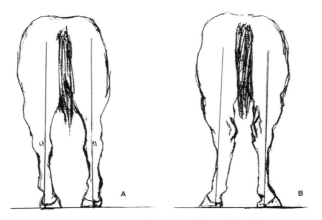

Figure A: Shows a horse with bowed hocks.
Figure B: Indicates cow hocks. Notice that the bowed hocked horse toes in,
while the cow hocked horse toes out.

Knocked Knees	Horse's forelegs bent in toward each other at the knee.
Bowed Knees	Forelegs bend outward at the knees.
Bench Knee	Cannon bone is offset.

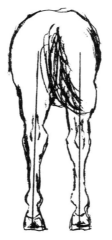

In the correctly built horse, a vertical line runs from the centre of the foot
up through the centre of the hock, through to the point of the quarter.

Relative Importance Of Size

* Is the horse too big? Will he fit into the show ring and be able to fit the correct number of strides in the lines? Will he appear awkward?

* Is the horse too small? How easily will he be able to make the lines in a future hunter class?

* Look at the amount of bone. Are the legs proportionate to the size of the horse? Does the small horse have fine bone which makes it appear too dainty and brittle? Does the big horse have so much bone that it makes him appear heavy and common?

Relative Importance Of Condition And Presentation

Several points of turn out will work to your advantage in the final analysis. Of course the horse must be spotless, trimmed at the ears, bridle path, muzzle and throat latch, coronet bands and fetlocks, with the hooves painted with oil. Give an overall picture of neatness. Always put the horse in a show bridle that is clean and conservative and fits well, with the bit polished. The mane should be braided in the traditional pencil-style hunter braids with dark wool, no ribbons or bows. The tail can be braided if it compliments the horse's conformation.

The handler's turnout is just as important. Dress conservatively and practically. A suit and tie is appropriate for a man. Clean, neat slacks and a jacket are suitable for a woman. Skirts and high heels are impractical dress, especially when you consider that you must jog the horse on a grass or dirt surface.

Whether you win or lose on the line, the training, discipline and experience you gain will no doubt benefit both yourself and the horse. It will assist you with future endeavors in the show ring where an extra edge of polish and professionalism will impress judges, spectators and potential clients.

*Note - A young horse that stands around and is not properly muscled up through conditioning will probably not move as well as a horse that is fit. Moreover, as the emphasis has been shifting to performance, the horse that has not been worked will be at a disadvantage. As with any performance horse, and because conditioning is involved, preparation of the line horse begins months and even years before the horse enters the ring. It is a relatively unsuccessful venture to pull a horse in from the field a week before the show and try to get him in the appropriate physical and mental condition. A lack of preparation, a rough coat, unpulled mane, or poor muscle tone, indicates a lack of confidence in the horse's quality and a lack of caring on the part of the owner, all of which will have a negative influence on the judge's opinion of the horse.

What is done to get the horse in top physical condition depends to a large extent on the horse's age. Three-year olds should be turned out for three or four hours a day, five days a week. If a young horse is quiet enough, longe him for a half hour at the walk and trot to replace ridden work. However, be very cautious about longeing as a horse can do himself a lot of damage if he acts up on the longe line.

Older horses can be kept fit by regular exercising under saddle and if the horse shows over fences, his show schedule will keep him in condition.

On top of a good exercise program, a good basic horse management program will ensure that the horse is healthy. Deworming, regular attention to teeth and a good diet of high quality feed will add that extra edge of brilliance to horse's condition.

Homework

With a young horse, preparation at home should involve teaching him to accept thorough grooming, which includes trimming with clippers at his bridle path, muzzle and legs. Unbroken horses should be taught to wear a bridle. In addition to exercise and grooming, the horse's preparation for the show ring should include walk and jog correctly on the line. You have to do your homework. The horse must lead properly and stand properly, remaining squarely beside you.

No matter how well-conformed a horse is, or how well it moves, the judge cannot see these qualities properly if the horse is acting up and will not stand still or jog quietly. You only have one chance to show your horse at the jog. It is important to teach the horse to obey on the line. If he is an aggressive, energetic animal, I advocate practicing with a chain shank. This will teach him to stay behind you rather than dragging you along from ahead. On the other hand, if he hangs back and will not step along beside you, rather than tugging at him to bring him along side, carry a long stick in your left hand. Reach back to tap him on the flank or quarters. Practice this along a fence or arena wall so he cannot swing his hindquarters away from the whip. He will have nowhere to move but forward.

It is very easy to teach a horse to walk and jog in a relaxed manner. At the walk, take a fairly firm but light contact on the reins behind the horse's chin. You should be positioned slightly behind his head. When you want to jog, loosen the contact by bringing the right hand out in front of the horse. This will be a signal to him to jog. Practice this at home. Tap him with the whip when you loosen your right hand to let him know you want him to jog. He will learn to react automatically to the loosened contact in the show ring and will pick up the trot easily. Bring your hand out in front of his nose at the jog so he can extend his head and neck. This will give him a nice top line, but remember to keep your body ahead of his shoulder and behind his head. This gives the judge the best view of the horse and leaves you in a position of control to easily bring him back to the walk. With sufficient practice at home, the horse will learn to walk and jog in a relaxed manner without leaning on your hand.

When the horse stand up before the judge, he should be positioned with his front legs almost side by side, and the hind leg nearest the judge (usually the left) a little to the rear of the other hind leg. This stance is accomplished by gently rocking the horse back and forth from the head, encouraging him to take small steps forwards or backwards until his legs are positioned correctly.

In the past it has been common to encourage a horse to stand with his neck long and low, making him appear very heavy over his front end. However, in the correct stance, the head is a bit higher than the wither and there is a slight arch in the neck. In other words, the horse should carry his head and neck as he would when being ridden so the judge can evaluate his presence as a riding horse.

Relative Importance of Movement

Always jog before lining the horses up. After you have done the individual inspection, jog all, then do your line. Very often you will note an exceptional mover with close conformation that you may move up a few spots. Perhaps the opposite, a very poor mover with good conformation, may have to be moved down. There is more and more emphasis on good movers. They seem to last longer, be sounder, easier on themselves, win more, and are more pleasant to watch.

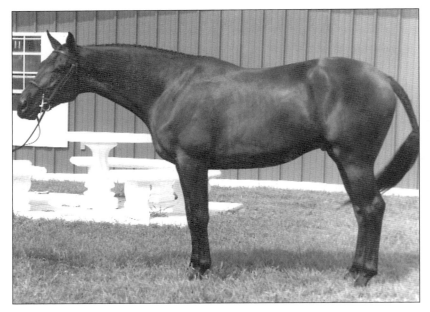

All The Aces

Marking The Card Symbols

A short description of the horse beside the number, e.g. #114 bay star, is very helpful. This is for easy, quick referral. This way you do not have to ask the handlers to turn their numbers. It is also a fast and easy way to discuss the horses when you are working with another judge.

Suggested Rating Of Symbols, From Worst To Least:

Fault	Interpretation
Ⓛ	Lame
CB	Curb
T → T ←	Toes out → Toes in ←
SPL ↑↓	Splint - ↑ high ↓ low
ANK	Ankles large
HKS	Hocks rough
PAST ↓↑	Pasterns ↓ short or ↑ long
K	Knees not correct
F	Fine bone
RG	Rough looking, course
U	Sway backed, inverted looking
Ⓚ	Klunky, heavy, common
WP	Windpuffs
P.G.	Pony gaited, short strided
TOP	Top line doesn't fit
B.M.	Bad mover
↔	Long back

H -	Head not appealing
NK -	Short neck, long, cresty or ewed
E	Eye small or white
W↑ ↓	Protruding wither ↑ or mutton ↓
ER	Ears too large
↑ ↓	↑ Too big ↓ too small
T.O. + -	Turn out + good - poor
G.M.	Good mover
+	Top one or top quality

Open Model

This is an Open Model class and as I look at entry #1, a chestnut horse with a blaze, I notice a prominent splint and a pair of curbs. I put his number down near the bottom on the left column. Entry #2 is a palomino, long backed, and has rough ankles. He goes just a little bit above the previous horse, but hopefully neither one will be in the ribbons. #3 is a dapple grey with slightly long pasterns. Better long than short, and he is beautifully conditioned and turned out. He is definitely a ribbon winner.

Entry #4 is a bay with white socks in front, short pasterns and rough, boggy hocks. With all of these serious faults I am going to squeeze him between the bottom two horses. Entry #5 is a small brown mare with a star, who appears light in bone but is attractive. She goes in the middle of my sheet on the left. She is standing second at this point, but a weak second. Entry #6 is a big, klunky chestnut horse with white socks and big ears. His top line is not wonderful, but he is clean legged. He will go behind the previous horse, #5. Entry #7 is a plain black horse with a low splint of no significance. I am a bit undecided; for now I place him just behind entry #5. Horse #8 is a roan horse that is clean (no obvious defects), attractive and nicely turned out.

Now I jog the class, noting that entry #2, the palomino, is a bad mover. Entry #4, the bay, is a good mover, and #5 is short strided. Entry #7, the plain black horse, is a very good mover. Just prior to lining up I switch #7 to pin ahead of #5, and switch #4 and #2, lining them up in that order. I look the group over one more time, making sure that I am satisfied with this order. I fill in my judge's card and hand it to the ringmaster for the announcement of the official results.

Judging A Model Class

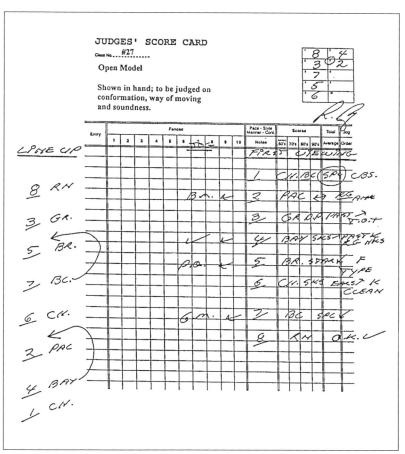

Positive Vs Negative Features

Positive Features

* Turn out.
* Manners.
* Organized, confident, calm handler.
* Properly fitted tack, clean and polished.
.* Handlers conservatively turned out and practical
* Interested and alert.
* Horse is conditioned, fit and is the proper weight.

Negative Features

* Poor turn out, rough coat, poor condition.
* Unruly behaviour, this makes it difficult to view.
* Over zealous, showy handlers (distracting).
* Poorly fitted tack, throat latch dangling, loose noseband, dirty bit, bit too low in the mouth.
* Handlers sporting flamboyant attire.
* Dull horse (possibly over-tranquilized).
* Coaching from the side.
* Poor condition and poor muscle tone, under weight or obese.
* Handlers who stare at the judge.

Do:

Re-jog if you question unsoundness or an inadequate trot

Don't:

Bend down and feel a horse's leg. This only draws unnecessary attention!

Don't study for a long time and write a story (judges who write a lot miss a lot!)

Winning On The Line - Ways To Move Up

Having the perfect horse won't guarantee a win. Turnout plays an important part in the results of the class. The horse should be spotless, neatly braided, with a clean, conservative bridle. It is the handler's responsibility to show off the horse. If they do the job correctly the judge will pick up on the horse's best qualities and may overlook subtle defects. If it is clean legged, attractive, in good condition and a good mover, then it has the makings of an ideal horse in the judge's eyes.

The individual temperament of the horse should determine what time you arrive at the showgrounds. If your horse is inclined to be lazy and dull, arrive just before your class is scheduled. The activity of the show will perk him up and give him a fresh, alert look in the ring. With the dull type of horse, get to the head of the line as you enter the ring so that the judge will see him at the beginning of the class. In this way, the horse will not have to stand around and become bored and dull before the judge gets a look at him. If a horse is the nervous or timid type, arrive at the grounds a few hours early so he has time to get used to the bustle and activity of the show. This will help to settle him before he goes into the ring. When you enter the ring, allow him some time to relax (it is probably best to get in about the middle of the line up). Pet him and encourage him to be calm. If he is still upset after awhile, give him a quick snap with the reins to remind him of his homework and put his mind on the matter at hand.

Remember that in a large class, the judge will have a number of horses to look at before getting to yours. Avoid standing the horse up as soon as you get in the ring. Do not attempt to pose the horse for a long time while the judge is looking at the other horses. Your horse may become bored and start to fidget. By the time the judge gets to you, he may be totally fed up and refuse to stand at all. Leave enough room between yourself and the next horse so that you may walk around in a circle. Keep the horse occupied. A minute or two before the judge gets to you, line your horse up. Remember to leave room between horses so the judge can walk around your horse without the fear of being kicked!

You Be The Judge

It is important to keep your horse away from you (say with the use of a crop) as the judge looks him over. Avoid letting him inch forward and end up against you.

Final Judge's Check List

* Plan your ring.

* Watch your ringmaster to be sure they are in the right order and he executes the right changes.

* Put the results of the model on a separate piece of paper, as the conformation division is often held over two days and you may need to refer to the order for the other classes in the division.

* Verify the percent of conformation in the division before moving any horses.

* Plan the jog so that the handler is on the opposite side of the horse you are viewing.

* Jog all of the horses in a class even though several will not get a ribbon - it is a part of the class!

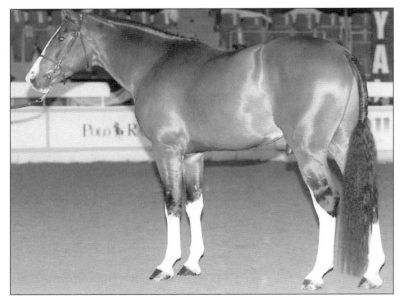

Popeye K

Questions & Answers

Q:Should you tranquilize a horse before you show him on the line?

A:No. Young horses should be trained and worked at home so that they are mannered in the show ring. Drugging the horse will make him appear dull and inhibit his movement.

Q:If a competitor jogs a horse into the ring for conformation with the number tied around the horse's neck, do you say anything?

A:No, but he should know better. It certainly detracts from the overall presentation.

Q:How do you deal with a totally unruly horse?

A:You don't need to deal with it. The horses in the ring need to be disciplined and have manners. The handler must do his homework and bring his horse to the ring ready to be a show horse.

Q:When showing a horse on the line, where should I stand?

A:Don't worry or dodge around the judge. Position yourself in front and away from the horse. You should be facing the horse at all times, making sure he is positioned correctly.

Q:Is it OK to look or smile at the judge?

A:It is not necessary - just get on with your job!

Q:Do you model a horse in the bit they show in?

A:Not necessarily, unless they show in a D-bit or plain full-cheek snaffle. They should not model wearing a pelham, wire bit or kimberwick.

Q:As a judge, what percentage do you think the conformation portion should be in a conformation class?

You Be The Judge

A: 25% - to encourage people to show in the division and keep it alive. There really is no need to move a horse more than one or two spots if he is the model winner, and the horse's performances are comparable.

Q: When do you jog the line in a class, before or after you judge them standing?

A: It is the judge's decision, but I recommend jogging them first, as after standing on the line for some time the horses tend to stiffen up and may make the jog look questionable.

Q: When judging a conformation class, can you ask a handler to move a horse or pony?

A: Absolutely, if you need a clearer view. Often they are so close to the next horse you can't get between them without the possibility of getting kicked, let alone get a good view.

Q: How do you feel about conformation disappearing in Canada, and what does this do to judges as you don't often get to officiate in these classes?

A: Conformation means the "beautiful, correct horse", and it is what we all strive for, so to lose the division would be a shame. Judging conformation becomes difficult as you rarely have the opportunity to do it, and then if you are invited to a U.S. show you have to judge many conformation classes. You need to rely on your basics and knowledge of the conformation faults and positive features.

Q: How do you remember the order of the model, to make any changes in the over fences and under saddle class of the conformation division?

A: At the completion of the model, make a list of the ribbon placings and keep it with you for the rest of the division, for reference. The division often goes over two days, and may be in two different rings, so you need to keep notes to refresh your memory.

*Q:*When you jog back a conformation class to stand for conformation, and one horse is lame, do you excuse that one before or after judging the conformation?

*A:*Definitely before, as he is eliminated at this point from further consideration.

*Q:*Are you always obligated to move up the model winner in the other classes of the division?

*A:*No. It depends on one of the following:

1/ Percentage of conformation (25%, 35%, 40%)

2/ Was model won by slim or large percentage?

3/ The difference between the performance in the class - was it a large or small difference that separated the horses?

*Q:*Do you judge conformation hunters differently than working hunters?

*A:*No. The only difference is that when they jog back into the ring, a percentage is awarded for their conformation and can be moved on the line accordingly.

*Q:*If a horse or pony wins the model do they have an advantage when the over fences or under saddle classes happen?

*A:*Absolutely not. The classes are run individually, and one has no bearing on the results of another. The model winner's only advantage is the possibility of moving up a place or two in the results after the performance placings are jogged in order.

*Q:*When a horse or pony in a model class are standing poorly, do you ask the handler to re-position the animal for a better view (i.e. resting a hind leg)?

*A:*It is preferable not to say anything as it is the handler's job to properly show their entries. With the children I don't mind saying something, but for the older handlers it is up to them to show their best!

You Be The Judge

Q: The class is lined up to judge conformation, and from the horses you have there appears to be no clear winner. What factors would be considered in order to designate a winner and place the rest of the class?

A: This is a very real and, sometimes, frustrating situation that judges must be prepared for. Each judge will have selected criteria that he/she can draw on to assign placings in this class. Conformation judging should relate what you see with performance expectations. This class should be sorted out by considering factors such as movement, soundness and type.

The athletic mover with the plain head and large ears would be a more functional and successful animal in the show ring than the short-gaited animal with a quality head. The horse with sound legs and feet would be placed over the better topped animal that paddles and has no length of stride. The 'carriage horse' type would stand behind the show ring 'hunter' type.

Placing such a group of animals is very subjective. Each judge will bring different priorities to the class, based on their experience and their preferences. Movement, soundness, and type related to function are criteria to be considered when faced with a class where there appears to be no outstanding winner.

Q: Should I show in the conformation division or on the line?

A: There are many factors to consider in order to determine if you should show a horse on the line or in the conformation division. Obviously, if your horse is a classic beauty and nearly perfect in all aspects there is no question in your mind. The uncertainty arises when there are small shortcomings.

The physical attributes of a well-built horse are documented in numerous equestrian manuals. To decide whether to show on the line you have to consider the individual's pluses and minuses. First and foremost a horse should be clean-legged and possess relatively correct angles and straightness. Some judges will forgive scarring from injuries but major faults such as a splint, capped hocks, cow hocks or back at the knee will cost you at least a placing or two.

174

Secondly, he must have an attractive appearance. He must have a smooth top line, a clean throat latch and an appealing, pleasant head. The judge's initial impression of a horse starts at the front end and continues along his top line. A beautiful body and great legs along with a large head, big ears, and a roman nose will probably not be the winner. Condition is obviously a factor of this first impression. If your horse is underweight or badly turned out he then must struggle to make an impression on the judge.

Another factor to consider in this first impression is your horse's temperament. If he will not show himself well and stand quietly there is little opportunity for him to be judged favorably. Movement is another quality a good conformation horse should possess. He should move straight and true with minimal knee action.

Judging conformation is not an exact science. The top six horses at any one competition will probably be in the top six at the next, but not necessarily in the same order. Basically a horse needs to be clean-legged, fairly physically correct, and attractive enough to make a good impression on any observer. He should be a good mover. The horse's condition and capability to show himself well are the responsibility of the owner/handler.

In addition, to show in the conformation division he must also be an athlete. If he jumps and moves well, he is less likely to be severely penalized for any faults when he returns on the line to be judged. If he has an obvious physical problem he should skip the initial model class and make his first impression on the judge as a well-turned out and very capable show horse.

Q: How much emphasis is placed on movement?

A: Now, more than ever before, the good 'looker' has to be able to move well to hold the top spot. We now jog before lining up to be assured of a good or reasonable mover winning. A rough, uneven or bad mover is subjected to much more wear and tear and is hard on himself physically.

It is difficult to watch a bad or offensive mover cantering around a hunter course. Movement is what you need to rely on when you have a tie or two horses that are close in conformation. You can never go wrong pinning the better mover.

Horses on the line ten years ago were mostly overweight and under conditioned, the emphasis is now on quality of movement; people want performers from the breeding divisions, not just a beautiful 'looker'.

Q: **How do you deal with awkward sizes, e.g. young horses that are higher behind?**

A: When looking at horses as a judge, or with the intention of buying them, I would make a note if a horse is taller in the haunches when compared to the front end, as horses should be proportionate in build. The croup and the withers should be approximately level with one another. In some young horses, the haunches will often grow more quickly than the front end. Therefore, when judging youngsters, one has to picture the end product and hope that they will continue to grow and even up. I don't tend to penalize this fault in immature horses as severely, as I would when judging an older animal.

Although there are exceptions to every rule, in many cases horses that are taller behind have the tendency to travel on their forehands. I have found that in more cases than not these individuals are not classic in their technique over fences, and further that their recovery from a fence is impaired. When trotting, they often trail their hind legs behind them. At the canter, their gait may be affected, appearing stilted, and they may have problems with their lead changes.

Horses with this disproportionate conformation are sometimes long in the back. You rarely see this problem in a short coupled horse. As a judge, one should remember that there are degrees of any conformation problem and that one should not dwell on any one fault. Remember to look at the overall picture and compare the degree of this fault with the rest of the competition to arrive at your final decision.

Q: **How far can you move a horse in a conformation class?**

A: First, how much does the conformation count? The percentages range from 25% to 50%. Second, how close or far apart were the horses by their performance over fences? Once you have taken these factors into consideration it will give you a good idea of how far you can move them.

Q:How much influence should the Model have in the division?

*A:*The Model should be quite important. This is the class that separates the conformation division from the working division. First and foremost, the horse must be a good jumper, a good mover and perform well in the ring. After this is decided, the top placing should then be arranged by conformation. If we do not stress this in our judging, then we lose all hope of maintaining our beautiful conformation hunters! It then filters down and takes away any incentive in the breeding industry to come up with these marvelous animals.

Q:How do you judge a class of beautiful, faultless ponies?

*A:*A trained eye, experience, and following a basic system as previously outlined helps you to determine an order. It also comes down to personal preference when there are no obvious faults or blemishes to separate them. Pick out one pony after you have looked them all over and start a line with the one that most catches your eye. This enables you to start with one and you will be amazed how the rest fall into place.

Q:How do you judge foals?

*A:*Generally speaking, these are the qualities which are always looked for in a foal:

- A lot of bone - a lot of substance

- A nice head

- A lot of front

- A short back

- A lot of depth through the chest

- Short cannon bones

- Depth at the quarters

- Straight movement

- Absence of cow hocks or sickle hocks

An early foal (February or March) stands a much better chance of doing well in line classes because of its extra growth and maturity.

Q: **As a handler, can I move my horse around if it moves out of a good stance?**

A: Yes. I give you time to do this, and you should make the adjustment and effort to stand the horse up properly (i.e. if a back leg is cocked or resting).

Q: **Do you want to see the tails braided?**

A: Absolutely. It is all about turnout.

Q: **If you suspect one of the horses is lame do you re-jog the entire line?**

A: I don't draw attention to it. I would discretely remove the horse. If you feel you must take a second look, you must re-jog the entire class. However, it is preferable and more professional to catch the lameness the first time, so there should be no reason to re-jog.

Q: **Can I let my horse move around when not being judged?**

A: Yes. Move around so your horse doesn't get bored, so that when you stand them up, they will stand properly.

Q: **Can you move a horse's tail out of the way if it is bushy and you cannot properly view the hocks or hind end?**

A: It is not a good idea. You can ask the handler to step the horse forward or back so you can view it better.

Q: **Should the handler talk to their horse?**

A: Quietly. If the horse is trained to the voice, quiet commands are permissible.

Q: **Have you ever asked an exhibitor to leave the ring if the horse is acting up or seems dangerous?**

A: I've been tempted! I would probably not excuse the horse, as the mishap would most likely happen when the horse is waiting to be looked at, and not being judged at the time.

Q: **When turning a corner, should the horse turn around the handler or visa versa?**

A: The horse should turn around the handler, making the larger circle.

Q: **Is a blemish (i.e. stitches scar) a serious fault?**

A: I can see through the blemish, and it is not as serious as a conformation fault, but it does not present the best picture. It is still unsightly - not perfection!

Q: **Do you judge a breeding class differently than a hunter model class?**

A: Yes. In breeding classes you need more room and time in the ring. This is their performance class, so let them perform!

Q: **If you don't think you will place in the model class but you are showing in the division, should you show in the model regardless?**

A: Excellent question. As a trainer I have dealt with this many times. I probably would not show in the model, and take my chances when the performance class is jogged back, and try to present my horse as well as possible. It is a difficult decision, as if you do model and do not place, does that mean you move down in the performance line up? It all depends on who is behind you in the lineup. If they are not model winners, you are usually safe.

Q: **Have you ever been kicked while judging a model class?**

A: Close, but no contact was made. I try to space the horses so I can stand well clear of the hind legs. On occasion you do have to do some gymnastic moves to dodge young horses, as they often act up on the line. I stand well clear of the ones acting up until all fours are back on the ground!

Q: **Would you ever say there is any danger involved in judging breeding classes with all of the young and high strung horses. What can you, as a judge, do to avoid any mishaps?**

A: I have often had to dodge away from some young, over-zealous breeding stock, and I would say that you need to make sure of the following to avoid any mishaps:

1/ Make sure that you or the ringmaster have announced that handlers line up their entries will spaced from the next horse.

2/ Make two lines when there are too many for one line.

3/ Jog breeding horses away from the ingate so the handlers will have more control and the horses will be less excited.

Q: **While judging a conformation class (green and regular divisions), specifically the Model class, an exhibitor showing a horse tells the judge that the farrier failed to show up to remove the bar shoes from his horse that morning. He wants the judge to be lenient when looking at these shoes because he didn't hold up the class to wait for the farrier. Is this allowed?**

A: When in the show ring - no talking! Bar shoes are a red flag, and the horse is moved down the line.

Q: **After a Model class, is it a good idea to keep the order of placing on your own judge's card, or on a separate notepad to refer back to?**

A: I always keep a separate list, as often the classes run over two days, and you need to check back to the original model order when judging conformation, just to be accurate.

Q: **If a horse has beautiful conformation, and he moves poorly, and another horse has fair conformation but is a beautiful mover, how do you pin them?**

*A:*I would go for the better mover, as they will probably last longer in the end, and win more, as movement is a large part of their performance.

Q:How close can you approach a horse you are judging?

*A:*As close as you are comfortable with, so that you can properly view the horse. Just be guarded around young and feisty horses, so that you don't get kicked!

Q:What would you do if a horse got loose in a model or breeding class?

*A:*Have the handlers catch the horse, and continue judging.

Q:How many times is a handler allowed to try to get his horse to jog properly?

*A:*Hopefully the ringmaster is there to help that situation, and encourage the horse to jog. Also, asking the competitors to jog towards the ingate, or towards the other horses, is helpful. Young horses are not experienced, and they need that ring education.

Q:Why are horses jogged in a model or breeding class?

*A:*The primary reason horses are asked to jog in confirmation classes is so judges can check their movement. Because a good mover is sounder, it puts less strain on itself and will win more classes.

"Notes To Judges"

When lining up the horses, two extra placings should be kept in reserve in the judge's mind in case one or more of the horses shows lameness at the job.

The top horses at the head of the line need more of the judge's attention. As a rule, those at the top should be left in position unless glaring faults such as lameness are detected. Judges should trust their first placing when looking down the second line up.

You Be The Judge

When judging on the line, several problems arise in different divisions. Yearlings, for example, often grow unevenly, so that their front or hind end is higher. Hence, a judge must rely more on movement and overall look. Sometimes, it helps to pick the best one and put it in front to compare the others.

All horses should be allowed to jog - the handlers have gone through the trouble of turning out their horses, so they all deserve an equal chance to show off their horses' movement.

Judges have to he wary of their own behaviour in the ring. Staring at and studying each horse for too long, or drawing attention to their faults is definite "don'ts" for a judge.

The first requirement is to line up the horses properly so they can be viewed fully. This involves spacing the horses off the rail and far enough apart so that they don't interfere with each other or the judge. The handler must also be on the opposite side from the judge to give him a total view of the horses. Handlers could be hiding a horse's faults if they are standing between the judge and the horses.

The individual inspection of each horse takes place from all sides of the horse. The judge begins on the near side of the horse, working from head to tail over the animal's topline. The horse's head and ears should not be too large, or out of proportion. Large eyes are an asset. The neck should be 'cresty' making the lower part look convex. From the neck, the shoulder should form a long, sloping line to the legs. The front legs should be square under the horse.

Continuing across the topline, the withers should not be high, or sloping like a ski jump, nor should they be concave or mutton, just sloping with simple definition. A short back without pronounced sway is ideal, leading into a high tail set that is not straight.

Next, the judge examines the horse's feet and legs more closely. The foot should be a fifty-degree angle to the pastern. The pastern itself should be long and sloping. The judge will mark down pasterns that are overly upright or short. Also, will keep an eye out for pinfiring.

The legs should be free from both structural defects and blemishes; however, structural defects are penalized more heavily because they affect the horse's movement and soundness. Blemishes such as scars only come into account in the event of a tie.

To win on the line, the trainer, the handler and the horse all need to have done their homework. There are a lot of things a handler or rider can do to mask the faults or enhance positive aspects of the horse but the bottom line for a conformation horse is its physical characteristics.

If I had to pick the ideal conformation horse, it would be around 16.2 to 16.3 hands high. A horse any larger will have too big a stride, will look awkward and be penalized. On the other extreme, too small a horse will have trouble getting down the lines because of its shorter stride.

"Now You Be The Judge"

Now it is your turn to test your judging skills. We invite you to judge three conformation classes. The following is an opportunity for the reader to practice putting the horses in order. The following are the instructions for your judging exercise:

1. There are three classes to judge. Take a sheet of paper and number the classes.

2. Look over the horses in the first group of three. Place these horses from first to third place, and make notes of why you placed them in the order that you did.

3. Once you have judged the class, turn the page. I have placed the horses according to my opinion. Now compare your results with mine. How did you do?

You Be The Judge

Class #1

Class #1

The bay horse will place first in this class, a good topline with a lot of neck and a kind expression.

Second in this class will be the chestnut horse with the white socks behind. He has a good shoulder, good legs and enough neck, but his back is a bit too long and his head is a bit high.

Third goes to the chestnut horse with the short neck and slightly long back, but again, good legs. A well deserved third place.

Class #2

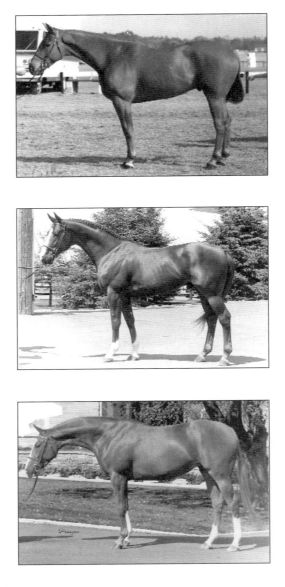

Class #2

The first place ribbon goes to the flashy chestnut with all of the white. This is quality, even with the slightly short and swanlike neck.

Second place will by given to the plain chestnut, who is pleasing to look at but has some minor faults. His topline could be a little more full, and he is short in the pasterns.

Third place goes to the big chestnut horse who just looks a bit course and has a slightly short neck, but has good legs.

Class #3

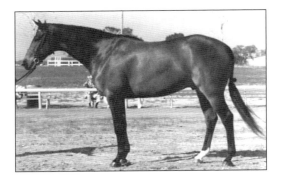

Class #3

This is a great class. It is always a pleasure to judge top quality horses. This is a difficult class, but I will give the first place ribbon to the bay with the white sock behind. This horse has an overall great look, and is a top model winner. You cannot go wrong with this one. He is very well proportioned.

A close second will be the dark grey horse. He is a beautiful type, with a great topline and good foundation, but he is just not standing as well in front, and I have to pin what I see.

Third, but not really last, goes to the bay in the D-bit. Maybe not as finished through his topline as the other two (he may be younger), but on a given day I could never dispute him being the winner! He has a good, solid look and is well-proportioned; a good shoulder, short back, nice neck and good hind end.

Summary

I hope you have enjoyed practicing judging and following through the placings of these top horses. I certainly could have elaborated on the details, but I wanted to show you how to actually sort through and pin a class.

As it is difficult to see small and detailed faults in a photo, I have not gone into great detail about those faults. You would certainly take note of all of the faults mentioned previously in this chapter, but in these photos I have basically clean legged horses and judging comes down to some of the finer points.

Probably the easiest and best way I can sum up this chapter on conformation is to first and foremost look at the legs, upon which the horse is carried. The foundation needs to be structurally correct before building anything, and so is the case in fact regarding the horse.

Therefore, no matter how beautiful the top line is, the legs have to be structurally sound. It is so easy to get carried away with a striking horse, but remember the legs and feet come first. The old saying, "no foot, no horse" rings true.

Chapter Six

Courses

A Hunter Course

Introduction

This chapter describes how to build hunter courses, which includes tips on dressing up the ring and how to make the jumps work for you. I will show you simple hunter courses along with more complicated equitation courses.

It is the course designer's responsibility to design and alter the distances. As the judge, if I feel a line or a jump is dangerous, or the ground line is on the wrong side, I will say something immediately. Most course designers will ask the judge during the day how the course is riding, and make the necessary alterations.

Good Designs

The following designs will help the horses go better and make the judge's job easier. Ultimately the **judge** should decide the best round - not the course.

* Make sure that the jump cup pins are secure. The rails should be firmly in place, helping to avoid knockdowns.

* Measure both sides of the jump as there can be quite a variance of distance from one side to another in a line.

* The fill, brush or box should be in front of a gate. If set behind, it can spook a horse and act as a false ground line.

* Extra rails can go in front of the jump or can be laid completely flat behind.

* For altering heights, extra rails can be stored at the jumps as mentioned above. Cups and pins can be attached to the standard below the supported rails and gates.

* Try to match lines. For example, have a white gate and rail line, followed by a brown ladder line, then a brick wall line.

* If rails are not matching in colour, make sure that the top rail is a brighter colour. This will avoid rubbing and rails down.

* Safety first! Lower the jumps, and close in the distances when the weather or the footing is bad.

* Avoid a lot of single jumps in the novice divisions - the distances are harder to find.

* A two stride 'in and out' is best. It is easier for the riders to adjust their pace if they jump into the combination incorrectly. It is also easier on the footing.

* Show where the ingate is located on the course plan.

* If you set the course the night before check the heights and spread distances again in the morning, as they may have been altered.

* You should plan for at least one lead change, and enough jumps on the course, the minimum being eight.

* In hunter classes, when numbering the jumps on the chart, the combination is '1' and '2', not 'A' and 'B'.

* The judge must be given a copy of the courses.

* All gates and walls should have a rail or a block on top, so that if a horse hits the jump it can fall easily.

* Be careful with boxes and flowers in front of oxers - keep them in tight. If they are left too far in front, the oxer may become too wide.

* Good fillers are necessary. The jumps should look solid. Good fillers are made of brush, straw bales, birch rails, plus the regular gates and walls.

* Vertical jumps need good advanced ground lines. You can use brush, boxes or rails.

* Broken lines should be used, with a minimum of six strides.

* Oxers always need the back rail higher than the front rail. This encourages the horse to jump.

* Try to avoid spooky colourful jumps - keep them plain and well filled in.

* The first jump into a line can often be one hole lower. This will encourage the horse to jump.

* Distances going away from the gate can be a little more lenient. They can be more 'forward' towards home.

You Be The Judge

* Similarly, oxer spreads going away from the gate can also be somewhat narrower and then toe to toe with the standards going towards the gate.

* Try to have a single jump (rather than a line) towards the ingate to start the course. This will get the horses started.

* The course should finish at the 'in' and 'out' gate.

* The distances should be altered in combined classes as the jumps are raised, and the lines should be changed accordingly.

* The distances vary with the quality of the show, footing, and the caliber of the horses.

* I am inclined to be slightly conservative the first day of the show until the horses are comfortable. I open up the lines as the show progresses.

* Try to move the jumps onto new tracks every day.

* Try to avoid two jumps directly beside each other (e.g. back-to-back classes). A horse can easily jump the wrong fence and it may go unnoticed.

* Leave as much room as possible at both ends of the ring. Allow the horse room to turn after they jump.

* Use coops and walls towards the ingate. Horses will jump them more confidently in that direction.

* Write in the distance that you are using on the course chart and the different distances that you are using in the combined hunter classes, as well as the small, medium and large ponies.

* Try to have an equal number of oxers and verticals on a course. If you are short standards, then obviously you have to go with more verticals. *Note - remember to put oxers at the end of the lines or by themselves.

* When measuring the distance between the jumps be sure to measure from standard to standard, and when measuring to an oxer, measure to the front standards.

Course Extras - *Dressing Up The Ring*

* Trees attached to stakes around the ring
* White portable picket fence
* Straw bales and flowers in the corners of the ring
* Brush and trees around the standards
* Potted trees and flowers around standards and on the jump
* Islands of flowers
* Barrels and flowers
* Arch wall and flowers
* Judge's booth outside the ring
* Tree and flower island

Building A Vertical

Well filled in with a generous groundline.

A Good Example Of A Beautiful Vertical

Building An Oxer

An oxer should be well filled in with the ground lines in tight to the base of the jump. The back rail is always higher than the front rail.

A Nicely Constructed Oxer

Hunter Courses

Course Equipment - Designing Needs:

* Clipboard to draw courses on.
* A plastic sleeve to hold the course outline. If you drop it on the ground, it is then protected from the rain and dirt.
* 100' or 200' tape measure.
* Small metal tape measure to measure jump heights.
* Eraser pen.
* Staple gun to post courses.
* Plastic to cover course sheet when posted.

  (Be sure posting board faces the same direction as the course Remember to show the 'in' and 'out' gate on the course plan)

196

Back To Back Classes

Low Hunter (1)   Low Hunter (2)

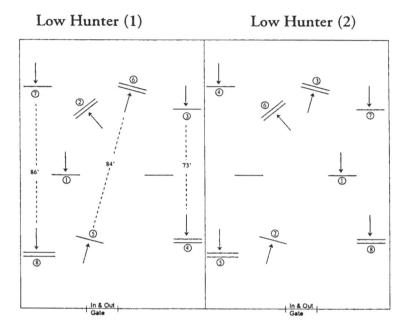

* Simple back-to-back classes.
* Two single jumps in the first class to get the horses going.
* Both courses have sufficient number of lead changes.
* A new first jump in the second class and less confusion for the judge.

You Be The Judge

Pony Hunter Class

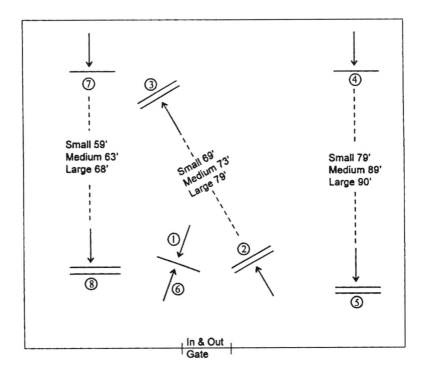

*   With the first line away from home, I use a vertical to encourage and help the ponies.
*   The oxers are at the ends of the lines towards home.

Junior Hunter Classic

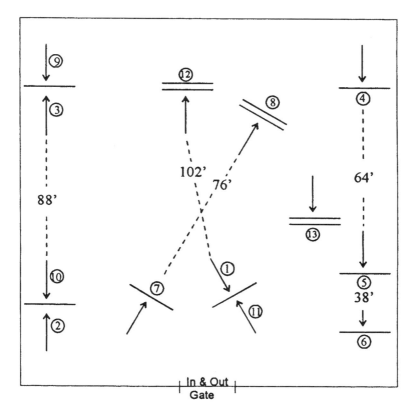

* Second round 1, 2, 3, 13, 8, 12 (reversed).
* Approximately 10 - 12 jumps for first round.
* Approximately 6 - 9 jumps for second round.
* Open up the lines to encourage the horses and riders to go forward.
* Try to introduce a broken line, 'in and out' and a single fence.

You Be The Judge

Handy Hunter Class

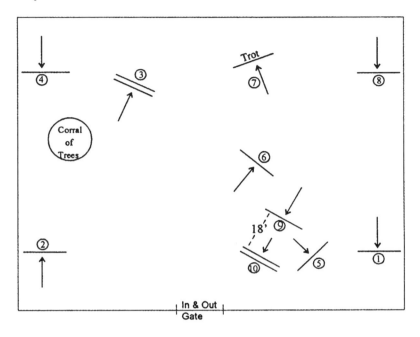

* A change from the routine classes.
* First jump option - a tight turn.
* No real distances, can gallop inside the pen (corral of trees) and do fewer strides, or outside the pen and get tighter turn backs to the next jump, or do both.
* Not for green horses or riders. This is designed for seasoned, advanced horses and riders that can handle the more difficult challenges.
* Some further ideas for handy hunter:
  - turn backs.
  - option turns.
  - trotting jumps or trot rails.
  - cantering rails on the ground.

- take your own line (riders walk a series of jumps placed in the ring and plan their own course of eight jumps).
- dismount and lead horse over a small jump.
- option jumps.
- option lines.
- open gate.
- drop a rail of a jump and hop over.
- bounces.

Good Designs

The first day of the horse show try to set most of the lines towards the ingate, as many of the horses are reluctant to go away from the gate in a new ring.

Second day of the show, you can set the lines away from the ingate, as most horses are comfortable enough with the ring and will easily travel away form the ingate.

All first jumps away from the ingate, and first jumps into the first line should be one hole lower, to make it more inviting for the horses, especially the first day of the horse show.

You Be The Judge

Variables

<table>
<tr><th>Adding Distance</th><th>Subtracting Distance</th></tr>
<tr><td>

- Downhill.
- Good footing.
- Large outdoor ring
- Open regular hunters.
- Hunter classics.
- Lines towards home or in-out gate.
- When the jumps are raised the lines should be opened accordingly.

</td><td>

- Uphill.
- Bad footing, deep, boggy, wet or hard.
- Indoors or small ring.
- Very green horses or riders.
- Lines away from the ingate.
- When the jumps are lowered, the lines should be shortened.

</td></tr>
</table>

Equitation Courses

C.E.T. Medal Class

A course of jumps of at least ten fences 3'6" to 3'9" in height, with spreads to 5'. The course must include a double and a triple combination with at least one spread fence in each. Two other spread fences are required elsewhere on the course. An eight foot water jump outside and/or a liverpool inside is mandatory. A time allowed must be established based upon 350 metres per minute.

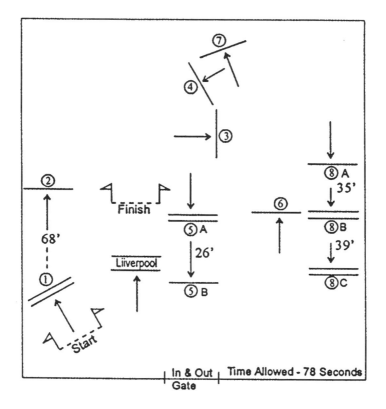

Ideas For Equitation Courses

* Broken lines.
* Option distances, long and short.
* Trot jumps.
* Bounces.
* Triple combinations.
* Skinny, narrow jumps.
* Liverpools.
* Coloured rails.
* Fan jumps.

You Be The Judge

* Swedish oxers.
* No ground lines.
* Slanted combinations.
* Altered distances at each side.
* Option jumps.
* Sufficient changes of leads.
* Square oxers.
  - Equitation courses need to be challenging enough to allow the best riders to shine.
  - Equitation courses should both test and teach.
  - Try to create difficulties on a course that bring out the best riders.
  - Be aware of the quality of the show and caliber of the rider so that it is not too difficult.
  - Courses should coincide with the quality of competitors.

Simple and Easy Courses:	Trillium shows, 'B' shows, schooling shows
Moderate to Difficult Courses:	'A' shows
Sophisticated:	Finals

* Judges should either walk or study the equitation course before the class so that they can plan a ride-off course prior to the class starting.

C.E.F. Medal Class

Figure eight course of not less than six jumps, 3'6" in height

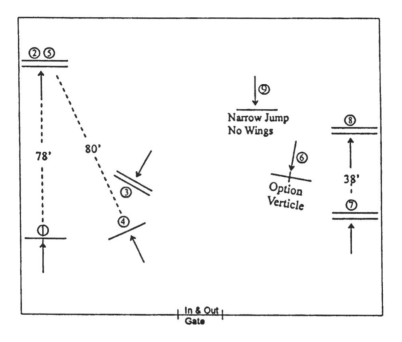

* Further testing: No schooling, canter fence 3, counter canter fence 4, halt and canter fences 5 and 9. Exit to the ingate at a sitting trot.

Note: New USA rule - "walk in, walk out".

Horsemanship Medal Class

Horsemanship medal horses and ponies to be shown over a course of eight of more fences with at least one combination, including an oxer, two changes of direction, plus two C.E.F. tests to be ridden as part of the course.

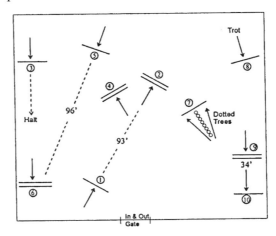

Simple Equitation Courses

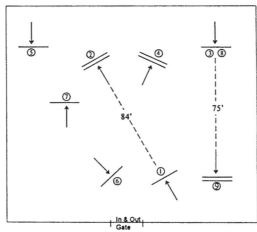

Further testing: Canter fence 1; halt; canter fence 9 and 7; trot fence 5 and 6; exit the ring at a sitting trot.

Questions & Answers

Q: When walking a Hunter Medal, what are you looking for?

A: Walking a medal course involves decisions that must be based on both the horse's and rider's experience and level of skills. If the horse is inexperienced (if riding medal classes, as a coach I would not recommend a green horse for this class) then the decision to travel the easiest and least complicated route will be the best. If the rider is moving up to the medals, then a decision must be made as to how much difficulty will be included in the trip.

For the experienced rider all options and difficulties will not be a factor, and the rider will be asked to put forward their best effort.

Course factors to be decided:

1/ Option turns (degree of difficulty).

2/ Number of strides (long or short).

3/ Entering and leaving the ring (presentation).

1. Not all options are 'do-able' - in my opinion as a coach, the rhythm of pace is the most important factor. In most cases, inside turns are the more aggressive options and should be attempted, provided the picture they create is pleasing to the eye of the judge. In some cases the turns are so difficult the rider may become rough and the horse may lose his rhythm and form. In my opinion, these turns should be avoided in most cases. A course designer should provide optional turns that do not require the rider and the horse to be put in this situation. An experienced course designer should be provided for medal classes.

2. The course should provide lines or distances that require the rider to lengthen and shorten his horse's stride. A course that shows only the rider's ability to lengthen the stride does not show the total versatility of the rider.

3. Entering and leaving the ring demonstrates the rider's commitment to providing a complete picture and should always be part of the coach's requirements for his rider.

Q: What do you expect from an equitation course?

A: When we walk an equitation course, we look for the same qualities that characterize the Grand Prix courses. Certainly they should be challenging - after all, the equitation division is the gateway for young riders to prepare themselves for the jumper divisions. But at the same time, it is important to remember that once a young rider is scared or discouraged it is difficult to build him or her back up into having a winning attitude.

What we want is balance. The course should not only produce results, it should produce riders - ones that can make an easy transition to moving on to bigger jumps bolstered by the confidence they have gained, the challenges they have successfully met, and the techniques they have perfected. As trainers we look at the course as a tool crafted by the course designers to prepare our riders and give them the challenges, experience and confidence they need to move on.

With so many young riders now competing in medal classes, it is important to avoid taking away their confidence or scaring the rider or the horse. Ideally, the course should produce a clear winner - but no losers.

This means having a course designed to test both the riders physical and mental strengths, with many areas in which riders can prove their accuracy. Narrow jumps are most effective at depicting the rider's ability to steer. Bending lines should challenge the rider to discern and display the best qualities of both the rider and the horse. A horse with a large stride can have more bend in a broken line. A short strided horse has the option of making a straight line between the jumps. Riders should develop the art of knowing their horses, and being able to show good judgment and accuracy in executing their ride.

Double and triple combinations allow riders to show off their good form. Although these combinations should be in placed so that are non-threatening, they should also show off the rider's ability to ride aggressively and accurately.

Options are crucial to allow riders to demonstrate those skills at which they excel. Scope should not be the only test, and the class should not be won or lost on the horse's length of stride. A rider should be able to decide whether to leave the stride out or to add it, to make an inside turn or go around. It is imperative that they be judged equally. If the tasks are performed well, the judge should not have to count the strides. Instead, they should only see equal jumps that match the whole course as a total unit.

Changes in pace offer an excellent way for riders an horses to demonstrate their control over the course. Forward options, followed by steady ones or vice versa, allow a rider to demonstrate great horsemanship skills.

Q: **When a halt is call for after a jump, where and how should you halt? When in a line, which lead should you pick up?**

A: The halt should not be an abrupt pull up. It should demonstrate control and the horse should stand still and squarely for a brief time without backing up or side stepping. The pull up and halt should be done at a reasonably close distance from the preceding jump.

This allows enough room to canter to the next jumps. When picking up your next lead, look ahead to the direction that you will be going and pick up that lead. When a halt is asked for after the end of a line, it should be done before the end of the ring. You do not want to use the barrier to aid the halt, you are testing the rider's control.

Q: **What happens when a jump is blown over while you are on course?**

A: The rider needs to pull up and wait for the jump to be rebuilt. As a rule, the rider would then start again at the point they pulled up. However, if the jump is the second one in a line then the rider should be able to re-ride the entire line. If it takes a lengthy time to repair or reset the jump, the rider should have the option of retaking the entire course with the judge's permission. There is no set rule; the judge decides where the rider will commence after assessing the situation.

Q: **How do you feel about triple trips, back-to-back-to-back?**

A: There are many pros and cons to the triple trips. For the course designer, the options may be limited. In order to achieve the optimum design, proper ring size and a large selection of jumps are necessary to set approximately twelve jumps in the ring. Without this requirement, the courses for triple trips may become very plain and simple. The same track being used twice within the division is an example. The design needs to be very versatile, utilizing lines with the fences which can be ridden in both directions and do not appear as if the competitor is jumping them backwards. This limits the number of oxers and combinations you can use within the course. As well, adjustments for bad weather affecting distances and footing become restricted to the division, as the classes are running simultaneously. From a course designer's point of view, the triple trips can be executed if required, but they are not the first choice based on the limitations that exist.

For the exhibitor competing in more than one ring, this routine can serve to expedite their time. However, it can also be an unfavourable situation for them if extra schooling time for improvement or correction is required from one class to another.

For the judge, working with three score cards can become an arduous task, especially when a large entry exists in the division. The ingate person and announcer must be on the job to help make this situation feasible.

Q: **What do you look for in a hunter course?**

A: Hunter courses should encourage the best performance from every horse entered. The judge, not the course, should determine the placings of the class.

Dimensions of the ring can vary, but a flat, rectangular field, ideally 150' x 250' - 300' is a workable size. The width of 150' allows for under saddle classes to be run without moving jumps, and permits the course designer to shift lines from day to day to allow for new footing. The length and width allows for good turns at the end of the ring, as well as a few variations in the number of strides between jumps.

Good grass footing is preferable, but sand rings are often used. The down side of grass is the maintenance. Often, grass rings are not properly maintained, and become hard, lumpy, etc. Most sand ring owners seem to want to torture their rings by harrowing with weighted teeth and therefore ruining the base. When a sand ring turns hard it is a positive sign. This is also very easy to correct, by simply adding one inch of 3/8 minus new washed sand. You will have a new surface with the cushion that you need to jump on. A regular watering program will help keep this new surface firm and relatively dust free.

The course designer must pay attention to the distance leading into (and off) the lines. It is very important that they be equal or that the distance going in is slightly longer. In normal hunter classes, especially those below the level or open or modified, straight lines are preferable. Bending lines and broken lines are better for more advanced divisions and medal classes. The distance between jumps is vitally important. For the 3' classes and lower, the lines should be conservative (11' to 12' strides). This gives the novice riders and green horses the opportunity to maintain control and accuracy. In more advanced divisions, lines can be pulled out to 12'6" to 13' strides to encourage a bold hunting pace and ensure that the best movers are not penalized.

Well built jumps are important, because good jump material helps train horses to jump well. Wide wings (3') are preferable, and are 5' to 5'6" high. The rails should be 10' to 12' long.

The jumps should be built to look solid and full. For example, there should be one top rail, with a solid looking 18" gate right below, with an 18" stone or brick wall below the gate and pulled out in front. To finish off there should be a take off brush or flower box 6" high on the ground in front of the wall. Trees tied to the wing standards, or potted shrubs in front and behind the wings, help to frame in the jump and add some decoration to the ring.

Colour and decoration play an important role in hunter courses. Coloured equipment is acceptable as long as it is painted in one solid "quiet" colour, such as green, grey, indian red, brown or white. Decoration helps take out the dull feeling in the hunter ring, but the course designer must be careful not to make the jumps too spooky.

Islands, built out of shrubs and bales can be used at the end of the ring, if the ring is a good size. They can help the less experienced horses and riders use the ends of the ring, and give the course designer some choices for creating turning options for a medal class.

Once the course is set, the course designer must watch and see how the course performs. Quite often it is this first class that will help him make adjustments (fine-tuning). This will help the horses and riders perform to the best of their ability. Keep it simple, keep it safe, and make everything look attractive.

Q: How do you feel about the dotted line on a hunter course?

A: The dotted line should be employed only if several factors have been considered. First of all, does the time of this designation fall within the show's program? If the dotted line is used in the first class of a division without a prior warm-up, the trips may not offer the best results for the judge nor the exhibitor. You are insisting that the younger or more amateur rider must ride the first line correctly, especially if it is a line away from the gate, in their first course, first class of the show.

If this format is a direction from the show management, hopefully the course designer has been asked for input in some way. Time is an important factor at a horse show, however often a good hunter course can be jeopardized because of the dotted line.

Q: When there is a dotted line on the course plan and there are no markers on the actual course itself, how do you judge it when a rider goes by the imaginary dotted line?

A: If there are no actual barriers, e.g. trees, rails, etc., I cannot eliminate a rider unless there is something visual to show a rider what line they cannot cross.

Q: **When a dotted line is in effect, does it need to be stated that it is in effect both before and after the course?**

A: There is not a rule regarding this, but it would be a nice reminder. Although it is seldom abused, some might not really be aware that at the end of the course you have to stay on the correct side of the dotted line.

Q: **On a broken line, are you penalized for adding a stride?**

A: At the very top level of "A" circuit competition, over a properly built course with safe footing, there should be no options. The horse taking the shortest, direct route should be used over those horses that add a stride.

However, at lower levels, riders may not be as well mounted, and other intelligent options should not be ruled out. For example, Rider 'A' on a drifting or short-strided horse who opts for a bending line, should be preferred over Rider 'B', on a similar horse who disregards his horse's problems and causes it to jump dangerously by trying for the direct route.

Q: **When a change of lead is asked for between two jumps, do you do a simple change or risk a flying change?**

A: Equitation tests are given to question a rider's skill. These tests require a strategy to give an appropriate answer in each competition. Each rider must examine the pertinent factors involved in executing the test before they calculate the risk of doing a flying change over a simple change. These factors include:

1/The reason (or goal) that each rider hopes to achieve.

    a)   Are they going for experience?

    b)   Are they attempting to qualify for a regional or finals?

    c)   Are they competing to win?

2/   What is the order drawn for the test? Do they go back first or last?

3/   How much room (distance) is there between the two jumps?

4/   Is the flying change easy for this horse or is it difficult? After weighing the factors involved the coach and rider will decide how much risk is required to succeed. They will make a decision on their strategy based on these factors, and then attempt the test.

Q: **What happens when, for example, a tree blows down in front of a jump that is set by the standard, and spooks the horse?**

A: I try not to hold it against the competitor, but I have to take it into consideration when I compare it to one that went well and didn't spook. I suggest securing the trees, etc., to the standards to avoid this from happening.

Q: **Do good courses make your job easier or more difficult, as the horses will all usually go well?**

A: Definitely easier, as this is what it is all about - good rounds and sorting them out, not pinning mediocrity but pinning excellence.

Q: **As a judge, do you ever walk a course?**

A: Not usually, but I will walk some equitation or medal courses when I have to design a ride-off, as it gives me a better idea of what will work or not work in a fair test.

Q: **If a horse jumps a jump backwards because it was not set properly, what do you do?**

A: The rider has the option of going again once they jump is set properly. If the rider pulls up on course before they jump the backwards jump, they then can continue from that point once the jump is properly set.

Q: **What would you do if equipment (e.g. standards, rails, walls, brush) piled outside the ring are spooking the horses and ruining your class?**

A: Suggest to show management that they store the equipment elsewhere. It would make for a better class, the exhibitors would be happy, and it would generally look better.

Q: **Can the judge ask for a course to be altered if it is not working or seems dangerous?**

A: If it is dangerous the judge should do something about it. To do this, he/she must contact the course designer and ask that the changes are made, or suggest what is not working and leave it to him to alter the course.

Q: **If you, as the judge, cannot see a jump well, what do you do?**

A: Move your chair to where you can see the entire course properly, or ask the course designer to move some trees or a jump if you still cannot see.

Q: **What is the minimum and maximum number of jumps that are required in a hunter course?**

A: The minimum is eight jumps and there is no limit to the maximum, but I would like to strongly suggest never use more that nine.

Q: **If a competitor jumps a jump on which a rail was not replaced after a previous knockdown, how do you score it?**

A: There is no rule for this, but you need to score it as if the rail was in place. If you notice it before the rider gets to the jump, you can stop them and have the rail replaced before they proceed.

Q: **How do you feel about 'in and outs'? I noticed that you don't use them a lot when you design courses.**

A: The following is a "yes and no" list for when to use 'in and outs':

Yes	No
- Later in the season	- Green horses
- Indoors in the fall	- Early in the season
- Advanced equitation courses	- Ponies
- Large rings	- Small rings
- When used with a jump into a line (e.g. jump - four strides to an in and out)	- Away from the ingate
	- Bad footing
	- Short stirrup or less experienced divisions

215

You Be The Judge

*Q:***As a judge, do you ever compliment a course designer?**

*A:*I certainly do, as it really makes my job easier, and just like someone telling me I did a good job a course designer appreciates positive feedback as he really works hard and wants the horses to go well.

*Q:***If there is something wrong with the course, do you say something?**

*A:*If it is wrong and illegal I say something, but it is really the course designer's responsibility to do his job correctly. I don't like to interfere with the course designer, but I have to bring it to his/her attention when something is built illegally.

*Q:***If the course height seems too difficult for the competition, can you lower the fences and still make the class legal?**

*A:*If it is solely the competitors that can't handle the height, and not because of weather or footing, then you need to maintain at least half of the jumps at the required height.

Summary

I hope you have been able to better understand what is involved with hunter and equitation courses, as I deviated from the judging trail in this chapter. I believe judging and courses are very closely related, as good courses make horses go well and judging is a lot better when you are separating and placing good quality performances.

Chapter Seven

From The Judge's Booth

Introduction

This chapter deals with some of the different issues revolving around judging. Different topics from the judge's viewpoint are of interest, as it enables everyone to better understand and appreciate the enormity of this position.

Back-To-Back Classes

Let's introduce you to a situation which occurs. The class has 60 entries and is a first year green division. The division is split even and odd numbers, and the classes are going back-to-back. Now, try to follow the entire procedure from the judge's point of view. There are roughly 30 even and 30 odd numbers, with each group performing twice. This means you have 4 cards to handle, which multiplies by 2, equaling 8, since each card has space for only 23 numbers. The first horse on course was at 8:10 a.m., and it is now 12:30 p.m. You are trying to capture a picture of the third horse in the odd numbers in the second class, in order to compare him with the 28th horse.

If you're confused, don't be! This is the judge's job. While the judge is attempting to recall and visualize this comparison through 110 rounds, you have to rely on the announcer as your cue to look up as the entry starts on course. You are busy shuffling cards, trying to keep some order to this card game. But the announcer happens to be busy doing the jog order for ring four. You happen to glance up, only to see a horse on your course cantering down to the second fence. Quick, is it even or odd? First or second round? How did this happen?

Would you like to keep track of 120 entries in four classes at one time, while the announcer is keeping track of four rings, and still pin 10 placings in each class? Most of the time the judges get the order right, but there are bound to be mistakes made. There is an answer to the situation. Two judges sitting together can easily remedy the back-to-back classes, with one doing the first round, followed by the other judging the second round. This allows the judges to draw a true comparison of the rounds, culminating in more accurate results. (P.S. That horse cantering to the second fence was off course! That was a life saver!)

Back-to-back classes, as you can see, are a lot to keep track of and you can easily get confused. Back-to-back in a small ring is more difficult as it all comes at you too quickly. There is not enough time to sort out the rounds properly. The triple rounds are even more confusing, as you have three jobs and for everyone it can be totally confusing as to what, which, and who?

These classes are time savers, and help limit rider/trainer conflicts, but you must be aware of the difficulties that go along with these popular back-to-back (to-back) classes! We still maintain and can enjoy the single rounds at the Highlight Show of the Year, the Royal Winter Fair. We can see and place each class as it happens with the rewarding presentations for great efforts and costs incurred.

Double Pinning

Double pinning is a wonderful system, as opposed to a split division, as the best two horses end up winning a class. When taking a chance on a split the caliber of the horses may end up unequal. Often it is uncertain if the division will be a split, so the class is run all as one. The judge keeps track of 16 placings instead of 8 and then goes down the list pinning two firsts, two seconds, two thirds, etc. If it is close, management will make the decision to split or not, and if it is, again the top horses have a chance of each winning a class.

This works well over the fences, but what happens in the under saddle? All of the entries are sent into the ring which can be anywhere from 40 horses upwards. You are then asked to pin 16 placings in two classes of 8 ribbons. Just writing down and finding 16 ribbon winners at one time on the flat is a major task. If you manage to find 16 ribbon winners you never have time to go back and compare your really top movers. They may make a mistake and then put your long list of numbers in jeopardy. The best movers are owed your concentration and you need to be able to watch them so that the top horses end up in the correct order. The difficulty of simply searching the 16 numbers all at once may rob the best horses of your attention. The solution to this, is to split the class in either even or odd numbers. Alternatively, line them up in the ring and divide them in half. Then run two completely separate classes and pin 8 in each.

Combined Hunters

This is the case where first year, second year and regular working hunters all show against each other in the same class. The seasoned regular horse would seem to have an advantage as he simply cruises around not spooking, simply doing his job like an old campaigner. However, the first year horse may have the competitive edge as he is a little more impressed with the jumps and may jump them a little more dynamically. The conformation division and regular working hunters are kept 'alive' by combining them. From the judge's perspective the combined hunter classes are bigger, more competitive, and easier to judge than pinning small mediocre classes. The edge is not always given to the seasoned regular horse. The green horse is still easily in contention as he is jumping a lower jump with easier distance between the jumps. Judging is made a lot easier when you have something to choose from and the combined hunters today provide that.

The "Prep" Classes

'Warm ups', 'add backs', and 'schooling' are all names for classes to prepare the horses for their recognized classes. They are judged by the show judge. These classes usually take the most time, and make the most money for the horse show. They start the day off and precede the real division. Besides being great money makers for the horse show, they provide preparation for exhibitors showing. On the other hand, judges are often tired, worn out and frustrated before the actual real day begins. Perhaps the show should commence a little earlier and have a small status judge to the 'prep' classes. This would give the 'prep' judge excellent mileage and would save the senior judge for the recognized classes. Although it is not always financially feasible, it is a nice thought to see the main judge saved for the recognized classes!

Lameness

Quite often the judge will notice a horse whose soundness looks questionable in the trotting circle. It is advisable to make a notation on the judge's card to pay extra attention to the jog, but the horse is definitely not ruled out at this point. Horses may look off when mounted and then fine when they jog in hand. Today the judge can make the decision on soundness and may excuse a horse for lameness, without a veterinarian. If lameness is completely obvious, the horse should be excused on the first jog. If it is questionable, have the line jog again. Once the judge decides to eliminate a horse, the ringmaster should be told. When the line-up goes by for their ribbon the ringmaster will simply state to the rider that he is excused. The announcer should also be made aware so that the excused horse's number is not announced as a ribbon winner.

Note: Any horse jogged back into the ring in a halter and not the bridle he showed in, is immediately excused.

Hunter Classics

When scoring Hunter Classics under the three judge system, it is imperative that each individual judge keep his own card as if he were judging all by himself. Score it as you see it, not the way you think others will.

Most often, horse show management asks two judges to sit together and come up with one score, which saves a lot of adding and averaging of scores. The problem with this is that it can cause a lot of discussion amongst the judges if they don't agree. Although this doesn't seem to happen often, if there is a difference of opinion a compromise can be met, which basically sets the score the same as if the two were sitting apart and their scores were averaged.

You Be The Judge

The class is run over two rounds, with the scores from both added together for a final score. The horses come back for the second round in the reverse order of placings, so that the best trip in the first round is the final horse to compete in the class. This format certainly adds a lot of tension and excitement to the class.

Although you don't see Hunter Classics at all horse shows, as the ring has to be large and the timetable light, they are held as special classes all over North America, with quite a lot of prize money involved. As they are held over two rounds (there are twelve or more fences in the first round and a shortened second round), they are a tough test for the horses and riders, but a thrilling class to watch.

"To Do" List

1/ When you arrive on the grounds to start your day of judging, make sure you are sitting in a place which gives you the best view of the ring. You should be centre ring on one side, preferably not facing into the afternoon sun. Keep in mind that the person setting up the judge's stand is not necessarily thinking of your needs. We have all dragged chairs around, moved pick-up trucks and made the changes necessary to ensure that our view is optimum.

2/ It is also imperative that you have a clear view of all the jumps in the ring. When organizing your seating, keep this in mind. If you cannot see a top rail (often due to large pillars or trees beside the jumps) ask the course designer to make the necessary changes so that you have a clear view. Remember, it is your responsibility to judge the class fairly and to the best of your ability, which you cannot do if you can't see the jumps.

3/ Ensure that you have all the equipment you need to begin, and end, your day. This includes writing equipment, extra judge's cards and paper, walkie-talkie (which is in working order), water and food, and comfortable seating. (You will be in that chair a long time!)

4/ Watch for illegal tack and equipment as each rider enters the ring.

It is a great time to do an overall check, so you don't miss anything.

5/ Find out if the class jogs.

6/ Ask how many horses are in the class and prepare your judges cards. Make sure you know how many ribbons are being awarded.

7/ Look over the course and make sure the jumps are all going in the correct direction (often there is an error), and the course is ready for the competition.

8/ Look at the specifications of the class, and prepare yourself accordingly.

"Qualities Which Constitute A Good Judge"

An Article By Peter Cameron

1/ Ability to judge the horse - not the person showing the horse.

2/ Ability to stand on his/her own convictions and judgment and beyond the influence of anyone.

3/ Ability to judge the horse as he/she sees them in each class on that particular day; not as he/she saw them in other classes on previous days, or as other judges have judged them. Judge only on what you see in the ring during the class.

4/ A person who reads and knows the rule book and uses it as their bible in judging classes.

5/ A person who does not leave themselves open for criticism, either in the show ring or outside by fraternizing with exhibitors at a show at which he/she is officiating by being wined and dined.

6/ The ability to use the ring steward to help him/her as a steward and not to advise him/her. To refrain from discussing or seeming to discuss the horses or exhibitors with the steward.

7/ A person who is neat, dignified, and businesslike.

8/ A person who shows confidence and firmness in his/her ability and decision.

9/ A person who looks at every horse in the ring and gives each one consideration.

10/A person who does not make embarrassing disclosures of defects towards any horse he/she is judging and avoids embarrassing situations both outside and in the show ring.

Questions & Answers

Q: As a horse show manager, where do I find a judge?

A: The national federation has an annual roster of all officials, which lists their accreditations, which horse shows they officiated at the prior year, and their addresses and phone numbers. It does not, however, rank their expertise in any way. This is best sought out by word of mouth.

Q: As a judge, can you call in or talk to an exhibitor about their negative behaviour or attitude?

A: If you feel the need to talk to an exhibitor about anything, call the steward to mediate the discussion. It is wise to have them there to witness the conversation, and deal with any further action needed.

Q: Can a judge be overexposed?

A: A judge can get to the point where they are seen too often in an area. Try not to do too many shows in the same area, especially within weeks of each other - you will be appreciated more. Horse show managers don't know who the other local shows hired, so use good judgment when accepting contracts.

Q: What is it that you most like about judging?

A: Judging and placing good rounds with quality horses.

Q: What are the top three priorities in judging?

A: 1/ Knowledge - know your stuff!

2/ Honesty

3/ A system you are comfortable with

Q: What do you do if an exhibitor or trainer makes a derogatory remark or gesture towards you while you are officiating?

A: If this ever occurs, report the incident to the steward immediately. This behaviour warrants an apology from the exhibitor or trainer.

Q: Do all good horsemen make good judges?

A: Even if the knowledge is there, the person must have the bookkeeping skills, desire, time to commit to the job and the patience to be a good judge.

Q: What does the judge say to the rider who asks how to improve their performance?

A: The judge is not hired to give a clinic. It is unfair of the exhibitor to approach the judge for this information. They should ask their trainer.

Q: Have you ever turned down a judging contract because you experienced or heard that the show was not up to your standards, and may be bad for you to be associated with?

A: Each individual has to make their own assessments. You have the right to accept only the shows you are comfortable doing. Keep in mind, though, that shows do improve with experience, and this may be a great year for that particular show.

Q: Do you vary your judging fee from show to show, or give some shows a deal?

A: Try to go with the standard fee, which varies between Canada and the US. Often the smaller shows have many classes crammed into a day and you will work a longer day than at a larger show, so giving a discount on your rate may backfire. Try to keep your rate the same for all shows - be consistent.

Q: Have you ever tried to get out of a contract for a better offer?

A: You may be tempted one day, but don't make this mistake. It is first come, first served in this business. Honour your contracts.

The horse world is a small one, and bad practices will come back to haunt you.

Q:Can I approach the judge to ask about my horse or rider, during the show?

*A:*Not without talking to the steward first. He/she will organize a meeting with the judge.

Q:What do you do if something happens on course that you do not see, and someone points it out to you (e.g. horse bucking in the corner)?

*A:*This is very difficult to swallow, but you can only judge what you see. However, you must use your own judgment (e.g. fall of a rider at the end of the course as you are watching the next horse go to the first jump - you would eliminate accordingly).

Q:What is appropriate dress for a judge?

*A:*Conservative, neat and tasteful. Men generally wear a suit and tie (with a baseball cap - very interesting fashion statement!), but the jacket can certainly be removed. Women wear suits, dress pants or skirts (not too short), and blouses or sweaters. Blue jeans, 'short' shorts, tank tops, etc., are not acceptable.

Q:Do you recall every losing your temper at a show?

*A:*Yes. Just keep it to yourself! Whether it is the overloaded schedule, slow jump crew, bad courses, talkative ringmaster or inept ingate person, just deal with it and do your job, with good manners and understanding. Tomorrow is another day!

Q:While judging a show, how much should you get involved in the other areas of the competition?

*A:*You are being paid to judge. This is your official capacity, not manager, course designer, steward or ringmaster. If you are asked your opinion, you may certainly give it, as long as it is constructive.

Q:What do you do during breaks in the ring?

*A:*Making a trip to the washroom is the first on the priority list. Take this time to eat something, read, do a crossword puzzle or stretch your legs. Keep the cellular phone in the car!

Q:Do you prefer to judge alone or with a partner?

*A:*It is usually easier to judge alone, as you don't have the issue of differences of opinion. Hunter classics are the only classes which recommend two judges, so it doesn't happen too often.

Q:Can an exhibitor or trainer complain about a judge?

*A:*The horse show office will provide you with a judge's evaluation form to fill out. You always have the option of not showing in front of a judge you dislike.

Q:How much outside assistance should you tolerate?

*A:*It is not necessary to eliminate the rider. However, it is truly unappreciated by the judge, and usually a message, via the steward, to the person and rider involved puts a stop to this problem. If it persists, the rider can be eliminated.

Q:As a senior recognized judge, do you ever judge permit or unrecognized shows?

*A:*It is not recommended for a senior judge, but a great place to get miles for a learner judge. Shows should be encouraged to hire learner judges for smaller, unrecognized shows.

Q:Is it different judging a 'big' show, and how does one handle the pressure?

*A:*You simply do the best possible job you can do. You were hired to do the job because you were thought to be competent. It is a thrill to judge the 'best of the best'. It is challenging, but very rewarding. Rely on your expertise to get through any 'jitters'.

Q:Can a judge bring action against an exhibitor?

*A:*A judge can file a complaint through the steward, which then goes to the Federation. It will take action accordingly.

You Be The Judge

Q: **Once you have signed the judge's card, can you change the placings?**

A: Pinned is pinned. If you make an error, you have to live with it.

Q: **If equipment breaks during a class (e.g. a martingale or stirrup leather) is the rider allowed to fix it?**

A: Unfortunately, you cannot stop to fix the equipment, or leave the ring and return for the same class. Your best bet is to proceed if it is safe, but if you feel it is unsafe, simply pull-up and wait for your chance in the next class!

Q: **Do judges need a ringmaster to assist them?**

A: No. Actually, this can become a distraction and a problem, especially if the ringmaster tends to make any decisions on his own regarding the running of a class or prize giving. A walkie-talkie with communication to the ingate and the announcer is all the help you will need.

Q: **If a rider wants to be excused from the ring for any reason, is it necessary to ask the judge's permission?**

A: During an under saddle class, the rider can stand in the centre of the ring until the class is over, or quietly (without disturbing the class) leave the ring when they pass by the ingate. If in an over fence class, a nod or wave to the judge will let them know that you are excusing yourself, and the judge can pass this information on to the announcer.

Q: **Is it proper to smile, salute or acknowledge the judge by saying anything?**

A: No, it is not appropriate in the hunter or equitation ring. Simply start your course - you won't be missed!

Q: **Have you ever had a cheque bounce from a show you judged? What can you do if this happens?**

A: First, call the horse show and explain what happened. If the show does not honour the cheque, send a copy of the cheque, contract and a letter to explain the circumstance to your national federation. They will handle it from there.

Q: **Is the judge the most important person at the show?**

A: Close to it. He makes all the decisions regarding the placings, and should be treated with respect. A good course designer is probably highest on the list for the success of a horse show.

Q: **Do you recommend other judges for shows you can't do?**

A: When asked, which is often, you can offer names of judges you would recommend for the job. It is a good time to refer new judges, as it helps them to break into the industry.

Q: **What do you do if the conditions make judging impossible (i.e. it gets dark, too dusty to see the horses)?**

A: You cannot judge what you cannot see! If this happens, you need to stop the class and talk to management to make arrangements to improve the situation. Watering a very dusty ring or moving the class to the next day will most likely be appreciated by all.

Q: **What classes do you jog?**

A: Any Equine Canada class which is recognized for a year-end award must be jogged for soundness. All classes other than miscellaneous classes.

Q: **Have you ever tried to get out of a contract to judge a show?**

A: Only under extreme circumstances. In case of illness, family emergency, or a matter of extreme importance. You should certainly try to help the show to find a suitable replacement.

Q: **How do you handle exhibitors coming to talk to you without the steward?**

A: Advise the exhibitor of the proper procedure, which is to approach the steward first, who will then make arrangements to mediate a discussion between the exhibitor and you. If the exhibitor acts unreasonably, you should take their name, and end the conversation. You shouldn't have a discussion without the steward.

Q: Do you need to carry any kind of insurance to be a judge?

A: As a recognized official of your Federation, you should be allotted some liability insurance, but it is wise to carry your own liability policy through an independent insurance company. You can be held liable in case of an accident in your ring, especially if it is due to a request made from you to the rider (e.g. switching horses).

Q: Does it bother you when riders you know come over and talk to you before or after their round?

A: Yes. This is business, not social. The rider needs to enter the ring and do their job - period. There is plenty of time for chatting at the end of the day.

Q: If you are judging with another judge, and you absolutely do not agree with each other, how do you handle it?

A: Good question. You pray this never happens, but it does. The best way to deal with this is to try to be as diplomatic as possible, and somehow both find a compromise. If you cannot come to an agreement, you may have to concede a few placings, and at the same time try to salvage the situation by not making a scene or getting upset. There is always another class and another show.

Q: You are in the middle of a class, and have to use the washroom. What do you do?

A: Don't suffer. Simply call to the ingate person and ask him to hold the next entry so you can quickly take a bathroom break. Make sure you map out the closest facility at the beginning of each show!

Q: If while you are judging a show, you see a horse that you may be interested in purchasing, what is the proper procedure?

A: Be aware that you must wait until the show is completely over to approach the owner or trainer. If you are unsure who to contact, find the contact through the show secretary . It would be best to try the horse a day or two after the show is over - and not on the showground.

Q: How do you deal with the pressure that goes along with judging?

A: Be confident that you know your job, that you are current, and follow the rules. Don't play games! Call it as you see it and as your expertise advises you, and you can't go wrong. You will not and cannot make everyone happy, so don't try to. It is not a popularity contest.

Q: Judging must be an exciting life with all the travel and meeting of new people?

A: Wrong! The travel is limited to the showgrounds, unless you take an extra day or two to see the local sights. It can actually be quite a lonely business. You sit alone all day and talk to almost no one, work very long hours, and then end up in you hotel room for the evening, usually with room service.

Q: In the horse world, as big as it is, you end up knowing a lot of people. Honestly, when you are judging do you tend to favour your friends or the ones you know, when the rounds are fairly even?

A: Personally, no. You must try to follow the rules and place the best round regardless of friends and who is who! Your judging career will be short-lived if you play that game.

Q: Do you have any tips on how to sit stationary for all those hours?

A: After each class, stand up and stretch or walk around. If you get a break, go for a walk. Try to get a comfortable chair at the start of the show. It also helps if you have a table to write on, so you don't have the clipboard on your lap. You may also stand up to judge the under saddle classes. If all else fails, you can bring a cushion with you.

You Be The Judge

Q: Does judging help you as a trainer?

A: It is a great opportunity to watch and learn different things to do with your own horses.

Q: Is the judge's decision really final? What if the steward arrives after a class and tells you that a rider who was pinned was off course or someone says a rail was down?

A: Pinned is pinned! If the judge did not see something and the class has been pinned, it is too late. It would have been preferable if attention was drawn to the incident before the class was pinned.

Q: Who makes the travel arrangements for a horse show you are judging?

A: Generally, you make your own flight arrangements, as you need to work the times into your schedule. You usually arrive the day before, as the first day of the show starts early in the morning. Departure time will depend on the show schedule, but normally you will fly out the evening of the last day of the show. Make sure you give yourself plenty of time to get to the airport and back, as you cannot leave the show before its over. Expect it to run late!

Q: Have you ever lost your luggage?

A: Yes. Usually it catches up with you in a day or two, but it is wise to take a carry-on bag with the essentials, so that you can last a day or two without your bags. For this reason, it is wise to travel in dress pants as opposed to jeans.

Q: Have you ever charged a show more or less than was in your contract?

A: Never charge more than your contract. If you feel the show was very light and management was losing money, you could be a kind soul and give them a discount, but you are not obligated to. A good deed is always returned!

Q: With videos being so popular today, I have heard so many say that they looked great, along with their trainer, and they

can't understand why they did not win. Would you care to comment?

*A:*First, perhaps they were good, but the others were just a little better. Second, the judge's view is a different one than that of the videographer, and it is possible the judge saw things the camera didn't pick up on. Video tends to slightly distort reality, smoothing things out, so it is not the most accurate tool.

*Q:*The judge is constantly on display. How does one avoid exhibitors, or is this something not to worry about?

*A:*It is wise to try to keep to yourself. Avoid walking through the food tent or attending exhibitors parties. You will certainly be 'nabbed' by some riders and trainers to give your opinion on something if you make yourself available.

*Q:*After the show is over, do you make any comments to the show management, or just leave?

*A:*Thanking them for inviting you is the first thing to do, as you close up you business at the show office. If your opinion is asked, you could make suggestions regarding scheduling, etc., or simply congratulate the show for a job well done.

*Q:*How hard is it for a young judge to cut into the judging circle?

*A:*A good judge will soon be recognized by show managements, as news travels fast. Most jobs are obtained by word of mouth, and your name will be passed on if you do a good job.

*Q:*What do you do if the show is running overtime, or the show adds unexpected classes to you schedule?

*A:*Overtime is difficult, but you have to deal with it. If classes are added, it is necessary for you to fulfill your duties, as schedule changes happen for a variety of reasons. You can only work, however, until the sun sets. After that, management should reschedule for the next day.

You Be The Judge

Q: **What is more difficult - judging hunters or equitation?**

A: There is no difference, as both classes are judged on the most even, effortless and best ridden round, whether it be horse or rider.

Q: **If you don't use the numerical scoring system all the time, how do you do it out of the blue for a hunter classic?**

A: Putting a percentage to a round takes practice, so you must use this system once in awhile to keep yourself comfortable with it. You will inevitably be asked to judge with a numerical score to be announced, as the hunter classics and many larger shows use this system.

Q: **How do you feel about posting your judge's cards?**

A: The judge is the only one who should have access to his cards. First, no one else would be able to understand them, as the symbols are shorthand in your own language. Second, it is not appropriate for exhibitors to see what you wrote about other exhibitors. This is not their business. If you are asked to post your cards, you have the right to refuse.

Q: **If it begins to pour rain, do you stop the class or wait for management to make that decision, even though both you and the riders cannot see properly?**

A: If you cannot see, stop the class (you may give the rider on course the option for a re-ride). There is also an issue of safety if there is lightning. The show should always be held up for a storm of this type.

Q: **Do you advertise your services as a judge?**

A: This is not generally done. The national federation annually publishes a list of all of their officials, and horse shows can use this book to find a judge. Word of mouth is the best advertising for your career, and doing a great job will certainly get you hired by other shows.

Q: **Do you ever take a break while judging a large class?**

*A:*Once you have a good list of ribbon winners on your card, and a horse makes a serious enough mistake to eliminate himself from that list, you can stop marking his round. Be subtle though. This is not the time to get up and stretch, or pick up your novel. People are watching, and don't know that their rider is out of the running.

*Q:*In the future, what do you foresee regarding judging?

*A:*I believe that numerical open scoring is making a comeback, as it is easy for the general public to follow. I also believe that rating of judges is in the future, and will be published. More judge's evaluation forms will be made available to exhibitors and they will be encouraged to comment.

*Q:*How can a judge stay current, and help to upgrade his skills?

*A:*By attending clinics; going to shows and watching; watching videos; reading articles and books on the subject; judging with good, current judges; attending the indoor shows and perhaps the winter circuit in Florida or California to watch the top performers.

*Q:*What can judging teach you?

*A:*To be more appreciative of judges, which makes you a better exhibitor. Judges have a lot of responsibility and a very difficult job. You have to admire the effort and focus they have, and we should applaud them rather than bad mouth them when we don't win.

*Q:*What do you think is a good format for a judge's clinic, so that people can get the most out of it?

*A:*The following format works quite well:

1/ Hunter over fences discussion, followed by questions and answers.

2/ Introduction to judging and marking the card.

3/ Watching video of an actual class, while practice judging.

4/ Hunter under saddle discussion, followed by questions and answers.

5/ Equitation over fences discussion, followed by questions and answers.

6/ Equitation on the flat discussion, followed by questions and answers.

7/ Conformation discussion, followed by questions and answers.

Q: **Judging has been referred to as both difficult and rewarding. Could you comment on this statement?**

A: Simply, yes. The difficulty lies in the hours of strict concentration. The reward is not the cheque at the end of the week, but watching so many wonderful horses and riders, and feeling competent to place them in order.

Q: **If you were called upon to make a statement about judging, how would you respond?**

A: Judging is an honour. The judge is in a position of high esteem and power, and it's a position that should not be taken lightly or abused.

Q: **What happens when, for example, a bag blows into the ring and spooks a horse?**

A: If it was a minor spook, try to ignore it . Use common sense.

Q: **If a horse is on course and you notice that there is a rail down on a jump the rider has not jumped yet, what would you do?**

A: The best decision is to stop the rider, via the announcer or whistle, and have the fence fixed. The rider may then start from where they stopped, and you judge their round from that point, or they could ask for a re-ride.

Q: **Can a judge's placings be overruled by the steward?**

A: No. The judge has the final say.

Q: **Does it bother you as a judge that there are so many low height divisions offered now, and does it make any difference when judging?**

*A:*This is a great question! Hunters as we know them, have been downgraded by the low height divisions. Pony hunters who jump 2'9" and 3'0" in the USA, jump higher than most horses do at a show. Horses do not really elevate over 2'0" to 2'9" heights. All of these low height classes are really programmed for the rider, so they can get around the ring, therefore when you are judging rounds at these heights horses are stepping over the fences or jumping flat or inverted. There are now divisions for every possible category. Perhaps the future should hold these classes as strictly 'rider prep' classes, and not be categorized as 'hunter' classes.

*Q:*Now that poling in the USEF rules has been eliminated, what difference do you think this will make to judging?

*A:*American judges will not hold rubbing a fence so hard against us. They will focus more on style and form. On both sides of the border I have often let good jumpers win with rubs.

*Q:*Cellular phones have become a part of many people's lives. How do you feel about judges carrying activated cell phones?

*A:*Turn them off, or leave them at the hotel! There is nothing more disturbing than watching a judge carry on a conversation while a horse is on course. You have been hired to give 100% concentration - cell phones are not part of the contract.

*Q:*Do you prefer judging or showing?

*A:*Both equally - they balance each other to keep me fresh and looking forward to showing and judging. Showing helps me to be a better judge, as I am more objective and understanding, and appreciative of the responsibility of judging. Judging helps me to come up with better ideas in regards to showing, and I have an appreciation for all that goes into showing.

*Q:*What do you consider to be the most important thing about judging, and what advise do you have for new and existing judges?

*A:*The most important thing is to be as fair and unbiased as you can by following the rules when coming up with the results. The challenge is to remain current. It is your responsibility to attend the shows and observe the winning performances.

*Q:***What do you feel constitutes 'current' in the judging world?**

*A:*Judging today's hunters and horsemanship classes is not always an easy task, as there are always flawless hunter rounds and expertly executed horsemanship classes. The smallest of dividers can end up splitting the performances, and I would never venture into this task unless I felt very current with all that is occurring in the hunter and horsemanship fields. By current, I mean constantly observing, whether officiating or not, exhibiting, teaching, training and working with horses. Outside of the local horse shows, an annual trip to watch the best quality hunters and competitors is a fun way to combine a holiday and your education!

*Q:***A question from my own experience! Recently, a rider came into the ring and proceeded to run her hand along the horse's neck on both sides, petting and soothing him all the way around the course. She did it very expertly and gently, and to add to it she had a good round. How will I deal with this?**

*A:*Well, I judged the round as I saw it, and called it as if the massaging and petting did not take away from the performance. Actually, it enhanced it as the horse responded. Therefore, whatever works!

*Q:***When you are judging and someone (e.g. jump crew) are in the booth with you and smoke or talk too much, how do you deal with it?**

*A:*Ask them to smoke elsewhere, and to please hold any questions and comments, as I need to concentrate.

*Q:***Does anyone ever tell you that you have done a good job?**

A: Rarely does anyone compliment you on your work. It is expected for you to do an outstanding job! As long as you know you have done it right, that's all you need. However, it is nice if you ever get a compliment, and is your end of the week bonus!

Q: **When will you stop judging?**

A: Hopefully before people start saying that I shouldn't judge anymore. I will know when the time comes, but not for awhile, as I really enjoy it and still feel competent.

Q: **I have noticed a lot of horses and ponies go with their ears plugged to quiet them down. How do you score them?**

A: Don't take off any points for it. It would be nice to see it as inconspicuous as possible, e.g. dark colour or put in far enough so that you don't really notice it. I do take exception and recommend to you not to plug the ears in a model class, as I feel it detracts from the best look.

Q: **This is a special question request from show management, for me to point out what a judge can do to expedite the show.**

A: Here are my ideas:

- have your results ready quickly after the flat class
- have the jog order ready as soon as the last horses exits the ring
- keep standby orders in large classes
- try to do you flat classes promptly (not too long in any gait)
- try to view your model classes as efficiently as you can
- ride-off tests should be short and meaningful

Q: **When you call in a standby order or the jog order, how do you assure that the right numbers are called?**

A: It is very important to listen to the numbers being announced. You should also ask the ingate or announcer to read back the numbers to you after you have called them over the walkie talkie. It is a mess and an embarrassing situation to have the wrong horses brought back into the ring!

You Be The Judge

Q: **If you were asked who is in you opinion the best judge in North America, who would that be?**

A: There are so many, but if I had to single out one individual it would have to be Rodney Jenkins, who is probably one of the world's greatest hunter/jumper riders as well. I have the utmost respect for him as a horseman, and I know when he judges that he is the best, qualified and respected.

Q: **Do you think you are a better judge because you are an exhibitor as well?**

A: I always feel that because of what the exhibitor has done to prepare themselves and their horses, they deserve my total undivided attention. I understand this commitment to do the best they can, as I know where they are coming from in all respects, mentally, physically, financially, etc., because I am in the same situation when I am an exhibitor. I believe this makes me a better judge, as well as a better exhibitor!

Q: **When you are acting as a trainer, do you focus only on your rider in the ring, or do you watch the judge as well?**

A: To be honest, I watch both. I watch the judge for two things - firstly that he looks at my entry before he gets to the first jump, so that he gets an impression of the horse or rider, that he is not spending a lot of time writing but watching instead. This is why it is so important to have easy short symbols so you can watch and not spend too much time writing.

Q: **If you have to eliminate a rider for three refusals, and they try the fence again, how do you eliminate or stop them from continuing?**

A: I do it via the announcer. I ask him to remind the exhibitors that they are excused and thank-you. Don't do it yourself.

Q: **From all of the judges you have worked with, could you share with us any comments that they may have had?**

A: Quotes from the pros:

"You always bring your own background and what's particularly important to you and your decisions, and that's going to come through."

Leo Conroy

"When you judge, you have to make up your mind what's going to be tie-breakers and what's going to be black and white for you. It might be different than for another judge."

Ralph Caristo, on how to penalize faults.

"If you think they did it, they did it."

Sue Ashe, on when a judge is not sure if he/she saw a fault.

"You have to learn when you're sitting with someone to give and take."

Linda Andrisani, on co-judging.

"They jump from the canter, not the trot. The canter is the most important."

Sue Ashe, on what gait is more important in the under saddle class.

"Trainers expect the judges to be professional, so I think trainers should act professionally."

Leo Conroy, on tardiness to the ring.

You Be The Judge

"Get to the point and get going."

Ralph Caristo, on riders who make long entrances.

"Most horses win classes with a score of 86 or 87. Usually 90 is 100, since so few 100's are given. But the score is insignificant. It just matters which horse is at the top of your card."

Leo Conroy, on numerical scoring.

Q: **When another judge asks you to recommend them for judging jobs, do you do so?**

A: Only if I have judged with them, or seen them judge, and I feel they are qualified. Judging is an important job. Judges will be hired by their reputation.

Q: **How do you feel about training a horse in the ring after the round, e.g. pulling up, backing up, spurring, etc.?**

A: I am glad someone asked this. Several judges, including myself, eliminate them from the ribbons regardless of the round, as I do not tolerate training in the ring. When you finish your round and you feel a need to discipline your horse, wait until you are out of the ring, as you may miss a good ribbon!

Q: **Have you ever refused to judge?**

A: Yes, once at a horse show where the rain was coming down very hard, and there was lightning. I was supposed to go out into the ring to judge a pony model class. I simply said that I could not mark my card in the pouring rain, and I couldn't see the ponies properly. Most importantly, it was dangerous for anyone to be in the ring while it was lightning. They stopped the show until the storm passed.

Q: **How do you feel about numerical scoring?**

A: Very strongly, for the following reasons:

- it is easy for the audience to follow.

- works well for the riders to follow as a standby list.

- keeps the judges alert.

- lets trainers and riders know how they are scored in good classes, even if they are not in the ribbons.

Q:Can you call off a class because of bad weather, e.g. lightning?

*A:*This is a horse show management decision. However, you may point out that the conditions are inappropriate, and contact the management to let them know that there are issues in your ring.

Q:If you overhear derogatory comments being made about the judging, would you do anything?

*A:*Absolutely. But only with the steward present. Approach the person responsible and ask for an explanation. If the person is persistent, there are certain ways in which the steward will inform you, to deal with the matter. At no time may an exhibitor approach a judge with any comment, unless the steward is with them.

Q:What do you think is the most important thing a judge needs to remember?

*A:*The most important thing is to be fair. Following the rules when making your decisions is vital. The challenge is to remain current. It is your responsibility to attend the shows and observe the winning performances.

Q:What is the one most important thing you would tell new judges?

*A:*Watch … and try to use the shortest symbols for your card, so that you can watch the round and not miss anything on course. The worst thing is a judge that spends most of their time writing and misses the beginning and end of the competitor's round.

Q:If a horse goes off course, and the judge has not noted this, is it up to the trainer or rider to point this out?

*A:*This does happen! There are many days when the judge is marking 4 - 6 cards at a time, a few with the same course and first jump, and they may miss the fact that a rider is off course. It happens rarely, but may happen. In this case, it is honest and forthright if the trainer or rider informs the ingate/judge about the error. The judge will take this into consideration and mark their card appropriately.

*Q:***If you cannot properly see a jump from your judge's booth, will you ask for it to be moved?**

*A:*Absolutely. A good course designer will look at the ring from your viewpoint. Large pillars as standards are not workable in the hunter ring, as they block your view. The course designer also has to take into account the trees and flowers. If you cannot see the course clearly, you must talk to the course designer at the start of the day and have thing moved.

Chapter Eight

Learner Judging

Introduction

The Equine Canada and USEF have a very specific system in place for obtaining your judge's card, but outside of this there are guidelines and responsibilities each judge must follow. Knowing the rules is imperative, but protocol is also vital to your success as a professional.

In this chapter, we cover the method of becoming a judge. As in any business, there are "unwritten rules" to be aware of. We offer the answers to most of these issues in this chapter, as well as suggestions to get you off on the right foot. As you gain experience you will create a want and need list of your own, and be able to pass this valuable information on to any learner judges you may work with in your future.

The Pros And Cons Of Judging

Pros

- Travel
- Exposure
- Contacts
- Satisfaction of doing a high pressured job well
- Judging makes you a better exhibitor
- Keeps you current
- Watching and comparing good horses and riders
- Makes you a better teacher

Cons

- There is no way to please everyone
- Hours of concentration
- Hours of travel time
- You are always on display and being judged as well
- Not a secure position or a career in itself
- Long waiting periods
- Definitely a high pressure position calling for total concentration for long hours
- Putting an order to mediocrity

Responsibilities Of Judging

* Arrive on time - a minimum of 1/2 hour before the first class.

* Be prepared - you are responsible to have your judge's cards, course plans, walkie-talkie, etc.

* Introduce yourself to your ingate personnel, course designer and announcer. You will need them!

* Good bookkeeping - logging details of all rounds.

* You have a responsibility towards the exhibitors, trainer and show managers - subjective decisions. You must have the confidence that you are making the right decisions.

* Exhibitors and horse shows are paying you to be representative of the system.

* Dress conservatively.

* Don't over-socialize.

* Watch and observe.

* Read the specifications of each class prior to the start.

* Keep yourself current - educate, educate, educate.

Judges must know the rule book thoroughly, as well as any rules that might applying the area where the show is taking place. Senior judges should go over the rule book each year.

The judge has a responsibility to pay strict attention. Everyone has an equal chance regardless of past or present performances. You have to call it as you see it!

Guidelines For Licensed Officials

We are becoming increasingly concerned about the way licensed officials are viewed in our sport. The following guidelines have been developed by the Licensed Officials Committee. While we take for granted that inappropriate or openly prejudicial behaviour is wrong, it is equally important to avoid the appearance of impropriety.

Some of our new members may not be aware of the traditions of our sport. It is important to educate the newcomers, and as officials, to set high standards of conduct.

Our sport has always been a 'cut above' when it comes to sportsmanship and accepting decisions handed down by show officials. On very few occasions have we resorted to verbal or physical displays of our emotions. The following guidelines should serve as a reminder to all of us to uphold the traditions of the show ring.

1. Officials must not blatantly disregarded the performance of horse and rider in favour of friends, associates, clients or would-be clients. This could hurt our sport and the reputation of all officials. Officials who take their assignments lightheartedly and continually 'cut up' in the judge's chair must understand that exhibitors have elected to show in front of them and are entitled to their sincere and undivided attention. It would be inappropriate for judges to continually make small talk, joke and laugh during performances.

2. Threats leveled at officials by exhibiting officials of equal stature, insinuating that they will have 'their day' when they sit in the judge's chair and reflect back on past decisions, should not be tolerated. The official who is the target of such threats must come forward and report it.

3. Some exhibitors have threatened and attempted to intimidate show managers. These exhibitors have made it clear to show managers that if certain individuals are hired to judge, the manager will lose their entries. When reported (in writing) by a

show manager, the situation will be thoroughly investigated and dealt with by the Association.

4. Vocal abuse of officials before the show, defaming the judge's character and questioning his/her competence seems to be on the increase. During and after the show, some exhibitors have verbally abused officials for their decisions in the ring. Again, the victim of this kind of slander has the right and the responsibility to report it. It is the responsibility of the exhibitor and trainer to set a good example of sportsmanship to others.

5. Officials must honour their contracts with shows, and those who break contracts will be dealt with on a firm basis. This means that you do not break the contract because you received a better offer. In the case of extenuating circumstances in which you cannot honour your contract, make sure that you contact the horse show manager immediately, so that they have the time to replace you.

6. Fraternization and socializing by officials with exhibitors, owners and trainers can become a problem. No one doubts the honesty of any official, but the appearance of favoritism is disconcerting to new entrants in the show world.

7. By dressing appropriately, you demonstrate your professionalism to your fellow officials, show management and exhibitors. Your standard of attire should be consistent, regardless of the show's rating. As stated in the Equine Canada Rule Book, Section A1402.9, "All officials must be appropriately dressed while on duty. Jeans, short shorts, tank tops, etc., are not acceptable".

The Judge's Wish List

The following list is a guideline for what is needed to enable the judge to do his job properly:

* Topping the list - a ride to and from the airport.

* A hotel room - not a room in someone's home.

* A comfortable chair.

* Privacy - the best spot for total viewing and quiet.

* Garbage can - the judge cannot walk around to find one and blowing trash from the judge's booth is messy and distracting.
* Cover from the sun and rain, or a pick-up truck to use in case of bad weather.
* Communication with the ingate and the announcer via walkie-talkie or runner.
* Copies of the courses.
* Extra judge's cards.
* Class specifications.
* Lunch and beverages, as you don't have time to get these on your own time.
* Close proximity to washroom facilities.
* The number of horses in a class so you know when to prepare the jog order.
* Timetable / schedule of events.
* Prize list to find out things such as the schedule, percent for conformation and number of ribbons in each class.
* Someone to organize payment of your expenses the day before the show ends, so that your cheque is ready for you.
* Rule book for reference if needed.

The aforementioned should all be provided by Show Management to insure the judge is comfortable and has everything he needs to perform his duties.

What The Judge Needs To Bring In A Carry Bag:

* Eraser, pen and pencil (pencils work best in damp weather!)
* Towel to wipe off rain or dust from your chair.
* Cushion for your chair.
* Rain gear.
* Rubber band to hold judge's cards down in the wind.

* Plastic bags to cover clipboard and judge's card (just in case you get caught in the rain and the class keeps going).
* Binoculars, to enable you to see far-away numbers.
* Hat.
* Sunscreen, sunglasses and bug repellent.
* Extra paper to write jog orders on or other notes.
* Extra pens or pencils.
* Your own Rule book (the horse show may not have a copy).
* Wet towellettes to freshen up, wake up or clean up with after lunch.
* Whistle (for judging jumpers) and stopwatch.
* Reading material to help pass the time between classes.
* Pullover sweater and gloves.
* 'Munchies', just in case you get missed for lunch orders.
* Contract.

Questions & Answers

Q: Where do I start if I want to become a learner judge?

A: Contact your National Federation, of which you must be a member in good standing, and ask for the criteria for the divisions in which you are interested. Your goal is to first obtain your recorded official's status. This is followed by the senior judge's status. The National office will provide you with all of the requirements to get you started.

Q: Do you allow learner judges to sit with you, and what would you suggest for them to get experience and advice?

A: A great question! First, I allow it but I am not overly excited about them sitting with me, first because it is only a matter of time before even the shyest one starts asserting himself. Second, they can easily glance at your card to get the order and therefore look proficient. The learner judge should sit on their own and compare results with the senior judge at the end of the class.

Q: **How do you deal with a learner judge who is getting too vocal?**

A: I would probably ignore it, but make a note of it in my comments on their report. Many judges would mention it to the steward or simply tell them to not make comments during the show.

Q: **How do you handle a learner judge who talks too much and disturbs your concentration?**

A: I would try to ignore it. It will be reflected in the learner judge's report, but as to how to handle it, I suggest saying that you have to hold your comments until the end of the class as it is difficult to concentrate on your job if you are having a conversation.

Q: **When you were a learner judge did you agree with or enjoy the entire process?**

A: Yes, I do agree that the process is necessary. I luckily worked with top judges, so I learned a lot - mostly by observing the way they judged the classes and pinned the best horses and riders. I suggest that you try to work with some of the top officials, as you will get more out of it, rather than doing it just as a part of the requirement to get accredited.

Q: **How would you recommend that a learner judge gains experience, other than judging with a senior and experienced judge?**

A: By going to the best horse shows and observing the hunter, hack and equitation classes - not keeping a card, but getting an overall impression of the classes, then working on symbols which will be the quickest and easiest for you to use. This way you can spend most of your time watching to evaluate the rounds. Judging is all about observing and not missing anything!

Q: **How do I obtain permission to be a learner judge at a horse show?**

A: You must first contact the horse show manager and obtain permission from him/her to use their show. The officiating judge must be contacted by you for permission to sit with them. The horse show will give you their address or phone number. You should contact them quite far in advance of the event you wish to attend.

Q: **Is there any paperwork that I need to send to the senior judge I work with?**

A: Not initially, but a thank you letter is very much appreciated. It is a courtesy that will not only make the judge you worked with feel their time was well appreciated, but will perhaps make the road a bit easier for the next learner judge that comes along to work with that judge. Good manners are always well accepted!

Q: **When a learner judge arrives at the show and is not properly attired, or is late, do you as the senior judge say anything to them, or mention it in the report?**

A: It would depend on how serious they are and how well they do. I will make allowances if they seem promising and serious, but will also point out proper attire and tardiness rules.

Q: **As a learner judge, how do I promote myself or possibly get some shows at which to learn?**

A: Make some calls to horse show managements that run schooling or unrecognized shows, to offer your services for experience. Talk to horse people and tell them that you are working on your judge's card, and if they hear of any shows that need a junior judge you would appreciate a mention in order to gain experience.

Q: **Do you think learner judges resent or accept the whole procedure to become a senior judge, and how did you feel as a learner judge?**

*A:*I believe that most people, as I did, accept the system as the only legal procedure to get your license. At the same time, I feel in reality people resent the time and money it takes, but we have to be educated to get a good job, and that is what the process is all about.

*Q:*As a learner judge, if I see something (e.g. a skip lead change or a spook somewhere) and the senior judge has not seen it, should I say something, or not?

*A:*My advice is to be silent and watch for the results. More often than not that horse will probably not place high as the judge has already penalized him for another error, so your observation would not really be appreciated. Your job is to watch, document, listen and learn!

Learner judges that sit with you will need to leave you a form to fill in and send to the National office. This is a confidential document, and requires that you give an honest appraisal of the learner judge's abilities and conduct. The learner judge may also ask for a letter of recommendation. You must use your own discretion in this matter. It is your responsibility to help to promote only capable and knowledgeable individuals, as they are instrumental in the future of our sport.

Summary

The road to becoming a proficient judge is one of time spent with knowledgeable horsemen. You can never spend too much time learning. In addition to the learning process, the candidate must have experience and knowledge as a horseman. The candidate must then apply this knowledge through the understanding of the rules, acknowledging the importance of honesty and integrity, and the skills of good bookkeeping.

Attending clinics, reading books, spending countless hours watching horses compete at quality horse shows are all time well spent. One of the most important qualities a good judge has outside of his/her knowledge and education is the confidence that he/she is completely capable of doing the best possible job for the exhibitors. The experience gained by judging with knowledgeable people is invaluable. Work with the best, and you will not be disappointed.

Chapter Nine

You Be The Judge

Introduction

Now it is your turn to judge both hunter horses and equitation riders. At this point in the book you should have a good idea what the judge is looking for. So without cheating by turning the page, study the three photographs as hunter and equitation rides and place them in your order. Then you may turn the page to compare your results with mine.

In some cases the results may alter slightly, so don't become discouraged if you do not have the same placings as I do with all of the examples. There are times when I could be convinced to alter my placings with sound reasoning from another opinion. Take your time to study the photographs and jot down the placings along with your reasons for placing them in your order. This will be a good reference when you compare our results. Remember to judge the class first as a hunter class, and then as an equitation class.

Hunter 1st   *Hunter 2nd*   *Hunter 3rd*

Hunter 1st

Winning this class is a great jumper with a great expression. The pony's knees are up and even and he is jumping nice and round. An overall enjoyable jump and pleasing to look at. In summation a good winner, you cannot go wrong pinning style like this!

Hunter 2nd

This bay pony places a close second! Just getting edged out by not having the identical relaxed and yet interested expression. The knees are square and high, perhaps jumping a little bit too much across the jump. In summary, all the ingredients to win and will!

Hunter 3rd

The grey pony places a very close third in this class. Her ears are a little half masted and somewhat disinterested - but at the same time a relaxed and comfortable expression. The pony is slightly uneven in front and a bit loose with the lower legs - meaning the knees could be higher and also seem to be jumping off to the right. A solid third place ribbon winner in a very competitive field.

Equitation 1st   *Equitation 2nd*   *Equitation 3rd*

Equitation 1st

Again I have the same winner, which often happens. When a pony or horse jumps beautifully it follows that the rider is doing the right release to get a good jump. The rider is a little roached in her back, but overall is an extremely pleasing winner.

Equitation 2nd

The grey pony places second on my card in this class. Her eye level is focused and she is right in the centre of he pony. She has allowed too generous a release, Her hand appears to be floating up in the air instead of pushing against the crest. Her stirrup is driven a bit too far back which puts her too far out of the tack. A shorter stirrup with the ball of the foot on the iron, would help her base of support, raising her leg and closing her upper body closer to the saddle. Overall, a very pleasant and concentrated look.

Equitation 3rd

Just behind the previous rider is the relaxed rider on the bay pony. She gives her pony lots of freedom to jump and is what we call a generous rider. Her fingers are opened up a bit too much and she is gripping with her knee which has made her leg slide back and toe out. Her upper body follows beautifully and she probably would be a good rider for a hot or tense horse!

Hunter 1st   *Hunter 2nd*   *Hunter 3rd*

Hunter 1st

First place in today's hunter class is the chestnut horse with the prominently white blaze. What an amazing jump, high, round and perfect front legs - square and high. I had a really good feeling about this jump, that their is lots of scope along with an enjoyable expression.

Hunter 2nd

The second hunter receives a well deserved second place for the grey horse with the white face. A very nice jump and a round, perfect front end. The chestnut has better scope and range. On any given day, however, I could be persuaded to place this nice grey in first place.

Hunter 3rd

The third place in this outstanding hunter event will be the dark grey horse. I really like this horse and his jump shows style and scope. He has perhaps jumped from a long distance, and is stretching his front end slightly in comparison to the others. This horse has an alert positive expression along with all the winning components.

You Be The Judge

Equitation 1st   *Equitation 2nd*   *Equitation 3rd*

Equitation 1st

First place in is the young lady on the grey horse with the white face. This rider has a look of total poise and confidence. Her leg is very good, but perhaps she is a little too far out with her toe. The young lady's fingers should be closed and pressed into the neck. These are very minor distractions from a near perfect ride.

Equitation 2nd

Our second place rider is on the dark grey horse. She looks very competent and capable. The rider is too far out of the tack (from the long distance) and her heel is up as a result of a pinched knee. She is off to the right instead of the centre of her horse. A competent rider, and a well deserved second place ribbon.

Equitation 3rd

This is an excellent ride. I like this young lady. She does appear to be a little less experienced compared to the other two riders. Her leg looks awkward with knees pinched and too parallel. Her release is floating, and her fingers are open, and low on the neck. This rider's position will improve with practice, and is a good ride overall.

This very nice group of horses and riders are to be judged as hunters and as equitation riders. They would be competing in the junior or amateur divisions, over 3'6" high fences.

You Be The Judge

Hunter 1st   *Hunter 2nd*   *Hunter 3rd*

Hunter 1st

Another class of top quality horses. The red ribbon performance awarded to the chestnut horse with the white star. A solid good jumper, knees up and even, with a relaxed look. Possibly one could say that he is jumping slightly flat across the jump but I am confident that he has ample scope and stride to handle the jumping efforts easily. A well earned red ribbon.

Hunter 2nd

An excellent second place blue ribbon is pinned on the bay horse with the white star and snip. He is magnificent with his head, neck and body. Round, high and scopey.

Hunter 3rd

A well deserved third place ribbon goes to the liver chestnut with the white star. Again, a beautiful jumper that is high, round and relaxed. His knees are perfectly square. The only slight error is that the right one is slightly lower than the left one. However, these three hunters, are not very far apart in their performance.

Equitation 1st   *Equitation 2nd*   *Equitation 3rd*

Equitation 1st

The young lady riding the liver chestnut will take top honours in our equitation class. She demonstrates style, confidence, and focus. Her heel could be a little deeper, but the rest is flawless. I can easily place her at the top of the class.

Equitation 2nd

The young man on the chestnut horse is going to be second place. He also shows polish, position and focus. I have a really good feeling about this positive rider. The second place ribbon is awarded as his stirrup appears to be slightly too far in front of his foot and is parallel with the ground. However, the rider has all the ingredients of a winner.

Equitation 3rd

Placing third is the rider on the attractive bay horse. She has a good upper body position and I like her generous release over the fence. However, the rider's lower leg has slipped back with a pinched knee against the saddle. This is easy to fix, and by the looks of this competent rider, she will easily remedy this lower leg and henceforth be in a winning position.

Another group of outstanding performers for you to judge. Pay close attention to the smaller details of the horse's jump and rider's positions.

Hunter 1st   *Hunter 2nd*   *Hunter 3rd*

Hunter 1st

This chestnut horse with the white, takes home the red ribbon. High, scopey and a good front end along with a good expression makes for a red ribbon performance. The horse may have 'stood off the base of the fence' too far, but he is handling it with ease and does not look quick or flat. A well deserved win to take home.

Hunter 2nd

Mr. Spot will be the second place winner. His front end is impeccable, up and square. He is alert and kind in his look. A second, because he is just stepping over this low jump, with his back legs still on the ground. He looks a bit inverted and flat. Again, as the jump is so low, little effort is required. A good front end, and he looks easy enough so 'blue' he will be.

Hunter 3rd

The third place ribbon is going to the liver chestnut with the white blaze. A nice look, easy and confident in an uncomplicated rubber bit. The front end is not perfectly square, slightly uneven (higher on the left), and reaching out. These are minor faults, but will serve to separate these three winning performances. I am confident that this sweet, good look will win many events in the future.

You Be The Judge

Equitation 1st   *Equitation 2nd*   *Equitation 3rd*

Equitation 1st

Mr. Spot's rider has a beautiful, effective and very solid leg. Her foundation is solid and firm. The upper body is centered and out of the saddle. The release is too 'fisty' and pulled back to her neck, and should be fixed by going up slightly with it ahead of her chin. All the rest 'is there' to win anywhere.

Equitation 2nd

In second place is the young lady on the liver chestnut. Her lower leg is excellent and she has a good enough release for this size of jump. The rider is looking in a little too early and has raised herself too high in the air as a result. She needs to close her upper body down and stay in the centre - all will then look like a 'photo finish'.

Equitation 3rd

A third place ribbon will be awarded to the man on the brown horse. He is an effective rider, getting the job done, but he is looking down and off to the left (he may be concerned about a lead). His leg has slipped back and he is gripping with his knee as a result. The low left hand is probably guiding his horse away from the right side. A very functional ride with good upper body control.

You Be The Judge

Hunter 1st   *Hunter 2nd*   *Hunter 3rd*

Hunter 1st

This is why I love judging - just look at the top calibre of horses' and riders. This is a true contest and I will award the red ribbon to the bay with the white face. A great jump - alert, around, even and very stylish. He looks like he really enjoys what he is doing and I will justly give him first place in our hunter class.

Hunter 2nd

A really difficult decision but just because he is so perfectly square with his front legs the blue rosette goes to the bay with the white stripe on his nose. A great expression, maybe a hair flat but a true athlete demonstrating a clear, comfortable jump along with a well-deserved blue ribbon.

Hunter 3rd

The plain bay goes home with the white ribbon for a great jumping effort. The tiniest of dividers separate this class. Because the horses' front legs are split higher and uneven, makes him third.

Equitation 1st　　　　*Equitation 2nd*　　　　*Equitation 3rd*

Equitation 1st

This boy shows it all - lower leg, upper body, release, hands, eyes - a definite red ribbon rider. Horses jump well and are happy when you ride this way and I felt really good with this first place win. As you can see when you do it right, the right things happen. Truly a great class and an exceptional winner.

Equitation 2nd

This girl is a good blue ribbon winner. I really like her upper body and the way she is focussed on the next jump. Her stirrups are slightly angled out, but her lower leg is excellent and effective.

Equitation 3rd

This girl makes her horse jump beautifully by the way she rides. However, for this equitation her fingers are open around the reins which works fine for the hunters but in the horsemanship classes you need to close your fingers. Her leg has slipped back as well as her knee is pinched. I think she make horses jump really well. Keep up the good work.

Hunter 1st   *Hunter 2nd*   *Hunter 3rd*

Hunter 1st

This chestnut with the white blaze is first. He looks happy and easy going. His knees are perfect, up and square. He is jumping a little flat across the jump, but appears a pleasant and relaxed look for an indoor performance. This 'easy' kind of horse usually comes through for the rider, is nice to work with, and easy to train.

Hunter 2nd

The second place goes to the dark brown horse. He is both high and square with the front end. He appears somewhat tense, inverted and jumping to the left. The rider is giving the horse a lot of release to stretch out his head and neck, but still he looks tense.

Hunter 3rd

The flashy chestnut with all the chrome is third in this hunter class. This horse is very attractive and well turned out but his jump makes him appear to be laying on his left side, making him appear twisted to the right, and uneven in front. He also looks a little 'ready and quick'.

You Be The Judge

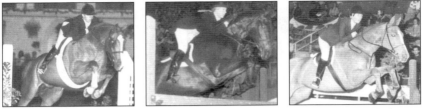

Equitation 1st   *Equitation 2nd*   *Equitation 3rd*

Equitation 1st

Another tough decision but I go with the rider on the flashy chestnut. She looks focussed and capable. I like her release and her upper body control. Her leg may have come back slightly, but it is correct length and solid. She is giving just enough for this jump, and looks very positive about her ride.

Equitation 2nd

On any day this young rider could be the winner. She appears confident and in control of the ride. Her lower leg puts her in second place, as she appears to be standing in her stirrup, with knee pinched and a little too high out of the saddle. Fix the lower leg, and this rider would go right to the top in any company.

Equitation 3rd

The white ribbon and third place goes to the young lady on the chestnut horse. A generous release and she is looking up and ahead in the direction that she is heading. Her upper body is excellent with a good follow through, and out of the saddle in proportion to the jump. The rider's problem lies with the over exaggerated toe out, and a gripped knee. With a relaxed knee, heel down, toe in, you would have a winning look.

You Be The Judge

Hunter 1st *Hunter 2nd* *Hunter 3rd*

Hunter 1st

First place in this hunter class is the plain bay horse with the gentleman riding. A classic look that is effortless, scopey, round and perfectly square in front and behind. A kind, easy expression and an 'A-plus' jump on my judges' card. This is what makes judging so enjoyable - to see such quality and an outstanding performance here.

Hunter 2nd

The second hunter is the plain bay with the young woman aboard. Again, this horse has a great expression and the look of a top quality show horse. He is placed in second place as he appears just slightly uneven in front and a little flat from jumping from too far a distance. He looks totally confident, capable and a pleasure to ride. This is an excellent group of horses and they would all be winners on any given day.

Hunter 3rd

The third place goes to the grey horse. He is quite scopey and very athletic. The only reason he is placed third is because he appears to be unfolding his front legs too early over the jump. He appears to be reaching for the back rail, most likely as a result of slightly long take-off. He definitely has the scope to finish the jump. He has a tremendous amount of winning ingredients.

Equitation 1st   *Equitation 2nd*   *Equitation 3rd*

Equitation 1st

First place in the equitation over fences is the young woman on the plain bay horse. She has great style and presence. The rider is totally focussed and appears square in the centre of her horse. Her leg is excellent, and there is an ample release for this size of jump. The rider is slightly ahead and too far out of the saddle for the jump, but this is a minor flaw for a winning ride.

Equitation 2nd

Our second place is the gentleman on the grey horse. A confident and capable rider, he appears to be at ease with his performance. He needs to stay closer to the tack and his leg will come underneath him with his heel down. He is looking to the left and down, and should be looking between his horse's ears. These would be easily remedied, for a winning ride.

Equitation 3rd

This is an excellent ride. This rider gets the best performance out of his horse. His knee is pinched which has caused his leg to slip back, and his stirrup is on the tip of his toe. Similar to the second place rider, he needs to shift his eye focus from the left and down to centre. When you see a horse jumping this well, you know that there is an accomplished rider on board.

Hunter 1st   *Hunter 2nd*   *Hunter 3rd*

Hunter 1st

The lop eared bay with the white socks wins first. This is a great effort. High, square and totally pleasing to watch, judge and reward with a first place ribbon. Judging is truly a contest with these great performances.

Hunter 2nd

Second place goes to the bay with the prominent blaze. An equally great jumper, he is high, round with an extremely pleasing expression. He is not as 'tight' with his front end as the first place horse. Without a doubt he would be a winner on any given day.

Hunter 3rd

Third could have been first as this is such a competitive class. The plain bay with the small star is a good third place win in this spectacular hunter class. He is a little flat and has opened up a bit early over the top of the oxer. Good scope and a lovely expression.

You Be The Judge

Equitation 1st   *Equitation 2nd*   *Equitation 3rd*

Equitation 1st

The plain bay rider has the best lower leg position and a generous release. She could be a little more in the centre of her horse with her head looking between his ears. She also needs to raise her eye level up and to the middle.

Equitation 2nd

The girl on the white faced bay is second. Both her upper body and eye level is good. She needs to close her fingers around the reins. he leg has also slipped back and she appears to be reaching for her stirrups. If the stirrups were a hole shorter, this would fix the problem. A confident, positive rider overall.

Equitation 3rd

Third place is the young woman riding the first place hunter win. From a style point of view she needs to look up, and she should be in the centre of her horse more. Her leg has come back slightly and she needs to improve her hold on the reins. She is holding her fist upside down and needs to fix this.

You Be The Judge

| Hunter 1st | Hunter 2nd | Hunter 3rd |

Hunter 1st

First place is the bay pony with the white face and legs. High, scopey, round, square and beautiful. This pony is a real athlete and uses all his parts to perfection. This is a joy to behold and a well deserved ribbon for his effort here. This group reflects one of the best pony classes judged in this Hunter section.

Hunter 2nd

The second place goes to the grey pony that has his ears back. He has a terrific jump that is high, and he is perfectly square with his knees. He is in second place because he is not as round through his top line and his ears are back. The bay pony in the first place has a more positive and alert expression. This grey would win just about anywhere on any given day.

Hunter 3rd

The grey pony with the 'flop' ears is our third ribbon winner. He has a terrific jump. The knees are up and even. He also has a relaxed good look. He is third in this class as he is jumping a little flat in comparisons to the first and second place winners. He may have jumped too long a distance, and may end up reaching for the back rail. The grey definitely would be a pony that anyone would want to ride.

Equitation 1st　　　　*Equitation 2nd*　　　　*Equitation 3rd*

Equitation 1st

The winner in the horsemanship equitation is the young lady on the grey pony. Her lower leg is excellent, heels are down, a proper length and correct angle. She is a bit too far out of the tack, up the pony's neck, and could be 'closer to the tack', but this is a minor fault.

Equitation 2nd

Second place goes to the girl on the bay. What a terrific solid lower leg. She has a relaxed, yet determined look. The rider is also too high out of the tack, and too forward. She needs to be closer to the saddle. However, the rider deserves to win second place in this top competition.

Equitation 3rd

The third place ribbon is given to the girl on the "lop-eared' grey pony. Her heel is riding up, and her knee is pinched which has caused her leg to slide back. The rider is also looking down. She is 'out of the tack' just enough and demonstrates a good following arm with her release. A well deserved third place ribbon in this fine company.

Hunter 1st   *Hunter 2nd*   *Hunter 3rd*

Hunter 1st

First place in this hunter class is the grey horse with the young lady aboard. This without a doubt is an exceptional jump. The knees are totally even and high, along with an alert and pleasing expression. There is a lot of scope here. This hunter is the real thing, a real athlete which obviously enjoys his job.

Hunter 2nd

The second hunter is the chestnut horse with the white blaze. He also appears to enjoy his job and has a relaxed expression. He demonstrates a great deal of scope and is quite round over the top of the oxer. His knees could be higher as his lower legs are dangling significantly. A minor flaw but that is all it takes to place him second in this excellent company.

Hunter 3rd

The third place ribbon will be pinned on the dapple grey horse. This is also another outstanding jumper with scope, roundness and a good look. His knees are high and up but slightly uneven, the right being higher than the left. The left leg is also twisted slightly to the left which again in this good group places him third, but an excellent placing in this quality event.

You Be The Judge

Equitation 1st   Equitation 2nd   Equitation 3rd

Equitation 1st

First place in the equitation class goes to the gentleman on the dapple grey. Without a doubt this rider looks positive, confident and totally in control. His leg is back a little but is totally effective. His upper body is doing everything in the right way, and there is a terrific forward focussed look. This rider gives a very positive feeling and is therefore out first place winner.

Equitation 2nd

Our second place ribbon in the equitation class is the young lady on the grey horse. She has an excellent lower leg and is square in the centre of her horse looking up and ahead. She could be a bit more 'closed' or closer to her horse with her upper body if her hand was not floating up in the air, but rather pushed down into the next, this would close down her upper body. And then voila, the winner of the class!

Equitation 3rd

This is an excellent third place ride for the rider on the white faced chestnut horse. A competent rider, today he has a few errors theat place him third. His leg has slid back and he is over his horse to the right. The rider should be centered in the middle of his horse. This fault is easily corrected and will lead to a better equitation ride and ribbon placing.

Summary

Do you feel more qualified and confident now? I hope that this has been an educational exercise in judging hunters and equitation riders. Judging is one of the most difficult jobs I have ever done, but I genuinely enjoy it. If you judge honestly, to the best of your ability and knowledge, you will not go wrong.

Chapter Ten

The Lighter Side
Of Judging

Introduction

Through my years of judging horse shows a number of amazing things have happened. I have enjoyed telling people about them whether it be just in casual conversation, or at a clinic. Several people have requested that I relate these experiences under title and incorporate them in the book. As I write down these experiences I will not refer to the actual show or the people involved. This book has been a formal presentation of judging. Now I would like to relate to you a lighter, more personal side of judging.

Most Aggressive Parent

The only judge's card I would gladly forget is the lead line card. In this particular class there were 75 exhibitors, and I could only place 6! Miraculously I somehow pulled out 6 from this fantastic turn out and placed them. Upon leaving the ring, I was approached by a lady who asked me why I did not trot the class. I pointed out that the specifications on my card said to simply walk. She then went one step further by saying that if I trotted the class, I would have eliminated them all. They simply couldn't ride.

At this point, the ring had been held up for over half and hour. We were waiting for a child from the pony ring who was catch riding. It is more than a coincidence that the particular child that we were waiting for, belonged to the aggressive mother who wanted me to trot the lead line so her child could stand out! You be the judge!

Most Allowable

Breaking the rules in an acceptable way. During a flat class, right in front of me a horse kicks out at another horse, and the kicked horse dodges away to avoid another attempt. Unfortunately the child fell off and I called the class to a halt. The horse was caught and the child remounted. The rest was up to me.

Since I witnessed the entire situation, and it was the last way of the ring at the last gait (note: the child who fell off was in contention for a ribbon), I asked the exhibitor who's horse kicked to line up in the centre of the ring, and the rest to continue at the last gait. The child who had fallen finished beautifully, so I lined them up and pinned the class with no reservations.

I might add that it was a short stirrup class, and the beginner levels need all the support and encouragement you can give them!

Most Ambitious

When I get the prize list from a show that I will be judging, the first thing I look for is the schedule of events. I usually look at the last day to see what flight I can make to get home. When I received this one particular prize list and I glanced at Saturday's list of events, I thought they had mistakenly put all six days of showing on one day. Well the schedule was real, and Sunday's was just as bad! As I had already signed a contract, I was committed to do the show, so I planned on coming home on the Monday. There were 49 classes on the Saturday schedule and 41 for Sunday, plus many classes with two phases or second rounds. It took two clipboards to hold all of the judge's cards!

Most Challenging

It was 8:00 a.m. and the fog was so thick that I could barely see. The first class was the under saddle and I had to judge it. This was difficult! I had to get very close to see how they moved and to see their numbers as they went by. Then the riders would be out of sight again. I could only hope that they continued to hack well. A second look was virtually impossible. It was one of the most challenging classes I have ever judged. I was unable to see adequately, it was such a guessing game. Luckily enough, there were no complaints.

Most Controversial

A rider on course suddenly pulls up in the middle of a line and announces that the judge is on the phone! The rider then walks out of the ring and goes over to the show manager to explains what has occurred. The manager approached the judge to speak to him regarding the use of cellular phones during officiating.

The rider was allowed to go again, and the judge was most apologetic. Again, I must impress on all judges that cellular phones have no place in the judge's booth. This was a classic example of a most awkward and embarrassing situation, which can easily be avoided.

Most Dangerous

If asked, I would have to say that judging as an occupation has a very low danger ratio. However, there are exceptions. This happened at an indoor show where the judge's booth is set up considerably high on the side of the ring. The judge actually looks down below to judge the classes, probably the safest and most remote place to be. Not so. A horse on course bucked so violently that he threw his hind shoe, which went into the air directly to the judge's booth, knocking the judge out cold. The judge, a good friend of mine, thankfully was fine, but ended up in the hospital with a concussion.

As I am writing about this episode, I am sitting in the same judge's booth at the same show. Believe me when I say that I rear backwards every time a horse kicks out!

Most Demanding

It was a two ring horse show and we all shared the same channel on the walkie talkie. I heard a call for the Junior "A" equitation on the flat to assemble in ring 1, and I was judging ring 2. I could not help but hear the commands and I do have to share them with you, as I have the other judge's permission to write about this, without mentioning his name.

The class is called to order on the rail to the left, at the walk. The best and most effective way to do this is to list the commands in the order they were called for:

1/ counter canter

2/ sitting trot

3/ drop your stirrups

4/ extended posting trot

5/ halt

6/ turn on the forehand

7/ counter canter

8/ canter (on the true lead, which meant a flying change)

9/ line up (at the canter, which meant cantering to the centre of the ring and halting)

This all, I might add, was asked for indoors at a B-rated horse show, and at the beginning of the year! I have no idea how they all executed these arduous commands, but I can just imagine how eliminating it was. I later asked the judge, why? He responded, "Just to get them thinking." I didn't disagree with the concept of testing and keeping them on their toes, but so many tests in a short span of time can eliminate all!

Most Destitute

I was alone in the back of a pickup truck, out on the side of a field judging a show. A storm started brewing and word spread that there was a possibility of a tornado. As the storm intensified and things got blacker, the showground started to vacate. I called the announcer - no contact, and not a single horse in sight! Things started to look bad, my first thought was to drive the pickup back to the office - no keys! I could not stay in the pickup and it was quite a hike back to the office against the rain and the wind. I was all alone and had to decide what to do next, and now! The only advice I could remember was to find a low area and lay down flat. I got into my rain suit and aimed towards the ditch. The sky at this point was so black that I was convinced that something was about to happen to break the intensity. Luckily, the tornado passed by without touching down on the show grounds. I crawled out of the ditch cold and thankful that it was over. It is amazing how you can adjust to adverse situations when you have to. Judging calls for all sorts of adaptability!

Most Difficult

The best way to describe this experience is simply that you cannot judge what you cannot see. I was forced to call a class to stop about three quarters of the way through it, as it was just too dark to see. Management should have called the class over and postponed it until the next day, but when they didn't I called the announcer over my walkie talkie, and then to the ingate person, that the class is now officially over, and to ask management what they would like to do. Either pin the ones that went or completely re-run the class in daylight. Besides the obvious (not being able to see), the safety factor overrides all, so the decision was made to stop for the day.

Most Eliminating

I was judging a pony conformation class in which they jump and then are called back to jog and then line up for conformation, which counts for 25%. I jogged the class back, and as I am inspecting each one I come to one whose noseband is undone, which is fine except that it is showing a healthy row of quite large studded tacks inside the noseband. What do you do? It is simple, as it is illegal. You have to eliminate the pony from the placings, and you should tell the steward what you have done so that they can deal with the trainer. This move backfired for the exhibitor, so remove it or better yet, don't use it!

Most Embarrassing

This of course happened at one of the biggest and most prestigious shows in the country. It was an equitation class, and I called in the numbers of the riders to return for the flat phase. Once the flat phase was completed I switched around the two top riders, and gave the new order to the announcer. I then went in search of a washroom (they always seem to be far away). The presentation ceremony was quite a big deal with a blanket of flowers, a cooler and a trophy. There were photos to be taken of the trainer beside the winner. From the distant washroom I heard the announcement of the winner and I was panic stricken! They announced the wrong one! (I might add, that strangely enough the top two riders had the same first name).

As fast as I could I made my way back to the judge's booth, grabbed the walkie talkie and halted the announcer. He was already at the fourth placing and the winner was there completely adorned with all the winnings. The announcer admitted that he had read the results of the original call back list. That was a tough one to weather, as they stripped the winner and re-assigned all the winnings to the real first place winner!

Most Exciting

This has to be the first time I was invited to judge the Washington International Horse Show. I was one of the first Canadians to judge there, and it was an honour and a thrill. My partner was Daniel P. Lenehan, one of the most honest, compatible and knowledgeable judges that I have ever judged with. It ended up being a fantastic week at a very high profile show.

Most Excuses

One exhibitor made the supreme effort to go to the steward with their list of reasons why they were unbraided and late, and if it would be alright to show! Let me now share with you the list of excuses:

1/ When we tried to load my horse first, he wouldn't load, and then lost a shoe.

2/ The braider never turned up.

3/ On the way to the show, we had a flat tire and no spare.

4/ I forgot my riding boots at home.

5/ My trainer was busy in another ring.

6/ Sorry, but I lost my number.

Well, she showed in spite of all the excuses, which I excused, and, as to how she performed amidst all of these mishaps, she did not make the ribbon list!

Most Frightening

This was at a winter show held in South Florida. I had just come out of the frozen north, so on my first day judging, I took my chair and my clipboard across the ring to sit facing the sun.

About halfway through the first class the announcer called me over the walkie talkie and said, "Randy, I don't want to panic you but something is wrong." I called back and said, "What could possibly be wrong. I haven't even pinned the first class!". He then said, "Sit absolutely still and do not make any moves". An alligator had climbed up out of the lake and was sunning himself right behind me. I not so calmly told the announcer to pull up the rider on course and that I was getting up and running across the ring. As I ran one way the 'gator' turned and crawled back into the lake. Now I have become very selective as to whom I sunbathe with.

Most Frustrating

Of course it was a major indoor show, and an evening side saddle class running on a tight schedule. I was asked to judge the class with a person I had never judged with before. We proceeded into the ring and worked on separate sides for the fist half. When we joined in the middle for the second half we compared numbers. I was panicked to discover my partner did not even have one of the ten numbers that I had! Whoa, where do we begin? I felt that I had done it right and somehow I was going to have to convince my partner that my order was right.

This proves the importance of good bookkeeping! We were able to determine that she had missed some of the things on my side of the ring. Using this procedure we were able to work the numbers into the proper order.

Most Heard About

I finished judging a pony under saddle class and the ponies were all lined up in the centre of the ring. I called the results into the announcer, and the ribbon lady was standing by the ingate with the ribbons. The announcer awarded the first place ribbon, and everyone was waiting for the rider and pony to move towards the gate to receive their ribbon. Nothing happened, and I instantly looked at my judge's card and then to the line up to be sure that it is the correct number.

It was correct, so I thought that the child perhaps did not know her number. As I looked again, I see the child trying to coax the pony out of the line up to go to the ribbon presenter, but there was no way that this pony was going to leave the herd. One can wait only so long, so I got on the walkie talkie and told the announcer to ask for second place and on to pick up their ribbons, hoping the first place pony would follow.

Luckily, the plan worked, and once again proved how determined ponies can be.

Most Humorous

There needed to be a video of this performance to truly visualize and believe this particular round. A very spooky green horse walked into the ring. He looked all around, and was herded forward by a very tough, aggressive rider. They both somehow managed to clear the first fence toward the in-gate and then aimed towards the line in front of me away from the gate. The horse hooked into the jump and fell down, the rider somersaulted off and away from the horse. The horse lay half down and half up, trying to decide what to do or not do next. The rider aimed at the horse at a run and jumped aboard. The horse leapt up and cantered down the line. They jumped the next fence, and by this time I am in total disbelief.

All is not over, as the horse jumped into the diagonal and came to a screeching halt at the next jump. The rider vaulted over the jump, landed standing and turned back to glared at his mount. The horse sized up the situation quickly - and jumped over the fence to stand beside his rider. Who says you can't make a horse jump?

Most Ignorant

I call this incident the most ignorant as I feel it was an overly aggressive display of intended intimidation. I was judging a large pony model class, and as we all well know, trainers station themselves around the ring and offer words of advice and comments, which is not appreciated nor tolerated. One overly aggressive trainer voiced out as I was viewing their pony, "Yes, just like that. Perfect. Don't let him move. That is just the way he stood when he won the model at the pony finals." Well, that was overboard, so just to demonstrate how I cannot be intimidated or directed, I easily found another pony to beat it in the model, as there were forty in the class.

To further support my feelings on ignorant behavior, I had the final ten ponies lined up (that pony was second) and I decided that I liked the third one more, switching the two. Aggressive comments will not be tolerated by any judge, and could be reported to the steward, so beware before you speak!

Most Independent

I believe it was a green pony class, and the pony stopped three times at the first fence. Finally, the rider slaps him with the stick and reacting as many ponies would, bucked the rider off.

Now the pony is free and running wild. He proceeded on his very own to jump all the jumps as if it was meant to be, and then to further add insult to injury, he turned around and ran back the other way, jumping all the jumps backwards (rub free, of course). When he finished this incredible display of jumping talent, he stood and allowed himself to be caught.

That was the first class, and the same combination returned for their second course. The pony once again decided not to perform. By the last class, however, the pony was convinced to perform with his partner, and easily won the class.

Most Incredible

It was May, I arrived out in Western Canada during a snowstorm and had to judge an outdoor horse show. The area receives over a foot of snow and the plows arrive. They plowed the rings and the show went on. It was an incredible feeling and sight sitting on top of a snow bank judging hunters cantering up and down the plowed laneways. They jumped jumps amidst a winter wonderland.

A true show of snow!

Most Inexcusable

On two different occasions I have had exhibitors try to jog back a substitute horse, which I have both times recognized and openly and instantly eliminated, reporting it to the steward as well. This is going too far. One time was in a large class which ended up being a poor class, so naturally a lot of horses were sent back to the barn and put away. I can understand this, so when called back the exhibitor simply needs to say they will not be jogged back, instead of grabbing any horse (not even the same colour!) and trying to pass it off as the one they rode. Since I note the colour and description of each horse on my card, I know what each horse looks like, so this does not work.

The second attempt at a substitution was for a horse that was lame. The rider found a similar looking horse and tried to pass it off. The possibility of getting away with this kind of action is small, but the consequences are great. Something never to do!

Most Knowledgeable

This is a personal sort of appreciation to some of the judges I have been honoured to have worked with. I know they were and are the best we have ever seen. I regret that some of them have passed on, so I would like to pay tribute to these remarkable judges that I was so fortunate to have worked with, and most importantly learned from.

I am assured that this list will go unchallenged by any horseman in North America, as showing under any of these judges was truly an honour and never questioned.

> Hunter - Daniel P. Lenehan
> Conformation - Gene Cunningham
> Hack - J. Arthur "Bucky" Reynolds
> Equitation - George H. Morris
> Overall - Rodney Jenkins

Most Laundered

This really happened, and I do not recommend anyone else trying it. A good friend of mine told me this story, which I found quite amusing. It was early morning, judging a model class in a grass ring, and this certain judge walked around the horses in a very damp ring. His shoes and socks ended up quite wet afterwards. He then proceeded to take off his shoes and socks, and draped them over the ledge of the judge's booth to dry.

This was quite an attraction to all, and in plain view, which I again say do not attempt to copy. I think the judge needs to be as inconspicuous as possible, and this definitely left him out to dry in public!

Most Lengthy

As a rule, judging is usually a full day, but when it goes into the evening it makes for a very long day and long hours of concentration. When these unscheduled evening performances happen as a result of an overly ambitious schedule and late entries, you simply have to go along and get through it doing the best job you can.

On one memorable occasion I recall judging all day and dark was coming along, with several classes left, and I noticed there were no lights around the outdoor ring. What I did not consider was the indoor arena, so that is where we moved to in order to complete the remaining classes. Probably the most irritating thing at this point was with the new location there had to be a warm up class judged, so the competitors could all become acclimatized to the new ring. I was there until past midnight, having started the day at 8 a.m., a very long day at the office!

Most Lost

I had been judging since 7:30 a.m. and it was now 9:00 p.m. I was judging an amateur hunter class indoors. The layout of the ring was constructed so that the stalls were around the outside of the ring, being two aisles of horses with gates that opened to give access to the indoor arena.

A certain horse was on course and went across the diagonal. With two jumps left he disappeared from sight as I was marking my card. I knew he had not finished his course as I still had two more spots on it to fill in before the end of the course. I know I was tired at this point, but I lost the horse. Then, he suddenly reappeared into the ring, jumping the last two jumps!

The horse had gone out of one of the open gates, down the aisle of stabled horses, back up the next aisle, and into the ring to finish his course. This unscheduled exit obviously eliminated the duo, but I still find it amazing and amusing that he was able to do all of this, and then expect to reappear and finish the course as if I might not have noticed his absence.

Most Memorable

Six ribbons, six competitors and a walk trot class! Everyone is at the walk and all looks fine. Now I call for a trot - I should point out that this is a grass ring and the children are mounted on ponies. One black pony is determined to get a mouthful of grass and, as he plunges his head down, the child falls off down the neck and over the head, landing easily on the ground. The father quickly leaps into the ring, helps the child remount and then jumps back out of the ring.

By the end of the class the count for this one particular child, was six dismounts. Around the ring were stationed the mother, sister, brother and friends, all of whom took turns helping the child. I actually judged this class under F.E.I. Rules - where a fall does not instantly eliminate! The child placed 6th and her entourage of helpers all thanked me for being so lenient as it meant so much to all of them. I suggested an overcheck might help the situation.

Most Mishaps

You may not believe that this actually happened, but I assure you, it did! In front of me in one class, a girl came into the ring riding a high-headed grey horse in a tight standing martingale. She picked up a canter and went up the first line of jumps. At the end of the ring the martingale broke and the horse's head went higher, which makes the rider have to look to the side to see where she is going.

She continued down the diagonal, and at the end of the ring hauled on the right rein to turn and get the lead change, at which time the rein broke. She kept going up the diagonal with leather flying in all directions. At the end of the ring and the last turn towards home, she stepped into her stirrup to get turned and the stirrup leather broke, but she brought her mount home in spite of all the mishaps.

I don't think much more could have gone wrong, and I do admire and give her credit for continuing, as she was determined to get around in spite of all her misfortunes.

Most Missed

I was judging a show in California, and Sunday night I took the red eye from Los Angeles to Washington, to start another show the very next day at 8:00 in the morning. When I arrived in Washington at 5:30 a.m., I was to rent a car and drive to the hotel for a change of clothes before heading to the show. I really prefer not to work at shows so close together, but the shows were at opposite ends of the country and the dates were open for me.

I was fast asleep when my plane landed in Washington. I did not wake up until we were back up in the air. I looked at my watch and noticed that it was now 6:00 a.m., I asked the flight attendant if we were late arriving in Washington. When she informed me that we had already landed and were now on our way to Dulles, I was shocked. Thank goodness we were not too far from the show, and I was able to rent a car and drive directly to the show, change my clothes in the office, and start working on time.

I now ask for a wake up call on flights when I need to sleep.

Most Obedient

This is a short story, but it definitely makes the top of the "most" list. I was judging an equitation flat class. Half way through the class I asked the riders to cross or drop their stirrups. To my astonishment one girl pulled her leg forward, pulled her stirrup off, and dropped it to the ground. I was convinced this was a mistake, but she then proceeded to do the same with the other stirrup.

What she obviously took "drop your stirrups" literally, and was quite serious about it. I asked the ringmaster to retrieve her stirrups, and I proceeded with the class. It was a good thing that I did not ask them to pick up their stirrups. I couldn't even imagine how she might have worked that out.

Most Painful

It was an outdoor summer show and I was standing in the ring judging the under saddle. Halfway through the class I felt a tickling sensation in my pant leg. I realized that I was standing on a clover patch and there was a bee in my pants. It was definitely there buzzing around, and I knew I was going to get it! I started to dance around in order to shake him out. He finally gave in to his captivity and laid his stinger into my thigh. I'm sure you can imagine the initial pain in such a sensitive area. The show must go on and I had to look cool, judge the class, and pin it. I beat the bee but did I pay later!

Most Patient

While judging a large green pony class, a certain large pony comes into the ring and does his first of the back-to-back classes, and goes very well. A few rounds later, he walks into the ring to do his second round, and the announcer announces his arrival.

After walking into the ring, the pony halts and stands still. I watch for something to happen but nothing happens. He simply plants his four feet on the ground and will not move one inch in any direction. The rider spurs, clucks, whips, drives with all her body parts, and resorts to screaming. Still, no movement. The pony has cemented himself into the ground. From the ingate comes all sorts of advice, and still no reaction.

Finally, when the announcer, who can't see the ring but assumes the pony has finished his round, announces the completion of the round, this is my cue to excuse the pony, as he has definitely gone over the time allowed to start and finish the course. When I have it announced that the pony is excused, the trainer has to come into the ring and lead the pony out. I felt very badly, but the patience limit had been reached.

P.S. I was later told by the apologetically by the trainer that feeding time was 3:00 p.m., and sure enough, he came to a halt precisely at 3:00 p.m. Mind the pony minded - they obviously have a mind of their own, and not much moves them when dinner is served!

Most Pleasing

My most pleasing judging experience is having put all my judging mileage in my book, "Here Comes The Judge". The next best thing was having it sell out. Rather than reprinting it, doing a new and revised edition is the result. This is very exciting as I have been able to include so many people's great questions and work with my co-author, Carolyn Vaillancourt, answering your questions. What could be more pleasing than finishing my fifth book, and looking forward to its distribution with enjoyment.

Most Questionable Answers

In the equitation division further testing often involves question and answer sessions. I use 'Q. & A.' on occasion. I believe it is good, as it makes the riders stay current and on their toes. Well some anyway - let me share with you some of the answers that I have been given in response to my questions.

Q: **Where is the dock?**
A: Where my father parks his boat.

Q: **Where is the poll?**
A: On the jump.

Q: **Point out the muzzle.**
A: It's what you put over the horse's mouth to keep him from biting.

Q: **Where is the crest?**
A: With my toothbrush.

Q: **Where are the chestnuts?**
A: In the trees.

Q: **Where is the gaskin?**
A: In the boathouse (thought it sounded like gas can!).

You Be The Judge

Q: Point out the hock.

A: Looks and point to the sky.

Q: Where is the curb?

A: On the side of the road.

Q: What's a hand?

A: She waves it at me!

Q: Where is the pastern?

A: Where my horse gets turned out.

Q: Where is the croup?

A: I got the crop flashed at me!

Most Repeated

I am judging a show way off the beaten track, somewhere early in my career, and it is an intermediate equitation class with about twenty entries. The class is nearing the end, and I have the distinct feeling that a certain plain bay horse looks really familiar, as if I have seen him recently. So just by chance I call for the steward and ask if she could go to the ingate area to ask the rider of the bay horse (#21) if by chance he was ridden in the same class by someone else. Well, the steward returns and to my astonishment she says that this was a fact, and the horse was also ridden in the same class by two other riders!. Whoa... I can't believe it. Furthermore, they say that they do it all of the time, and why can't they continue this way?

I know there is a rule, but I simply state that if I called for a ride-off either on the flat or over fences, how could they possibly all come in riding the same horse? They accepted this, and all but the first rider were eliminated. If this were allowed, I could simply open a booth at the ingate and rent my horse out for all to ride!

Most Reassuring

Probably one of the best things about judging, is that at the end of a long day or a long show knowing that you did the best job possible. I keep saying that judging is one of the most difficult things I do in the horse business. The long hours, the pressure of peak performances and the total concentration that is called for. You know that as a judge you try to do it right, and it's not just the cheque you receive at the end of a show, but the seldom thanks from management, trainers, parents or exhibitors means a lot. There is always someone who seems to have a nice word to say to you about your judging at the right time, which really reassures you that you did it right.

Most Regrettable

While watching for the return jogging order for a green class, one of the riders was jogging back his horse when the horse reared and bolted. I had experienced this before, and the horse had been caught, jogged again and then pinned. Here we have quite a unique situation, as the horse ran and jumped out of the ring over a low enclosure, and was long gone!

I was very sorry, but jogging back for soundness is required. If the horse had actually jogged before leaving, I could have let it pass as he would have fulfilled the requirements of the class. No jog - no ribbon. The saddest part of this instance is that this horse was the winner of the class!

Most Remarkable

I climb into my judge's booth in the morning and set up all of my things around me and on the table. Into the day the wind started up and it was blowing quite strongly by midday. I started to question my housing situation as I felt the shakiness of the booth. I was about to call the announcer and ask him how it looked from his position when I felt the booth toppling over! Dropping everything I jumped out the side entrance to about 10' below and watched as the booth blew into the hunter ring and crash landed. I now always check out the stability of my housing before moving in!

Most Reminiscent

I was invited to judge Harrisburg Pennsylvania National Horse Show, which was quite an honour as I was the first and only Canadian to have been invited to judge the hunters. Along with this prestigious honour it was quite a trip down memory lane for me. The last time I was at Harrisburg Horse Show I had worked as a groom for George H. Morris. I recall sleeping on the tack room floor, as the evenings were so late and the mornings so early it was impossible to get back and forth to the hotel. Now, here I am all dressed up and judging what I used to take care of. I just goes to show that if you work hard enough you can make it. I am very proud of all the background I experienced, and appreciative of where I am today.

Most Rewarding

Early in my career I was asked to judge a show in the Midwest. The show was great and all the people involved were extremely courteous and helpful. The show ran well and was really fun to judge. At the end of the show as I was leaving the grounds the announcer came over the loudspeaker and congratulated the judging. This was followed by applause from people around the rings. I was really moved by this and have always enjoyed judging that particular show.

Most Ridiculous

One show tried this, and I was one of the two unlucky judges to have to deal with it. It was supposed to be a "horse saver" plan. Two judges sitting together, judging (in a sense) two classes - one each. Let me try to explain. The courses were exactly the same, with the exception being that the second course had one additional fence added on to the end (jump #9). Simply, the idea here is that the first course ends at fence #8 and the second course at fence #9. The first judge was to judge the first course only, and the second judge (me!) was to judge the second course.

Two different rounds, but the horse only had to jump the round one time. To make it more confusing, the rider had the option of jumping fence #9 after the first eight fences if he thought all has gone well and he wants the one round to count for both classes. If by chance something goes wrong, he has the option of finishing the course over fence #8, and coming back to jump the second round later.

As the second judge, I ended up judging twice, as I didn't know if the rider was on the second course until he was finished. I am sure you can see why this ended up making the most ridiculous list. Luckily this didn't become a trend, and was never seen again!

Most Rude Awakening

It was mid-afternoon on an incredibly hot day and I was sitting in the judge's booth, halfway into a low hunter class, when a black horse started on course. He jumped the first jump reluctantly towards home and then came to an abrupt, but predictable halt on the line away from home. The rider then used his crop. The horse over-reacted by bolting off. He ran to the end of the ring, jumped out of the ring over the rope enclosure, galloped up the bank and halted before the high wire fence. The announcer, unaware of what had happened, announced over the loudspeaker that there was to be no riding permitted on the bank around the hunter ring.

The rider turned around, picked up a gallop and headed back down the bank. He jumped back into the hunter ring and down over the line of jumps towards home and then out of the correct in-out gate! I might mention that the two best jumps for the horse were the two undesignated jumps out of and into the ring. I might also add to the incredible situation that the ingate personnel, seeing no one on course, had sent in the next horse. They were on course, as the black outlaw galloped back onto the scene. This definitely detracted from the legitimate horse's performance and I allowed that one a re-run!

Most Solicitous

One thing I wish is that exhibitors would not talk to me while I am judging a model class. I need to focus and concentrate, and not be distracted by talking.

On this one particular occasion, the handler proceeded to tell me all of the following listed below, during the time I walked around and judged his horse's conformation:

- How much the horse had won
- How much the owner paid for the horse
- How beautiful the horse was
- What a good mover he was ("Wait until you see him move!")
- How well he jumps
- How he has never been defeated on the line!

Unbelievable! And guess what! That day he was beaten. He was not the best model and I did not appreciate all the uncalled for comments. Just leave me to do my job, which I am capable of doing without any assistance, especially from an exhibitor.

When this happens, you really have to ignore it, and as I always say, do what you think is right and you can't go wrong!

Most Soothing

I thought I had seen it all, and then just this year I have one for the book! A rider did her first back-to-back round and had trouble with her horse's lead changes, as he would run after she asked for them. Well, she comes back into the ring for her second class, petting and massaging her horse's neck, and proceeds to do this around the entire course. She reached up and patted his neck after all the lead changes, and amazingly so, it worked every time as he went around smoothly, and jumped well. The challenge for me was how to judge and place her. I placed her second, as after all, it is a hunter class and I am judging the horse. Furthermore, it beats spurring and whipping around the course. Her gestures, although different, made it work, so I justly rewarded her.

Most Aggressive Trainer

I am judging a back-to-back pony hunter class, and a pony goes around in the first class and every time he goes by the ingate he bolts ahead while getting a lead change. I am really quite suspicious of this as the trainer seems to step into the ring and then backs away after the pony goes by. The round was a good one otherwise, but curiosity gets the better of me so I ask the jump crew sitting beside my booth to go over to the ingate when the pony comes back for the second round and see if he notices anything happening at the ingate. The report I got back was that the trainer had a high powered water pistol that she was blasting the pony in the sides with, in order to get the lead changes.

This certainly has to be one of the ultimate aggressive techniques I have experienced while judging. What did I do? I called for the steward for obvious reasons - the pony is eliminated for outside assistance. Furthermore, I informed the steward that if there was any resistance to this I could pursue it further, as such acts of aggression will not be tolerated. I was certainly happy I noticed what was going on, as not acting on it would have set a bad example for the other competitors watching this performance.

Most Uncomfortable

Judging in Florida where it is supposed to be warm, however on this day I am on top of a hill sitting in a chair in the open, with the wind blowing and the temperature just above freezing. There is no way to get a vehicle up on the hill and there is no cover, so it is just shake and bear it!

My feet had started to freeze and feel numb, so the only way to start up the circulation is to alternate sitting on each one with my shoe off, and massage my toes with my free hand (which also kept my hand from freezing!). When not writing, my hands dove for my pockets to get warm. It is a very difficult thing to concentrate, write and watch when you are so cold.

I did survive the first class, but then announced that I needed new heated territory in order to continue. You must always be able to do you job, so these needs come first!

Most Unconvincing

On a number of occasions with all the travelling I do, and the connections, my luggage often does not catch up to me until a day later. Well, this is a memorable occasion, as I was travelling in shorts, a T-shirt and running shoes, and that is all I had to wear for the first day of judging.

I arrived at the gate of the fairgrounds where there was a security guard looking quite officious. I announced to him that I was the judge, and tried to explain that my luggage was lost, and I need to be admitted as the show started in ten minutes. He took one look at me and said, "I don't think so, and to try another occupation, perhaps a groom", and maybe I would have a chance of admission.

There is no alternative now as the judge is the real story, and Mr. Security Guard is not going to buy it. Well, off to a phone booth I go, to call the horse show office and have someone meet me at the gate. When it was all over I had missed the first class, which the other judge officiated. I must admit that as frustrating as it was, I do respect the guard for sticking to his guns as I definitely could not pass for a judge by the way I was dressed!

Most Unreasonable Request

At a certain show the ingate girl came over to the judge's booth and asked me if I would hold seven judge's cards at once. Three different age groups of children's hunters to go twice, with approximately twenty entries in each, and a medal class card with most all of them in it, followed by required further testing.

The medal course was the same course as the first of the back-to-back children's course, to make it even more confusing. This all together with an incompetent in-gate person, who repeatedly never told me about what class and what number was on course until after the round. Need I tell you more...that I would not do!

Questions & Answers

Q: **Has anyone tried to cheat in front of you when you were judging?**

A: I interpret that as meaning what is obvious, e.g. substituting a horse. Yes, I have seen a horse jog back which is not the one I watched perform. Also, someone has tried to show a horse in the rest of a division that another one started, and a horse showed in the hack that did not complete a course over fences. In all instances, elimination was the answer!

Q: **Have you ever spooked a horse, or been asked to move from where you are sitting?**

A: Yes and no. I crossed my legs once while a rider was making a pass in front of me, and the horse spooked causing the rider to fall off! They did not get a re-ride. It is part of the game! I have never been asked to move, and would not even if I was asked.

Q: **Have you ever jumped out of your booth or chair?**

A: Twice - once to save myself when the judge's booth blew over, and once to save a rider when she fell off a pony, taking the bridle with her and ending up with her foot caught in the stirrup. I was the closest to them and without hesitation I jumped into the ring and wrapped my arms around the pony's neck, as it was about to bolt.

Q: **Have you ever made a mistake when you were judging, and will you share it with us?**

A: Yes I have, but the good news is that in all my career I can remember them as I am really conscientious and work very hard to get it right. Mixing up the dates, I have arrived a day early for a show (having to spend the day at the pool), and have arrived a day late, luckily being saved by a fill-in judge and schedule change to correct the problem.

One time I forgot to jog a horse for the ribbons, and it was the winner. I had put it far on top on my card, and had missed its number for the call back. I held the class until the horse was found and jogged.

Even though these are the ones I recall, there may certainly have been other incidents I am unaware of. Afterall, we are only human!

Q: **Have you ever had anyone apologize to you for an awful performance?**

A: One exhibitor once asked me to forget and forgive his awful performance, which was quite unforgettable. Yes, it was not good, but I tried to reinforce the positive and encourage the rider that the next time there was room for improvement.

Q: **I know judging is very serious, but when something really amusing happens what or how should you react?**

A: Enjoy the moment without too much expression, or as I am doing in this chapter, write it down to share with all!

Summary

I hope that you have enjoyed these personal experiences as much as I have enjoyed writing about them. These types of situations make a 'day at the office' interesting and unpredictable, and certainly keep me smiling! Every horse show brings its own flavour and moments, and has helped to make this side of the horse business a wonderful part of my career.

Chapter Eleven

About The Authors

Randy G. Roy

An Interview With Randy G. Roy

The following is an interview with Editor in Chief of Horse and Country magazine, Judith McCartney, which offers insight into the life of the author, Randy Roy.

Q: **How do you find time to write?**

A: I make time, early mornings are the best. At home while I am mucking out I think a lot and keep mental notes, then I write them down after. When I am on the road, while I am jogging in the mornings again I keep mental notes and then write them down when I get back to my hotel room.

Q: **From all the careers you pursue, which one do you prefer the most?**

A: Let me answer that with a diagram I want you to picture. In the centre of the diagram is the word training which is the career I enjoy the most. I feel all of the other careers that I pursue feed into the training career:

Judging - Viewing and learning from the best performances which helps give you the winning edge.

Clinician - Educating horses and riders.

Course Designer - Making horses and riders go well.

Manager - Show and home, organizational skills and delegating jobs.

Q: **What would you say is the highlight of your equestrian career?**

A: All of it - just being able to do what I love is a highlight as it has all been so rewarding. If I have to single out one outstanding highlight it would be having been invited to judge the three prestigious indoor shows: Pennsylvania National, Washington International and The National; being the first and only Canadian to officiate judging the hunters and equitation.

Q: **What is the biggest honour bestowed upon you in your career?**

A: It would have to be the recent 2006 Jump Canada Hall of Frame of Hunter Just Cruising (Sham) being the first Indictee along with the jumper "Big Ben".

Just Cruising

A "jack-of-all-trades and a master of one" is an apt description of hunter legend, Just Cruising. During the 70's and 80's, he captured championships across North America at such prominent horse show destinations as Palm Beach, Devon, Upperville and Ox Ridge.

His is a true Cinderella story. Foaled in Spain, the thoroughbred gelding was sent to Argentina to play polo. At 16 hands, he was purchased by Jerry Laframboise and sent to Hudson, Quebec, to be a hunt horse. When he failed to live up to expectations, he was sent to a dressage barn where, yet again, he was deemed unacceptable. He finally found a home in 1978 when he was purchased by Randy Roy and his wife, Cathy, who were based at Dwyer Hill outside of Ottawa.

The plain bay gelding had finally found his niche, excelling in the hunter ring with Cathy. In their first year alone, they claimed zone championship titles in three divisions - Green Conformation, Green Working Hunter and Amateur-Owner. While pregnant with daughter, Ryan, Cathy leased Just Cruising stateside where Leslie Howard took over the ride. Other riders who successfully showed Just Cruising, known as "Sham" around the barn, included Mac Cone, Jamie Mann and Ian Millar.

In 1980, Cathy and Randy moved to King City to start a new business, Hunter's Glen. Although they had many offers, the Roy's decided to keep Just Cruising and Cathy won many championships at Toronto's Royal Horse Show and on the Florida circuit. In 1982, Just Cruising was sold to Carl and Martha Lindner of All Seasons Farm in Cincinnati. After many more championships in the Amateur divisions, Just Cruising was retired to California.

You Be The Judge

Just Cruising is remembered for many reasons - his struggle to find a career, his dominance once he found his calling, and his remarkable longevity.

Q: What is the lowest point of your horse life?

A: Having to make the decision to put down two of my most favorite animals, Another Brother (Earl) and Polaris Starship (Eugene). They were both such winners that I valued so much, they showed and won right to the end. Although they never were retired, I believe they were truly happy showing and doing what they did best right to the end. I need to add here that both Earl and Eugene were afflicted in such a way that they could not be retired to pasture. My only consolation here is that they went as peacefully as possible and they are always in my thoughts.

Q: Where do you think the industry is heading?

A: That is a loaded question so I will be somewhat guarded. There are now divisions at the shows that cater to everyone. Sometimes I feel we are coming close to burying the jumps. What I mean by that is, hunters now jump 2'3" which is lower than ponies jump; and jumpers jump such low heights that running can be dangerous as there is nothing to slow them down. I know it fills the divisions at the shows and allows a lot of riders and horses to show, but I just cannot help feeling that we are getting away from the real divisions! Now on the positive side I think horse shows have definitely upgraded insofar as footing, jumps, courses, officials, scheduling, and management is concerned. This is a big plus for the industry as all shows need to keep upgrading to attract exhibitors. I think the horse industry is booming forward with all kinds of promising aspects.

Q: Besides horses is there anything else you like doing?

A: Actually, lots of things. I really enjoy reading now that I am an author and I can really appreciate other authors. Canoeing has become a great pastime as I recently purchased an old wooden canoe which I put on the roof of my truck and off the lakes I go! Cooking, now that I am single I have no choice! Let me indulge a little here and share with you my favorite recipe. This can be a meal or a side salad with dinner. With my schedule, it often ends up lunch and dinner. This recipe is light, healthy and most important easy.

Marinated Vegetable Salad

Chopped (uncooked) - broccoli, cauliflower, carrots, sliced mushrooms, celery, black olives, tomatoes

Salad dressing - 1/2 cup wine vinegar, 1/4 cup vegetable oil, 1 chopped red onion, 1 chopped clove of garlic, 1 tsp. basil, 1/2 tsp. oregano, 1/2 tsp. sugar

Mix salad dressing and pour over chopped vegetables, leave in refrigerator overnight as it tastes better the next day.

I like working out along with jogging and swimming. When I am at home I muck out, which is equivalent to an aerobic workout. I ski both downhill and cross country. Writing is a major part of my life now that I write monthly articles for Horse Sport, along with finishing this book. I might add here that all these extra activities are a good break from horses; and it all only fortifies you when you go back to your horse duties.

Q: People call you the pony king. Why is that?

A: I guess because I have so many ponies and young children showing. I also own a number of ponies that I lease out, that show with me and I assume that is why so many people associate me with ponies. I really enjoy working with the young riders and I especially appreciate my ponies who will be with me hopefully to retirement.

You Be The Judge

Q:Why didn't you go into business with Ian Millar when Dwyer Hill folded?

*A:*I felt it was time to go alone. At this point in my career I had a lot of exposure and I felt there were several avenues I wanted to follow. Also I had a wonderful opportunity waiting for me in Toronto with the Collard family and Hunters Glen Farm. Ian and I had an amazing successful time together and we both agreed it was time to pursue our own careers. So we parted the best of friends and we still consult on a regular basis.

Q:Why do you prefer hunters to jumpers?

*A:*I don't. It is simply because I have more hunters than jumpers and people assume that's what you do better. I really like doing the jumpers and if more opportunities arise, that will be great.

Q:What do you think is your biggest drawing card?

*A:*For openers, not my riding. I think it is the success ratio I have with the numbers I take to the shows. Doing well is your mark of success and henceforth your drawing card. I try to mount my riders with what will not only teach them but win as well.

Q:How do you handle a bad day at the horse show?

*A:*There is always tomorrow. I try to analyze what went wrong and what I can do differently. If I have a difficult horse I will consult with other horsemen as to what they would do. That is what is so good about the business, being surrounded by experts, and as long as you are open minded the answer is usually right there. The best advice I can give you is try to be positive and things will surely improve.

Q:How long do you see yourself being in the horse business?

*A:*Hopefully for a long time. I plan on always having a barn with horses and ponies of my own. Showing will probably slow down, but feeding, turning out, mucking out, and caring for my horses and ponies will always be a part of my life as long as I am able.

Q: Do you get attached to your horses and ponies?

A: Remember that I do this because I love it, and believe me they are not just machines to me. When they are sold or pass on I always have the memories with me and that's what I try to focus on while continuing forward. It is more difficult with the children and very often it is their first horse or pony and they get quite attached, so you need to handle it carefully when you tell them they have to move on. Having a replacement right there really helps the transition, and finding a good situation for the previous one is a good cushion.

Q: What would you say is your biggest contribution to the horse industry?

A: I'm still working on it with my horses and riders that I am helping. Quality horses and ponies, along with upgrading riders is what I am contributing to the horse industry today. If you make me single out one thing that I consider to be my biggest contribution, that would have to be my first book, "Here Comes The Judge", which is a guideline for all as to what the judge is looking for.

Q: Is there anything you regret during your years with horses?

A: Yes, probably the time I travelled excessively judging and during my U.S. partnerships. I was away for months at a time when my children were very young. What I realize now is how fast they grow up and while you pursue your career, you never get back that time with them. Today, I realize how much they mean to me and I organize my career around them.

Q: What is your favorite time with horses?

A: When they are all settled in the barn and I am doing night check, watering and haying. Just listening to them contentedly munching on hay, warm, comfortable and relaxed; it makes it a great time to reflect on the day and really appreciate all you have to be thankful for.

You Be The Judge

Q: What motivated you to become a judge?

A: It always fascinated me how one person could sort out all those amazing performances of horses and riders. Now that I do it, I appreciate it even more. I thought judging could be one of my best contributions to the sport, as I always find myself studying horses and riders, to be more competitive and always trying to improve.

Q: Were you ever nervous or overwhelmed by a situation, and if so, how did you handle it?

A: Many times I have been overwhelmed and apprehensive, but one time comes to mind is when I was invited to be a panelist for the A.H.S.A. judge's clinic in Oklahoma City. This was to be a first for a Canadian and believe me, I was somewhat nervous, especially speaking in front of all those senior judges. I overcame it by relaying on what I knew. I started by saying that I was aware that a lot of people were there because it was mandatory, so I would try to make it as bearable as possible. I was also aware of the fact there were several senior judges who had been at it a lot longer than I, and who was I to be telling them how to do it. I pointed out that I was not about to tell anyone how to judge, simply suggest and discuss different techniques that might be helpful. I relied on simplicity and honesty for my presentation and ended up well received and applauded!

Q: What in the hunter world is the weakest area?

A: Probably how boring it is to someone who knows nothing about the sport. Anyone can relate and get excited with jumpers going around jumping coloured jumps and running fast in the jump-off. Hunters however, jumping plain jumps totally under control is far from exciting. I might suggest numerical scoring along with announcements of high and low scores, and repeated referrals as to what the judge is looking for to spark up more interest in the hunter world.

326

*Q:***Do you enjoy course designing?**

*A:*I do, because I like to design courses that can make the horses jump well and the riders ride well. I feel comfortable and confident. It is my goal to encourage, not discourage, and that is a challenge.

*Q:***How do you handle the pressure at the big shows, and all of the excellent rounds. Do you find it intimidating?**

*A:*I rely on knowledge, good bookkeeping and honesty. Then I can't go wrong or become intimidated.

*Q:***How do you choose the best movers in a large class, in a short period of time?**

*A:*How long do you think it would take me to pick out the prettiest girl in the room? They simply stand out to a trained eye, and all I have to do is write down their number (back number that is, not telephone number!)

*Q:***Is there anything that you would like to change or add to the hunter division?**

*A:*Yes.

1/A conformation division at the 3'6" height, open to all horses, judged 40% conformation and 60% performance.

2/One class in the pony division to be judged 25% conformation, to teach young riders how to stand up their ponies.

3/Handy hunters in the junior and amateur divisions, with optional turns and "take your own line" options.

4/End low, schooling and preparation classes. They should run the day before the show starts, or very early in the morning with small "r" or learner judges judging them. This saves the senior or "R" judges for the real classes.

*Q:***What do you consider your biggest contribution has been thus far, to the horse industry?**

A: I feel that it could be a new book, and the title would be "Horses Make The Person", not the way you would obviously think, that the person makes the horse. I believe that my biggest asset is that I act as a spokesman for the horse, as they cannot speak for themselves. I feel that I am able to think like a horse, and I try to understand them first, and then try to match them up to a rider. I deal with short stirrup riders learning to jump, to grand prix riders with Olympic goals, and I have always taken the horse's side to be able to work with them to suit the rider.

Hopefully, I have been able to make people's lives better as they try to reach their goals, and I hope that I have helped horses by not over facing them and realizing their limitations, so they compete at the right level.

Q: **If you were to ask yourself one question about your life with horses, what would that be and how would you answer it?**

A: Without even thinking about it, the question would be, "Are you happy?". Happy for me is being thankful for my two children Ryan and Colin, and being able to enjoy what I do, a successful life with horses.

Q: **Do you have any suggestions or guidelines for new clients?**

A: Hunters Glen Greeting List - here is a list of things that will help everyone get along:

- If your horse makes a mess in the aisle, please clean it up.
- When you have finished riding don't leave your horse on the cross-ties.
- The staff feeds at certain times - do not give your horse extra feed.
- The indoor arena can hold only so many horses, so please use good judgment as to how many riders should be in the arena, and wait your turn.
- Horses are fed their grain at 3:00 p.m., so we ask that everyone time their arrive accordingly.

- Make sure when you leave the barn the area you leave it as neat and tidy as when you arrived.

- Ask permission before borrowing tack; clean and return it to its proper place.

- The last person in the barn should make sure all of the lights are turned off and all tack room and barn doors are closed.

Thank you!

Q:Do you have any tips for staying on top?

A:Throughout the years in the horse business, I have learned to value some things that have helped me to achieve success. These headliners may help you with some of your situations. This "alphabet to success" has really helped me to maintain my status and encouraged me in the horse world. In no particular order, these are some priorities and ingredients you need to consider to stay on top:

A/ Hard work - there is no substitute.

B/ Stay involved - keep track of all details, e.g. touching base with all parts of your operation.

C/ Know when to move up and when to back down, with both horse and rider.

D/ Whatever your function at a show, be it trainer, course designer, judge, etc., try not to interfere with other functions. Concentrate and focus on your own responsibilities.

E/ Make losing work for you - learn from mistakes.

F/ Watch and learn from other trainers, riders and horses.

G/ Keep current - be around the shows whether observing or exhibiting.

H/ Plan goals for the year - know where you want to be at the end of the year with riders and horses.

I/ Good help makes it all run smoothly.

J/ Find and develop quality horses and ponies.

K/ Promote yourself and your product.

L/ Be aware of the competition and deal with it.

M/ Take a break whether it be a vacation or just a movie - you'll be better for it, and survive longer.

N/ Stay positive - there are always many ways to succeed. It is never easy being on top but it's worth it! A prosperous attitude wins.

O/ Be decisive. Believe and be confident, and you will either immediately or ultimately have the answer.

P/ Remember how you got to the top and don't take anything for granted.

Q/ Don't quit - persistence pays off.

R/ Staying on top means being very tolerant at times and requires amazing flexibility.

S/ Be aware that less is better - underdo rather than overdo.

T/ "Slow and steady wins the race".

U/ Maintenance is of utmost importance - consider the physical, for without soundness you have nothing.

V/ Winning means earning it every time.

W/ Read - horse literature, magazines, etc., to stay abreast of new trends and ideas.

X/ Have respect for your colleagues.

Y/ Back to basics - remember simplicity is the key.

Z/ Integrity and honesty are always the best policy and will keep you on top longer!

Q: **Could you share some of your goals with us?**

A: Certainly. Some of my goals are:

- To produce top riders and horses.
- To create and maintain a friendly competitive atmosphere.

- To educate riders in horsemanship and care of the horse.

- To develop an appreciation of the horse in others.

- To keep horses and ponies as content as possible, with turnout, feed and care.

- To develop good sportsmanship and a sense of values with people.

- To give young riders a sense of responsibility and identity - belonging and participation.

- To make showing as enjoyable as possible.

- Finding young horses to develop and sell, and for my daughter, Ryan, to show.

- Becoming more involved, to improve the horse industry, e.g. being a voice in horse organizations.

- Retiring and breeding my top show ponies, Dawnwatcher, Sir Lancelot and Braveheart.

- Stage a video "You Be The Judge" - actual classes; hunter, hack, equitation and conformation, that all can watch, judge and learn from.

Q: **What are your secrets to success in the show ring?**

A: Some of my secrets to longevity and things that I have learned that have helped me may also help you along the show road. They are as follows:

A/ Do your share around the stable. This insures awareness of the horse as more than a vehicle and helps performance in the ring.

B/ Train at home or in the schooling ring - not in the show ring.

C/ Come to the show prepared, do your homework at home.

D/ Don't waste winning jumps in the schooling area - know when to stop!

E/ Reward your horse for a job well done.

F/ Try new equipment at home first- tack, bits, etc.

G/ Always jog your horse, regardless of your placing.

H/ If your horse does not trot well, walk into the ring, then canter.

I/ If you have an unruly horse in a flat class, avoid traffic or excuse yourself.

J/ Always finish your course with the correct lead change and a nice circle - the judge is watching and you are still being judged! Don't ruin a good round with a rough exit.

K/ Try not to do a lengthy grand tour of the ring before starting your course.

L/ If you have a single jump towards home as the first jump, no opening circle is needed.

M/ Three refusals and you must leave the ring; if you fall off you also must leave - that is the rule.

N/ Upgrade yourself and stay current by attending clinics and observing the schooling area and winning performances.

O/ Make the most of you and your horse's turnout. This is your moment.

P/ Try not to keep the judge waiting, as it does not work in your favour, and time is always a factor in a successful presentation.

Q/ It is better to underdo than overdo.

R/ Good sportsmanship goes a long way - remember it is easier to be cordial. I always remember the nice people.

S/ Maintenance of the horse - grooming and physical condition - is of utmost importance.

T/ A sense of humour makes showing a lot more pleasurable.

U/ Read and understand the Equine Canada Rules and class specifications before competing and complaining.

V/ It never hurts to congratulate the winner - you know how hard it is to get there and when someone acknowledges you, you always remember it.

W/ A little appreciation and acknowledgment of staff at home and shows can give you that little extra edge and support when things get tough.

X/ Cooperation with show management makes for happier competitors and a better show all around.

Y/ At the end of the day, regardless of the day's events, your horse comes first.

Z/ Remember to be nice and acknowledge everyone on your way up the ladder, as you will meet them all again on your way back down!

Q: **Who in Canada do you admire the most, and why?**

A: Most of all of my horse compatriots have helped me in some way in my horse ventures; but some stand out, and I will simply list them in no particular order, and what impresses me most about them. They are all quite remarkable in what they have accomplished and how they have contributed to the horse world!

Gladys Adam - Horsewoman extraordinaire with unlimited knowledge

Ian D. Millar - Winning!

Bobbie Reber - Her connection and relatedness with people.

Wayne McClellan - Thoroughness and what he produces.

Mac Cone - Dedication and hard work.

Jill Henselwood - Studious and directed.

Patty Markell - Loyal friend.

Donna Gramling - Conditioning horses and turnout.

Peter Stoeckl - Disciplined.

Robert Meilsoe - Promoter.

John Allan - Patience.

Ronnie Davidson - Showman.

Torchy Millar - Motivated.

You Be The Judge

Jane Fleming - Class.

Jim Elder - Respected.

Ron & Marg Sothern - Unparalleled in show development.

George & Diane Tidball - How the west was won!

Ainsley Vince - Positive.

Cheryl Lanctot & Sonny Brooks - Team work.

Eric Lamaze - Talented.

Dee Walker - Polished.

Debbie Garside - Outstanding teacher.

An Interview With Carolyn E. Vaillancourt

Carolyn E. Vaillancourt

Q: How did you and Randy come together to write "You Be The Judge" ?

A: Randy and I have known each other both personally and professionally for many years, and have that we have very similar thoughts and opinions. This is the third book that Randy and I have written together, and I am very excited about our literary partnership.

Q: Are there other things than horses that you enjoy doing?

A: Actually, yes. I also work as an interior decor consultant. I have enjoyed and worked in this area for many years, and continue this fulfilling part of my life along with my judging career.

You Be The Judge

Q: **Do you enjoy judging, and where do you think it is going in the future?**

A: I enjoy judging very much. You have to, as the hours are extremely long and often uncomfortable, and you must be very committed to your work to do a good job and stay current. I think that judging will not change that much in the near future. Certainly, there are slow changes within the industry, but our job remains the same - to reward the best competing horses with ribbons that they deserve to win, and to help promote the horse industry.

Q: **As a senior judge, do you have to work at staying current?**

A: I believe that in any line of work you need to stay current and on top of changes in the industry. I travel throughout North America to watch horses and riders compete, and find this a fun and educational experience. I encourage all judges to spend time at the show ring when they are not working, to watch and experience different levels of competition. It is also important to attend clinics and seminars, not just because they are mandatory to retain your card, but because they are a wonderful place to discuss issues which arise and talk amongst other professionals about your line of work.

Q: **What part of the horse industry to you enjoy the most?**

A: I really enjoy the hunter and equitation classes, which is obvious as this is what I judge most of the time. A great performance by horse or rider is a beautiful thing to witness, and a thrill for me to judge.

Q: **Have you and Randy ever judged together? If not, how do you think you would get along?**

A: Actually, Randy and I have judged together, and it was always a wonderful experience. Randy if a terrific horseman, and sitting with him is always a learning experience. We tend to share the same views and opinions, therefore making it quite easy to work together.

Q: **Did you have goals and a plan at an early age to become a top equestrian judge?**

A: No. At a young age I was just thrilled to go to the barn everyday, show during the show season, and learn all I could from the great teachers I was so fortunate to have. I didn't decide to start judging until I was in my early twenties. My decision to do so was based on my love of hunters and equitation. I could sit all day and watch great hunters jump, and I was fortunate enough to be able to turn that into a career.

Q: **As a role model to young riders, what would you suggest that they place emphasis on in their daily training and life experiences?**

A: It would be wonderful to see young riders have fun at the horse shows. I feel that there are times that the young riders are under too much pressure to win, and this can take away from the enjoyable experience of riding and showing. Yes, it is a competitive sport, but at a young age, and for new riders to the sport, they should be happy with their personal goals being achieved at each show, which may not be only by winning a first place ribbon.

Riding consistently and successfully doesn't happen overnight. It take years of time and dedication, and a true love for the horse and the sport. There are more rewards to take home than just a championship cooler!

Q: **What does the future hunter/jumper circuit look like to you? In other words, where is the industry heading?**

A: I have had concerns in the past few years about the number of lower height divisions that seem to appear each year, in order to placate a large population of exhibitors. When the jumps become too low, not only is it somewhat dangerous (I have seen more accidents at the low heights than the divisions at 3'6"), but the horses do not jump properly over these small jumps. I would like to see more strength in the "regular" height divisions, where horses jump 3'6" and higher. Also, by having so many low and schooling divisions the days at the show can be very long, which is hard on the officials, trainers and the exhibitors. Unfortunately, these lower divisions are big money makers for the shows, so I don't see them disappearing too soon!

I think it would be fantastic if we could divide the recognized horse shows into training shows and separate shows for the higher level horses. This may solve some of the current problems, and allow the trainers to spend more time concentrating on their own stock separately from training customers and horses in 3 or 4 rings at the same time.

Q: Do you often share opinions with other judges?

A: Yes I do. I would like to share some of these opinions with you, so I am now including some questions directed to some of our country's top judges.

Q: Do you have any advise for new or learner judges?

A: I pass this question onto one of the premier judges in the USA, Linda Andrisani, a good friend and superb judge:

"It takes time and practice to become comfortable with your judging. It is very important for you to establish a style of judging that is consistent and easy to follow. Always show respect and interest for the exhibitor in the ring. Be courteous, responsible, attentive, and treat everyone equally."

Linda Andisani

USEF 'R' Judge & Equine Canada Senior Judge

Q: How do you respond to the popular comment that judging is political?

A: I will again pass this question on for Linda Andrisani to answer:

"I truly believe that we have improved our judges in the last ten years. I also believe we suffer more from judges being intimidated than from being political."

Linda Andrisani

USEF 'R' Judge & Equine Canada Senior Judge

Q: **What articles should you bring with you for a day of judging?**

A: Your extra all-weather gear, the prizelist, rule book, whistle, pens, stopwatch, clipboard, scrap paper, sun protector and snacks. You might also bring your copy of the horse show contract.

Marjorie R. Dennis

Senior Equine Canada and FEI Judge

Q: **Any suggestions on dress code?**

A: I believe judges should keep up a proper dress code. We are representing our Federation, show management, sponsors and exhibitors, all of whom deserve respect. I would strongly recommend that learner judges adhere to this code as well. I do not appreciate those who show up in jeans, shorts and T-shirts, no matter what level of horse show.

Cathy Harper

Senior Equine Canada judge / Horse Show Organizer

Q: **Do you prefer judging alone or working with another judge?**

A: Judging alone is fine, but I enjoy working with another judge, especially for hunter classics and equitation finals. Two sets of eyes are better than one! If I am judging with a second judge, I prefer to sit together rather than apart.

Debbie Garside

Trainer and Judge

Q: **In your opinion, what is the most difficult and most enjoyable part of judging?**

A: The most enjoyable is to judge nice horses and riders. The most difficult is finding ribbon winners when your standard of competition is mediocre.

Peter Stoeckl

Equine Canada Senior Judge

You Be The Judge

Q:Do you have any advice for new or learner judges?

*A:*Learner judges - Junior judging is an opportunity to educate yourself with the best horsemen and horsewomen in the business. Try to junior judge at the best shows with the best judges and spend the entire show (not just a few classes) immersing yourself into their ideas and scoring systems. The knowledge they can provide will give you the confidence you will need when you judge that first big show alone.

New Judges - Remember you are an employee of the show and a very visual representative of the Federation and our sport. Always err to the benefit of the exhibitor and remember that you have a huge responsibility to work as quickly and effectively as you can. A good or bad day of judging can greatly affect the spirit of a show and the exhibitor's attitude towards show management.

Evie Frisque
Equine Canada Senior Judge / Course Designer

Q:Suggestions on dress code?

*A:*With regard to a dress code for judges, remember you are a professional and a representative of the association, so dress appropriately. Be neat, well groomed and comfortable. Weather conditions may change, so be prepared. Rain gear, cold weather and war weather attire can be easily carried in a small bag if you are travelling. Flamboyant or loud attire, or very casual attire, should be avoided. Remember, you are not going to a Hunt Ball or the beach.

Carol Coleman
USEF 'R' Judge & Equine Canada Senior Judge

Q:In what direction do you believe judging is going?

*A:*Judging has already taken off in a direction which has left our present rules behind. The vast majority of classes we see today consist of fairly novice riders on horses with limited abilities in movement and jumping technique, competing over jumps 3 feet or lower. These classes are not really hunter classes, because we are unable to judge the horses as such, it is a contest of who can find the most jumps. Our judging emphasis has been forced to shift from the horse to the rider. This is not necessarily a bad thing, it just means we need to design the classes and the courses to be a more appropriate test of the rider's style and efficiency. There should still be classes in which we judge the horse's style but they should be a showcase for breeders to advertise their young horses.

Ann Hodgson
Equine Canada Senior Judge / Trainer

AND GOD SAW
THAT IT WAS GOOD